PENGUIN CLASSICS

TRAVELS WITH A DONKEY IN THE CÉVENNES
AND THE AMATEUR EMIGRANT

ROBERT LOUIS STEVENSON was born in Edinburgh in 1850. The son of a prosperous civil engineer, he was expected to follow the family profession but finally was allowed to study law at Edinburgh University. Stevenson reacted violently against the Presbyterian respectability of the city's professional classes and this led to painful clashes with his parents. In his early twenties he became afflicted with a severe respiratory illness from which he was to suffer for the rest of his life; it was at this time that he determined to become a professional writer. In 1879 he travelled to California to marry Fanny Osbourne, an American ten years his senior. Together they continued his search for a climate kind to his fragile health, eventually settling in Samoa, where he died on 3 December 1894.

Stevenson began his literary career as an essayist and travel-writer, but the success of *Treasure Island* (1883) and *Kidnapped* (1886) established his reputation for tales of action and adventure. *Kidnapped*, and its sequel *Catriona* (1893), *The Master of Ballantrae* and stories such as 'Thrawn Janet' and 'The Merry Men' also reveal his knowledge and feeling for the Scottish cultural past. Stevenson's Calvinistic upbringing gave him a preoccupation with predestination and a fascination with the presence of evil. In *The Strange Case of Dr Jekyll and Mr Hyde* he explores the darker side of the human psyche, and the character of the Ma[ster in *The Master of Ballantrae* (1889) was intended to be 'all I [ ] Devil'. During the last years of his life Stevenson's cr[ ] developed considerably and *The Beach of Falesá* broug[ ] the kind of scenes now associated with Conrad and M[ ] the time of his death Robert Louis Stevenson was work[ ] *of Hermiston*, at once a romantic historical novel and a [ ] reworking of one of Stevenson's own most distressing [ ] the conflict between father and son.

CHRISTOPHER MACLACHLAN was born in Edinbur[ ] Ph.D. from Edinburgh University. He is a Senior L[ ] School of English at the University of St Andre[ ]

editing Matthew Lewis's *The Monk* for Penguin Classics and an anthology of eighteenth-century Scottish verse, he has published articles on a number of English and Scottish authors, including Robert Burns, David Hume, John Buchan and Muriel Spark.

ROBERT LOUIS STEVENSON

Travels with a Donkey in the Cévennes
and
The Amateur Emigrant

Edited with an Introduction and Notes by
CHRISTOPHER MACLACHLAN

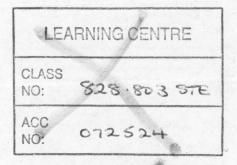

PENGUIN BOOKS

PENGUIN BOOKS

Published by the Penguin Group
Penguin Books Ltd, 80 Strand, London WC2R ORL, England
Penguin Group (USA), Inc., 375 Hudson Street, New York, New York 10014, USA
Penguin Books Australia Ltd, 250 Camberwell Road, Camberwell, Victoria 3124, Australia
Penguin Books Canada Ltd, 10 Alcorn Avenue, Toronto, Ontario, Canada M4V 3B2
Penguin Books India (P) Ltd, 11 Community Centre, Panchsheel Park, New Delhi – 110 017, India
Penguin Group (NZ) Ltd, Cnr Airborne and Rosedale Roads, Albany, Auckland 1310, New Zealand
Penguin Books (South Africa) (Pty) Ltd, 24 Sturdee Avenue, Rosebank 2196, South Africa

Penguin Books Ltd, Registered Offices: 80 Strand, London WC2R ORL, England

www.penguin.com

Travels with a Donkey in the Cévennes, first published 1879
The Amateur Emigrant, first published 1895
This edition first published 2004

5

Introduction and Notes copyright © Christopher MacLachlan, 2004
Extracts from *The Cévennes Journal*, ed. Gordon Golding, copyright
© CLUB CÉVENOL (Jacques Poujol-Gordon Golding), 1978
All rights reserved

The moral right of the editor has been asserted

Set in 10.25/12.25 pt PostScript Adobe Sabon
Typeset by Rowland Phototypesetting Ltd, Bury St Edmunds, Suffolk
Printed in England by Clays Ltd, St Ives plc

ISBN-13: 978-0-14-143946-4

Contents

Chronology

1850 13 November: Born Robert Lewis Balfour Stevenson in Edinburgh, only child of Thomas Stevenson, lighthouse engineer, and his wife Margaret. Stevenson is a sickly but precocious child, much influenced by his nurse, Alison Cunningham (known as Cummie), who fills his mind with stories and with fears of damnation.

1861 Attends Edinburgh Academy, but leaves after two years and thereafter educated privately.

1866 *The Pentland Rising*, an essay on the 1666 defeat of the Covenanters in the Pentland Hills south of Edinburgh, privately printed by Stevenson's father.

1867 November: Enters the University of Edinburgh to study engineering, in order to follow in the family tradition of lighthouse-building.

1871 April: Abandons engineering to study law.

1873 31 January: Confesses his religious agnosticism to his shocked parents. July: On a visit to cousins in England he meets Frances Sitwell, an older, married woman, and begins an intimate friendship with her; also meets Sidney Colvin, who will marry Fanny Sitwell in 1903 after her husband's death. Colvin helps Stevenson to find magazines that will accept his essays. November: Physical collapse, with threat of tuberculosis. December: First publication, 'Roads', an essay, appears in the *Portfolio* (journal).

1874 April: Goes to Menton in the South of France for his health. May: 'Ordered South', an essay on his Menton trip, published in *Macmillan's Magazine*. 3 June: Elected to the Savile Club in London. August: 'Victor Hugo's Romances', first essay in the *Cornhill Magazine*, edited by Leslie Stephen.

1875 February: Meets W. E. Henley in Edinburgh. July: called to the bar in Scotland but does not practise as a lawyer; returns to France, where his cousin Bob Stevenson introduces him to the colony of artists at Grez, near Fontainebleau.

1876 August–September: With friend Walter Simpson, makes a canoe trip along the canals of Belgium and northern France; returning to Grez, he meets Fanny Osbourne, a married American woman with two children who has come to France to study painting.

1877 Relationship with Fanny develops as he pursues his ambitions as a writer. October: First short story, 'A Lodging for the Night', published in *Temple Bar* (journal).

1878 April: *An Inland Voyage*, account of the 1876 canoe trip. June: Acts as secretary to Professor Fleeming Jenkin at the Paris Exposition. August: Fanny Osbourne rejoins her husband in California. September–October: Travels with his donkey Modestine through the Cévennes mountains in south-central France; returns to Edinburgh by the end of the year, when *Edinburgh: Picturesque Notes* is published.

1879 June: *Travels with a Donkey*. 7 August: Sails for America to join Fanny without telling his parents and against the advice of most of his friends; after an exhausting journey, reaches Monterey, California, to find the question of Fanny's divorce still unresolved; immediately sets out on a lone trip in the Santa Lucia Mountains, nearly dying of exposure; recovers at Monterey, then moves to San Francisco. December: Sends first part of *The Amateur Emigrant* to Colvin.

1880 March: Falls seriously ill; has his first lung haemorrhage, usually taken as confirming tuberculosis. Colvin receives the second part of *The Amateur Emigrant*. April: Thomas Stevenson forgives his son for going to America and promises to send him an annual allowance of £250. 19 May: After bouts of illness on both sides and a suitable delay after her divorce, Stevenson and Fanny are married; they spend the summer, with Fanny's son Lloyd Osbourne (her daughter Belle had eloped with Joseph Dwight Strong in 1879), at the abandoned Silverado mine in the Napa Valley. 17 August:

Stevenson, Fanny and Lloyd sail from New York for Scotland.

1881 April: Volume of essays, *Virginibus Puerisque*, published; for the sake of his health Stevenson, Fanny and Lloyd go to Davos in Switzerland. August: Begins writing *Treasure Island* at Braemar in the Scottish Highlands. October: Returns to Davos.

1882 February: *Familiar Studies of Men and Books* (literary essays); July: *New Arabian Nights* (short stories). September: Goes to France for the winter, but falls seriously ill in Marseilles with continual haemorrhages. December: *Deacon Brodie*, play written in collaboration with W. E. Henley, first performed at Bradford.

1883 March: Stevenson and Fanny move to Hyères in the South of France, where they remain until July 1884. July: 'Across the Plains' published in *Longman's Magazine*. November: *Treasure Island*.

1884 January: *The Silverado Squatters*, his account of his honeymoon in California. From January to June his health is bad. An outbreak of cholera at Hyères drives the Stevensons back to England; they settle in Bournemouth.

1885 March: *A Child's Garden of Verses*; November: *Prince Otto* (novel).

1886 January: *The Strange Case of Dr Jekyll and Mr Hyde* becomes a bestseller in Britain and America; July: *Kidnapped*.

1887 8 May: Thomas Stevenson dies. 21 August: Stevenson, Fanny, Lloyd and Stevenson's mother sail for New York, where Stevenson finds *Dr Jekyll and Mr Hyde* has made him famous and brings him several lucrative contracts; he agrees to write twelve monthly articles for *Scribner's Magazine* for $3,500. October: Stevensons settle at Saranac Lake, near the Canadian border.

1888 June: *The Black Arrow*. 26 June: Stevensons sail from San Francisco for the South Pacific islands: the Marquesas (July–August); Paumotu (September); the Society Islands (October; when they arrive in Papeete, capital of Tahiti, Stevenson is so ill a doctor says that his next haemorrhage will be fatal); Hawaii (December). Journey partly financed by an agreement to write fifty letters for the New York *Sun* for $10,000.

1889 May: Stevenson's mother returns to Scotland. 24 June: Stevensons sail from Honolulu for the Gilbert Islands. September: *The Master of Ballantrae*. 7 December: Stevenson, Fanny and Lloyd reach Samoa, where Stevenson buys some land.

1890 February: They visit Sydney, Australia, where Stevenson has a serious attack of lung disease. April–August: Makes his third Pacific cruise, to the Gilbert, Marshall and other islands, then returns to Sydney. October: They return to Samoa, where Stevenson begins building his house, Vailima.

1891 January: Goes to Sydney to collect his mother and escort her back to Samoa. February–December: *In the South Seas*, his book on the history and customs of the Pacific Islands and his travels amongst them, published in instalments in America.

1892 April: *Across the Plains*, a collection of essays including a version of the second part of *The Amateur Emigrant*. July–August: 'The Beach of Falesá' (South Seas novella) in the *Illustrated London News*. August: *A Footnote to History*, a survey of Samoan history and politics.

1893 January: Catches influenza, which brings on his first lung haemorrhage for some time. April: *Island Nights' Entertainments*, short fiction set in the South Seas. June: Civil war breaks out in Samoa. September: *Catriona*, the sequel to *Kidnapped*. Stevenson visits Hawaii.

1894 July: *The Ebb-Tide* (South Seas novella), written in collaboration with Lloyd Osbourne. 3 December: Suffers a cerebral haemorrhage at Vailima and dies within a few hours; next day his body is carried up Mount Vaea and buried at the summit.

1895 January: *The Amateur Emigrant* published, edited by Sidney Colvin, with many omissions from the manuscript version. October: *Vailima Letters*, also edited by Sidney Colvin.

1896 May: unfinished novel *Weir of Hermiston* is published.

1897 14 May: Margaret Stevenson dies in Edinburgh. October: Stevenson's unfinished novel *St Ives* (with an ending by Arthur Quiller-Couch) is published.

1914 19 February: Fanny Stevenson dies in Santa Barbara, California.

1915 June: Fanny buried with Stevenson on the summit of Mount Vaea, Samoa.

Introduction

Robert Louis[1] Stevenson is today a writer known around the world. His most famous works are household names and, thanks to their success in other media, have escaped from a purely literary context. Through countless representations on stage and screen, *Treasure Island*'s heroic villain, Long John Silver, is now the archetype of the piratical rogue, and the phrase 'a Jekyll and Hyde character', again largely because of repeated versions of Stevenson's story in the cinema and on television, has a currency well beyond the text that spawned it. Less well known, perhaps, is the outline of Stevenson's own life: his upbringing as a sickly child in Edinburgh, his rebellion against his father's wish that he follow family tradition and become a lighthouse engineer, his determination to be a writer and traveller despite ill-health; and then his escape to the Pacific in search of a kinder climate, enjoyed for just a few years before his sudden death and his romantic interment on a mountain-top in Samoa.

All this makes it difficult to imagine what Stevenson's reputation and prospects amounted to before he became world-famous. It takes a mental effort to construct the sort of writer he was before he made the trip through the Cévennes that he describes in *Travels with a Donkey*, and the subsequent journey across the Atlantic and America described in *The Amateur Emigrant*; but to appreciate the significance of these two works it is worth thinking back to the stage in his career Stevenson had reached in 1878.

In April of that year he had published his first book, *An Inland Voyage*, the account of a journey with a friend by canoe from Antwerp to Pontoise north-west of Paris, a short, rather precious piece of travel writing to which reviewers readily applied the word 'charming' as well as commenting on Stevenson's literariness and quirkiness. The book brought him some attention but little money, and did not sell very well. It is quite consistent in style and tone with his previous writing, pieces for various London literary magazines. Having satisfied his parents' desire that he should have a profession by completing his law studies in 1875 – the compromise reached after he refused to continue studying engineering – he had soon begun establishing the London literary connections that he would need for a life of writing. He had been fortunate to attract the attention of several useful figures in the literary life of the capital, and they had encouraged him as a young man of promise and given him the openings for the publication of his first works. These were mainly essays, though he had written a few short pieces of fiction, too.

Stevenson thus became acquainted with such figures as Andrew Lang, Leslie Stephen, Edmund Gosse, William Henley and Sidney Colvin, who would in time become something like his literary agent, and his executor. These late-nineteenth-century men of letters are now little remembered; indeed some, like Colvin, are memorable only for their connection with Stevenson. But at the time he was undoubtedly glad to be associated with them. Typical of this period of his life is his election to the Savile Club in 1874. He was then surely much in danger of becoming part of the late Victorian world of gentlemanly clubs and literary periodicals.

No doubt the attraction of this world was the contrast it offered with life in Edinburgh. Like many Scots, and many Scottish writers, he escaped from his native country and the restraints of family expectations and respectable customs to the south, making the move that James Boswell had made a hundred years earlier when he attached himself to the circle around Samuel Johnson. There were near-contemporaries of Stevenson who made a similar escape: J. M. Barrie, George Douglas Brown, Andrew Lang himself, Arthur Conan Doyle and, a little later, John Buchan. Of these, two were knighted, and the last was ennobled to become Governor-General of Canada. If Robert

Louis Stevenson could have survived British winters and stayed to cultivate literary fame in London, like Barrie and Conan Doyle, or even if he had lived long enough in Samoa to reap rewards from his international prominence, what honours might not have come to him?

Since Stevenson's health had such an influence on his life it is necessary to say a word or two about it. Although at first a healthy child, he had at an early age succumbed to chronic chest ailments that had given him many nights of breathless nightmare and left him as an adult astonishingly thin. In his early years he seems to have suffered from asthma, periods of breathlessness leading to severe weakness, though interspersed with periods of health and energetic activity. But colds and fevers plagued him, and often laid him low. Because these ailments affected his chest both Stevenson and his doctors feared that what was really wrong with him was pulmonary tuberculosis, although the full symptoms, such as lung haemorrhages, were slow to appear (in fact, not until he reached San Francisco, after his terrible journey across the Atlantic and America). It was the fear of tuberculosis that made his doctors advise Stevenson to seek what was then regarded as the best treatment, a change of climate – though opinion differed as to whether that should be a warm, mild region such as the South of France, to which he was sent in 1874, or a cold, mountainous one like that of Davos in Switzerland, where he went in 1881. It is not clear that either of these really helped, but in any case tuberculosis was in Stevenson's time incurable and the best that medicine could offer was palliative treatment. The result was a life lived always on the edge of collapse into utter weakness, when Stevenson would be forced to take to his bed in a darkened room, forbidden to write or speak or even to be spoken to, although mere hours before he might have been riding or canoeing or leading his friends and family in lively games. Such swings of physical condition relate to the author's mercurial moods, and his hunger for life and sensation.

Yet even if his health had allowed him to follow the same path to prominence as his fellow-countrymen it is arguable that Stevenson would not have emulated them. The crucial difference between him and the writers mentioned above is simply that he went further south. London and its literary life was not the end of his quest. Once he had discovered France he returned there again and again, driven, certainly, by his search for a comfortable climate, but also by that part of him that did not want to conform. In France he found, in the artists' colonies south of Paris, the sort of mildly Bohemian society that always attracted him. For one thing, it was a lot cheaper. In 1878 he was in his twenty-eighth year but still dependent on his father, the father with whom he had been fighting a running battle for more than a decade over his seriousness, or lack of it, about life, and especially about religion. There was not much money in the kind of occasional writing that Stevenson had been doing up to this point, and only seemed likely to do in the future. There is a hidden but worrying contrast between the smoothness and insouciance of his early writings, his elegantly written essays reflecting on what little of life he has seen, and the precariousness of his finances. His letters home frequently touch on his need for money, and elsewhere his correspondents hear of the stark calculations he has to make about the duration of his trips to London and France. Stevenson's situation in the 1870s is very revealing of the tension between the manner and lifestyle expected of a literary man and the harsh economic realities he actually faced.

The conflicts inherent in this situation are one key to understanding Stevenson's life in the two years, 1878–9, covered by the texts in this book. *Travels with a Donkey* and *The Amateur Emigrant* belong to what must be seen as the beginning of the critical phase in his life – a phase rather than a point, because what begins in 1878 extends beyond the next year and the journey to America. Arguably the process of change and self-examination never ended, and what Stevenson embarked on when he trekked with his donkey into the Cévennes continued at least to Samoa, if not to the end of his life. The beginning of this process, however, can be clearly marked by one event – his meeting with Fanny Osbourne, the woman he would marry. This was the making of Robert Louis Stevenson as a writer different from the one he was becoming in London in the early 1870s.

His first meeting with Fanny in Grez, near Fontainebleau south-east of Paris, in 1876 has been subsequently romanticized, even by the participants, into love at first sight. There is some reason to doubt this, though the truth is probably impossible to establish. Some evidence exists that Fanny was more interested in Stevenson's cousin Bob, Robert Alan Mowbray Stevenson (to whom *The Amateur Emigrant* was dedicated in 1879). He seems to have been a man who made an immediate, pleasing impact. Louis, however, had more staying power and in time became Fanny's more constant companion. He spent the summer of 1877 with her and her two children, for some of the time as an invalid, thus setting a pattern of dependence on Fanny which would characterize a large part of their relationship. He, in his turn, would be much concerned by her health, and at times the roles of nurse and patient would be reversed – theirs was a marriage based on a mutual pathology. In 1877, however, they could not properly be married, no matter how domestic their existence, since Fanny already had a husband in America, and for that reason – and also perhaps because she was ten years older than him – Stevenson at first said nothing to his parents about her. He had enough to contend with in the coolness of his literary friends to this new relationship.

Then, in August 1878, Fanny returned to the USA. Biographers claim that she did so to seek a divorce from Samuel Osbourne so that she could marry Stevenson, but the evidence for this is slim, and it is strange that she seems to have made no attempt to institute proceedings until later. It is not implausible that she left for other reasons, perhaps even out of frustration or dismay at the intractability of her relationship with Louis, who could offer her nothing but devotion, and certainly no direct way to a secure and prosperous future for herself and her son and daughter. Stevenson, of course, was left with the other half of this bleak assessment: a future in which personal loneliness was added to the prospect of a slow grinding out of a bit of ill-paid literary fame. His immediate response was to head for the hills with a donkey.

On the face of it this was a reversion to type. As he had done before, he set out on a short journey with a view to writing a

book about it. In an otherwise sympathetic study of Stevenson
David Daiches bluntly states that 'the trips he describes in *An
Inland Voyage* and *Travels with a Donkey* were made simply
in order to be written about when they were over'.[2] This is quite
true, although not perhaps, in the second case, the whole truth.
For one thing, the second trip was to be made alone. It would
involve rather more hardship than the first, since it meant travelling over steep mountains and empty landscapes. The weather,
as it turned out, was not a problem, but Stevenson was setting
out quite late in the season. It could be argued that he had
decided to cross the Cévennes because they were neither well
known nor much visited, but that leaves the question of the
more personal reasons for his decision. If one of the answers is
the religious history of the region, that in turn raises the question
of why this man, who had quarrelled with his father over his
refusal to share his religion, sought out a place so associated
with a tradition of faith. Thus, though in many ways *Travels
with a Donkey* is a book that in form and substance harks back
to Stevenson's earlier work, it is also a text in which one might
seek for signs of something new, some seeds of change.

Stevenson set out from Le Monastier-sur-Gazeille in the
Haute-Loire region of France on 22 September 1878 and
reached St-Jean-du-Gard on 3 October. He had travelled over
two hundred kilometres in twelve days, crossing several high
ridges and climbing to the highest point in the Cévennes, the
Col (he called it the 'Pic') de Finiels, at 1,702 metres. He had
spent four nights sleeping in the open air and for most of the
journey had been unaccompanied except for his donkey. As well
as fending for himself and Modestine he had also kept a journal,
much of which would find its way with only slight adjustment
into the published form of *Travels with a Donkey*. All this was
quite a feat for a man whose health was precarious. Richard
Holmes, in the most stimulating essay on the *Travels*, his
account of his own 1964 journey in Stevenson's footsteps,
describes it as 'a physical trial, a piece of deliberate "adventur-
ing", a bet undertaken against himself ... His ill-health, his
struggle against consumption, together with the real wildness

of the Cévennes ... made this trial a genuine enough affair.'[3] But the trial was not just a physical one.

Consider, for instance, Stevenson's references to the women he meets on his travels. There is the incident at Bouchet-St-Nicolas, in 'I Have a Goad', where he has to share the bedroom at the *auberge* with a young married couple. Stevenson's polite expression of embarrassment has an erotic frisson because of his protestation that he saw 'nothing of the woman except that she had beautiful arms'; in his journal he added: 'whether she slept naked or in her slip, I declare I know not; only her arms were bare'.[4] This suggests that whatever he did or did not see he certainly imagined more, and hints at a sexual undercurrent to the feelings expressed at this point in the journal and not quite expunged from the published *Travels*.

Blatant, and rather coarse, sexuality is quite evident in a later incident, in the public house at Le Pont-de-Montvert, where Stevenson plays the gallant with three women at the dinner table, and then comments on the physical charms of the waitress. 'I had not seen a pretty woman since I left Monastier,' he says, as though he had been on the lookout, and his failure to find any explains his eagerness to admire the first tolerable examples he meets with. Certainly his remarks on Clarisse the waitress are notably crude. In the journal he compares her to 'an educated cow',[5] which becomes the scarcely less unflattering 'performing cow' in the *Travels*, and in both texts he tells us: 'Before I left I assured Clarisse of my hearty admiration', which brings to mind Squire Western bestowing a hearty kiss on a serving-wench, or Lord Byron on his travels, taking advantage of a chambermaid. This raffish tone seems like an attempt by Stevenson to disguise with male sexual bluster his actual frustration, what Richard Holmes calls 'his intense sexual loneliness and longing for Fanny Osbourne'.[6] Uncertainty about his own sexual future leads to unsteadiness in his tone when he writes about women in the *Travels*; he writes like a man who has recently become aware of his erotic desires but has yet to discover how they may be satisfied. One need not go all the way with Holmes's thesis that *Travels with a Donkey* is largely the cryptic record of

Stevenson's yearnings for his future wife in order to agree that one of the things that concerned him during his journey, and that is apparent in his account of it, is his relationship with Fanny, as well as the larger question of his sexual life.

Stevenson said after the book was published that 'lots of it is mere protestations to F'.[7] One of the climactic scenes, 'A Night among the Pines', bears this out. Leaving Le Bleymard in the evening, he makes a start on the steep climb towards the highest point of his journey and pitches camp, under the sky. After a few hours' sleep he wakes, and lies looking at the stars and listening to the sounds of life around him. Tranquillity brings spiritual thoughts, but even as they arise Stevenson admits to feeling a certain lack: 'I wished a companion to lie near me in the starlight ... to live out of doors with the woman a man loves is of all lives the most complete and free.' It can hardly be doubted that he is thinking of Fanny here. Yet he does not make anything explicit, even in the slightly wordier version of the passage in the journal, but instead turns his thought into a generalization on the link between a moment of communing with nature and romantic love. Given the uncertainty of the future of his relationship with Fanny, the expression of desire for female companionship carries with it a foreboding that he himself may not be destined to enjoy it.

Such melancholy feelings of exclusion are also conveyed by one late instance of encounter with the female. Towards the end of 'The Heart of the Country' (and towards the end of his travels), Stevenson descends through the trees to St-Germain-de-Calberte and hears 'the voice of a woman singing some sad, old, endless ballad not far off. It seemed to be about love and a *bel amoureux*'. Holmes is correct, surely, in seeing this moment as a parallel to Wordsworth's poem 'The Solitary Reaper' (which, intriguingly, has a Scottish setting), even although in the *Travels* the text adds a diversionary reference to Browning's Pippa.[8] Stevenson, like Wordsworth unable to communicate with the singer in person, elaborates for himself on the meaning of her song: on how the world 'brings sweethearts near, only to separate them again into distant and strange lands'. That remark, added to the journal as Stevenson was transforming it into the

Travels for the press, surely looks forward to his next journey.

There are signs, then, that beneath the surface, and sometimes hardly that, *Travels with a Donkey* is not just a charming counterpart to *An Inland Voyage* – at any rate in terms of Stevenson's biography. The polished appearance of the text covers a struggle in the writer over his hopes for the future. In this context his remarks about the people he meets, and especially about married couples, take on significance. They also reflect his attitude to himself, or rather the studied emptiness of his self-projection in the book.[9] The narrator in *Travels with a Donkey*, and later in *The Amateur Emigrant*, is very much an unformed character, one who adapts himself to varying circumstances without really committing himself fully to any. We have already seen him playing the man-about-town, the shy bachelor, the scholar gypsy and the Wordsworthian passer-by. There is a great deal of role-playing in Stevenson's presentation of himself in the *Travels*, which possibly reflects the author's experimentation with life itself. Alone and among strangers, Stevenson could try out various personalities, free of the expectations of those who knew him. Yet if *Travels with a Donkey* is a record of some of the ways he sought to deal with his troubled feelings by performing different versions of himself, there is no reason to doubt that the feelings themselves were genuine. It seems that he made his solitary journey at least partly to give himself the chance to consider what he was going to do about his life.

But if one of the dilemmas that Stevenson agonized over in the Cévennes had to do with his fears that he had lost both Fanny and his best chance of sexual fulfilment (bearing in mind that, knowing his own constitution, he could hardly count on a long life in which to meet another woman like her), that is not the only issue raised between the lines of *Travels with a Donkey*. Although he had set himself at odds with his parents by declaring his disbelief in their Christianity, Stevenson chose to go to the Cévennes because of their association with the Protestant Camisards, whose early-eighteenth-century struggle against state persecution parallels that of the Scottish Covenanters a few decades before. Since the day in January 1873 when he had candidly confessed to his father his lack of belief there had been a gloomy and sometimes quarrelsome difference between them that may be hard to understand in the twenty-first century, when religious differences are for many of relatively low importance. Thomas Stevenson was deeply dismayed by the atheism of his only son and felt that it rendered his own life meaningless; Louis, on his side, was depressed to find that he had ruined the happiness of the two people in the world who cared most about him, and almost wished he had not told them the truth. Thomas, however, had not ceased to support his penniless son, even after Louis's determination to become a writer had ended any hope that he would take up a respectable profession. One can imagine that, because he was still so beholden to those he had insisted on offending, mingled with Stevenson's continued love and respect for his parents were more galling feelings. Intellectual independence came at a price he could not really yet afford.

The frequent references to religion in *Travels with a Donkey* suggest that it was a gnawing anxiety in Stevenson at this time. Yet he seems to have gone out of his way to rouse it. The central episode of the first part of the book is the visit to the monastery of Our Lady of the Snows, to reach which he had to leave his main route and make a deliberate detour. Of course, to one brought up in the Presbyterian Church of Scotland a Trappist monastery may be an exotic curiosity well worth a detour, but Stevenson's account of his visit is not merely touristic. His encounter with the retired French soldier and the local priest who, on learning that he has been brought up as a Protestant, attempt to convert him to their Catholic faith, brings out Stevenson's uneasy spiritual state in the *Travels*. Having put himself in the weak position of not initially admitting his beliefs, he not only fails to deny that he is some sort of Christian but ends up hotly defending his right to hold the faith of his father and mother.

Equally significant is the context of these debates. Stevenson's account of the life of the monks is not without admiration on his part and a sense that he is assessing their way of life with respect to his own. We ought to take seriously the last line of the epigraph preceding the section 'Father Apollinaris' in the published version, from Matthew Arnold (another questioning Victorian): 'And what am I, that I am here?' In the journal his analysis of the monastic life leads Stevenson to end the section 'The Monks' with serious reflections on the nature of prayer, and three prayers of his own.[10] All this was kept out of the published *Travels*, however, where instead he blesses God that he is 'free to wander, free to hope, and free to love', three quite unfocused desires. A comparison of the two passages suggests not only that the prayerful text of the journal 'was just too personal and . . . part of an emotional "autobiography" he was not prepared, at that date at least, to deliver up to his readers',[11] but also that Stevenson's mind swung between a serious desire for the spiritual comfort of religious belief and an often rather jeering rejection of religion as a delusion, a distraction from the real pleasures and struggles of life. The point is that at least at this period of his life the issue was not fully resolved. It might still have gone either way.

Another sign of this is his encounter, towards the end of 'In the Valley of the Tarn', with the old man on the road to La Vernède who asks him, 'Do you know the Lord?' Stevenson's answer is equivocal and leads the man to think he is a fellow-believer. This is, as Stevenson admits, in questionable taste, and not made easier to understand by his addressing the old man as 'father' and continuing with a complicated argument intended to excuse his deception as forgivable because he hopes that we shall all in the end 'come together into one common house'. It is hard to deny that for a while that morning Stevenson indulged himself by imagining a Christian fellowship with the old man, a fulfilment of a Protestant ideal of companionship in life's journey that picks up the allusions in *Travels with a Donkey* to *Pilgrim's Progress*, John Bunyan's famous allegory of a Christian's journey through life. (There is a prominent reference to Bunyan (1628–88) in this very passage.)

A few pages later, in the town of Cassagnas, Stevenson once again finds himself with Protestants, who deplore the case of a Catholic priest who has renounced his vow of celibacy and settled down there with a schoolmistress. Public opinion is against the ex-priest, holding that 'It is a bad idea for a man . . .

to go back from his engagements.' In the journal Stevenson comments that perhaps 'the bad idea was to enter into them at the first',[12] but this was omitted from the published version. The relevance to his own situation of the argument about changing one's beliefs is, however, clear enough. Conversely, there is the slightly earlier encounter with the Catholic shepherd in the valley of the Mimente who makes no shame of his religion, despite living in a Protestant region. Stevenson says of him that 'he could not vary from his faith, unless he could eradicate all memory of the past, and, in a strict and not a conventional meaning, change his mind'. He cannot have written this without being conscious that he himself had varied from his faith, and must therefore not only have changed his mind but in some sense altered his memory of the past. It is striking, then, that this, as a note to the 1978 edition of the journal points out,[13] is the only paragraph in it that refers to the Camisards.

As mentioned above, one reason for Stevenson's choice of the Cévennes for his journey was the Camisard revolt of 1702–05. After Louis XIV's renunciation in 1685 of the Edict of Nantes, which in 1598 had granted a measure of tolerance to French Protestants, efforts to impose Roman Catholicism on the people of the Cévennes had provoked an armed uprising. The war was notable for bloody deeds and bloody reprisals on both sides, accompanied by official incompetence, political and military, until Marshal Villars, by a combination of good tactics and effective diplomacy, defeated the rebels and pacified the region. Protestantism there was suppressed, but survived clandestinely until it achieved some legal recognition in 1787 at the time of the French Revolution, although some restrictions were to remain until 1950. For Stevenson the Camisards were a fascination because of their resemblance to the Scottish Covenanters, those Protestants, mainly in the south-west of Scotland, who for almost thirty years were persecuted for their refusal to accept Charles II, after his restoration to the throne in 1660, as head of the Church. Among Stevenson's juvenile writings had been an account of the Battle of Rullion Green in 1666, where an early rising of the Covenanters had been defeated in the Pentland Hills just south of Edinburgh. So pleased had Thomas Stevenson been with this essay by his son that he had had a hundred copies printed and bound as a small pamphlet.

This sufficiently illustrates the connection in Stevenson's mind between the Covenanters and his father, but it should be added that they had a much wider significance in nineteenth-century Scotland. The Covenanters, who had chosen prosecution and sometimes death rather than compromise their religious principles, had become recognized as the martyrs of the Scottish Church. Their heroic resistance to attempts by the state to impose its will on the Church was held up as an example of true allegiance to religious principle and of the independence of Church and state. These matters had come to a head again in 1843 with the Disruption of the Church of Scotland, when a large number of ministers and congregations had split away to form a separate body calling itself the Free Church of Scotland. Quite apart from the social and political aftermath of the Disruption, Stevenson would have been familiar with the earlier controversy caused by Sir Walter Scott's novel *Old Mortality* (1816), which had portrayed the Covenanters as wild fanatics and their opponent, James Graham of Claverhouse, as a dashing cavalier – not 'Bluidy Clavers', but 'Bonnie Dundee'. Scott's contradiction of Presbyterian iconography (he himself was an Episcopalian) had provoked literary and other responses on behalf of the Scottish martyrs. More generally, Scott's revisionist view of the Covenanters broaches the issue of what a nation takes from its past to construct its sense of itself. For Stevenson as a Scot the historical meaning of the Covenanters and the Camisards raises not just the question of his relationship with his father but also that of his nation's past, and more personally his own attitude to that past. How much was he, like his fellow-Scots, including his father, dependent on the received traditions of his country? One way to answer this question might be to look at a similar case in another country.

In expanding his journal with the history of the Camisards for the published *Travels*, Stevenson was not simply 'filling it out with historical details', as Ian Bell says,[14] but trying to make the connection between the country he had traversed and the history that had made its people. Hence his allusions in these later sections of the *Travels* to the Covenanters and his interest in the attitudes of the people he meets to their religion and to that of others. Hence also his religious role-playing, his experiments with himself and his beliefs. Partly this stems from a sense that beliefs can be altered by circumstance, but it is also an attempt to see what becomes of one's self if one tries to change from what one was brought up as. The Camisard revolt had been about a fierce resistance to forced change; two hundred years later, what had changed?

Richard Holmes concludes that for Stevenson 'the whole Cévennes experience was a kind of initiation ceremony: a grappling with physical hardships, loneliness, religious doubts, the influence of his parents, and the overwhelming question of whether he should take the enormous risk of travelling to America and throwing his life in with Fanny's'.[15] What is not so clear is how far Stevenson had resolved his problems. There is a sense of haste at the end of both *Travels with a Donkey* and the journal on which it is based which seems to reflect his anxiety to end his journey and reach Alès: his eagerness centres on the letters he expected to be waiting for him there. Perhaps he hoped for something in them that would settle some of his doubts and signal his way forward, but if so he seems to have been disappointed, to judge by his actions over the next year.

He had returned to England by November 1878 and was in Edinburgh for Christmas. Besides working on *Travels with a Donkey* he was also collaborating with W. E. Henley on a play, *Deacon Brodie* (published in 1892), based on the life of Deacon William Brodie, the Edinburgh magistrate and burglar who was eventually hanged on a gibbet of his own devising. This project was intended to make money and was clearly driven for Stevenson by his desire to fund a new life with Fanny, or at least pay for a journey across the Atlantic and the USA to be with her. In the event the play, although it was to see performance, was not a success and certainly no money-spinner. Henley's part in persuading Stevenson to put so much energy into an abortive drama at this time is suspicious, as he was one of the friends most opposed to his relationship with Fanny and to his joining her in America. Stevenson's state of mind in the first seven months of 1879 must have been unpleasant. He could not speak openly of his hopes and feelings with his parents, and his literary friends were almost to a man silently wishing that the separation from Fanny would become permanent and that Stevenson would return to being the bright young man of letters they thought was his destiny. The letters he received from America were of little comfort, providing no clear indication either of what Fanny wanted him to do or of an end to her marriage to Samuel Osbourne.

Travels with a Donkey was rapidly finished and published in June 1879, less than a year after the journey it describes. Reviews were generally favourable, though some felt the book had more style than substance.[16] Sales were not great. Stevenson received £30 and thought he should have had £50; he had told Henley that he needed to make £350 for the year. He was desperate enough to apply to the London *Times* for some sort of journalistic employment. Possibly he hoped the paper would pay for him to go to the United States, but if so he was disappointed. Then, at the end of July, he decided to go to Fanny in America. It is said he took this decision after receiving a telegram from her while he was staying with his parents at their out-of-town house at Swanston, south of Edinburgh. What the telegram said nobody knows; biographers have speculated that it brought bad news about Fanny's health. At any rate, Stevenson now made hurried arrangements to leave for America, although he said nothing of his plans to his parents. The few friends whom he did tell tried vainly to dissuade him. On 7 August 1879 he sailed from Greenock for New York on the Anchor Line steamship *Devonia*.

He went under the inadequate pseudonym 'Robert Stephenson', paying eight guineas to travel as a second-cabin passenger, two guineas more expensive than going steerage, for which he received the privileges he describes in 'The Second Cabin', at the beginning of *The Amateur Emigrant*. One real advantage for Stevenson was access to a table at which he could write, for he intended to use the voyage to complete at least one story and to write the notes which would in time become 'From the Clyde to Sandy Hook', the first part of *The Amateur Emigrant*. It is reasonable to conclude that, quite apart from economizing, he chose to travel in this way for the purpose of reporting on the experience of crossing the Atlantic on an emigrant ship, in the hope that ultimately the trip would pay for itself.

As Stevenson's remarks on his fellow-passengers make clear, by the late 1870s transatlantic emigration had entered a phase rather different from its heroic, pioneering image. The emigrants on the *Devonia* were not young and vigorous individuals rising to the challenge of a new continent. As Stevenson says in 'Early Impressions', relatively few were young, some were indeed 'already up in years', and most were 'people who had seen better days'. They were not going to America because of a yearning for adventure or to create a new life but to escape adverse economic conditions at home. Stevenson clearly saw that most of his fellow-passengers were part of the growing stream of unskilled, mainly urban workers, shaken out of their jobs by recession in Europe, that was now flowing to America – and like as not flowing back again, since the demand for unskilled labour there was also low. Later in *The Amateur Emigrant*, in 'Fellow-Passengers', Stevenson will note that as his train moves west towards California it is passed by others moving east, also laden with emigrants. And even in his 'early impressions' of the *Devonia* he concludes: 'We were a shipful of failures, the broken men of England.'

It is noticeable that Stevenson seems to include himself in this description. The tendency evident in *Travels with a Donkey* to identify with the people he meets is apparent in *The Amateur Emigrant* too. He has to begin the text with his explanation of the difference between steerage and second-cabin passengers because otherwise the reader would undoubtedly feel he was one of the former, of whom he goes on to say so much. Indeed, even after he defines himself as not a steerage passenger, it is difficult to keep a hold of the distinction as one reads on. Of course, due credit should be given to Stevenson's desire to give a voice to the poorest emigrants, to describe the voyage from the point of view of those making it in the cheapest and most underprivileged way. Commentators on *The Amateur Emigrant* are right to see it as at least in part a social protest at the treatment of steerage passengers,[17] but Stevenson's readiness to include himself in the 'company of the rejected' on the *Devonia* confirms that he made the journey in the lowest spirits.

Significant, too, are some of the kinds of people he dwells upon. In one of the longest sections in the book, 'The Stowaways', Stevenson gives extended character sketches of the men he calls Alick and 'the Devonian'. The first, 'Scots by birth, and by trade a practical engineer', bears more than a slight resemblance to Stevenson himself – perhaps an imaginary Stevenson of a later date, plausible, eloquent, humorous and reduced to living off his wits, having no settled place in society. Alick conjures up an image of Stevenson's fear of a future in which he has lost his connections with friends and family and become a drifter. His comments on Alick's natural talents, and his abuse of them, betray Stevenson's own anxiety about the outcome of the adventure he has embarked on, and that, if things go badly wrong, he might become such another habitual middle-aged sponger.

The other stowaway presents a more immediately relevant image, but no less disturbing. The Devonian is a young man well down on his luck, driven by poverty down the social scale to the point of so far losing the appearance of respectability that he becomes unemployable, despite a genuine willingness to work. Compared with the unscrupulous Alick, the Devonian comes across as a man of principle and goodness of heart, modest and willing to serve. As such, however, he is easily exploited by Alick and seems to exemplify the vulnerability of innocence in the world. Again it is possible to imagine Stevenson thinking of himself here. He is nearer in age to the Devonian than to Alick, and the former's outcast state must have felt close to his own as he sailed into an unknown future, having, he had to suppose, broken the link with his family by not telling them that he was going, or why. If his mission should fail, if Fanny should reject him and he was left to fend for himself in a world where he had deliberately cut himself off from those who had previously supported him, then he too might become just another young man trying to climb back up the social ladder. Stevenson's acute awareness of the nuances of status on the

Devonia, in his comments on how the first-class, or saloon, passengers and the ship's officers treated the steerage passengers, and even second-cabin passengers like himself, demonstrates his sensitivity to the risks he was taking in allowing himself to slip down the social scale.

It hardly needs to be said that in this and in a multitude of other respects *The Amateur Emigrant* is a book centred on liminality. As Andrew Noble puts it, 'this is a book concerned with crossing multiple, interconnected boundaries: from Scotland to America; from being an upper-middle-class, slightly spoiled writer to mixing with a far lower social stratum; from being single to becoming married'.[18] *Travels with a Donkey* also has liminal themes, both geographical and social, as well as personal. Both texts attest to Stevenson's sense that he was facing a life-changing crisis in these years, but *The Amateur Emigrant* is the more pessimistic. His fellow-passengers clearly do not support the easy notion that change of place will bring about change of fortune.

Stevenson's liminal state in *The Amateur Emigrant* is most clearly seen in his role as narrator. As in *Travels with a Donkey* there is a distance between him and those he moves amongst, for all the signs of sympathy with them. Although penned up with his fellow-passengers on board ship and then train, he retains his anonymity. However spuriously, he maintains a sense of individuality at the centre of his being, refusing to do things exactly as others do. On board the *Devonia* he insists on fresh air and sleeps on deck. He refuses to divulge his profession, preferring to remain a mystery to his companions. His use of a pseudonym seems to have been part of a much more elaborate attempt to mask himself, as though he was both unwilling to own up to his past and yet equally reluctant to commit himself to the present and the future. Instead, he passes through the scenes he records as an undefined observer.

Once in the United States he seems even more alienated from other people. Hardly anyone he meets is given a name and no sustained relationships are described – naturally enough, given that more often than not he leaves behind any acquaintances he makes, or they get off at the next station. By the end of the journey the narrative has shrivelled to a series of place-names and remarks on the landscape. This was undoubtedly due to Stevenson's physical state by this point. Ill enough when he landed in New York, after several days in the cramped and evil-smelling railroad cars of the emigrant trains he had lost all appetite for food and sleep and was barely keeping himself alive with the hope of seeing Fanny at the end of the journey (though she is never referred to in the text, even indirectly – she remains a personal secret). Yet the list of place-names is evocative in itself. So many of these towns had hardly existed a few years earlier, before the railway had reached across the continent, and they must have seemed almost unreal to the traveller in the sudden newness of their sparse buildings, appearing for the most part in the middle of nowhere. A feature of the account of the rail journey across America is the sense Stevenson gives of the stark contrast between the signs of human activity and the vastness of the land itself, most strikingly at the beginning of 'The Plains of Nebraska': 'It was a world almost without a feature; an empty sky, an empty earth; front and back, the line of railway stretched from horizon to horizon, like a cue across a billiard-board; on either hand, the green plain ran till it touched the skirts of heaven.' No wonder if in such an arena Stevenson felt even more helpless and alone.

Of course, the tone of *The Amateur Emigrant* may be as much due to his state when he wrote up his notes as to his frame of mind when he made them en route. When he reached California there was no easy end to his troubles. Fanny had moved from San Francisco to Monterey, about a hundred miles down the coast. When he finally arrived, worn out and ragged, a scarecrow of a man, Stevenson found the woman he had come so far to be with oddly undecided about what she wanted of him. Typically, he took himself off on a lone camping trip, despite his weakened state, and nearly died of exhaustion. He was brought back to Monterey, where he found new friends to take care of him, living separately from Fanny and her children, trying to write to make some money. By the end of 1879 he had moved after Fanny back to San Francisco. At last her divorce from Sam Osbourne had been completed and it was but a matter of waiting a decent interval before they married. They still lived apart, until illness intervened again. Stevenson began bleeding from the lungs, the first real sign of tuberculosis; it is difficult not to think he had brought this on by his terrible journey from Scotland to San Francisco. Now Fanny took him in and became his nurse.

The turning-point was a telegram from Thomas Stevenson in April 1880 promising his son an annual allowance of £250. How he had learned of Louis's plight is unknown; some biographers have surmised Fanny wrote directly to him. The message meant that not only was Stevenson reconciled with his family but also that he could afford to become a married man. On 19 May the wedding took place in San Francisco. Partly because it was cheap, and partly because the high altitude was thought good for Louis's lungs, the couple spent their honeymoon, with Fanny's son Lloyd, in the abandoned buildings of the silver mine which is the main setting for Stevenson's next travel book, *The Silverado Squatters* (1883). A few months later they all set out for Scotland, and hardly a year after leaving it Stevenson returned to the land of his birth, with a wife and a stepson (his step-daughter had married before he did, after eloping with a painter, Joseph Dwight Strong, in early 1879).

'From the Clyde to Sandy Hook' was sent to Sidney Colvin in December 1879. Stevenson had therefore been writing it during the period of illness and uncertainty at the end of that year. No wonder, then, if it seems gloomy and pessimistic, though this accords well enough with the subject-matter. But the change in tone and content from his earlier writings alarmed Colvin and others who saw the work, and they tried to discourage its publication. A few months later, but before his marriage, Stevenson sent Colvin the second part of the book, 'Across the Plains'. This was more favourably received, although there were still passages that were found offensive. Stevenson had fleshed out the account of the later stages of his journey across the United States with essays reflecting on the treatment of what he called 'despised races'. Just as with his comments on the way the Anchor Line treated its steerage passengers, there was much here to alarm his friends. The plain-speaking social conscience Stevenson had acquired on his journey seemed to them to threaten his reputation as a writer of agreeable essays and travelogues.

Nevertheless Stevenson persisted, if only because, until his father renewed his allowance, he could not afford not to try to publish all he wrote. He was, however, willing to compromise for the sake of publication and agreed to a number of cuts in both parts of the book, removing almost a third of the first, though less of the second. In this form the book was almost in the press when, convinced by Colvin that it would damage his son's reputation, Thomas Stevenson insisted on paying for its withdrawal from the publisher. Although a version of 'Across the Plains' would be published in 1883 in *Longman's Magazine*, and with other essays in book form in 1892, *The Amateur Emigrant* as a whole would not appear, even in its bowdlerized form, until after Stevenson's death.

A very significant element was therefore missing from the picture of Stevenson that his works presented to the world after his death. It is well known that his widow did her best to protect and project her view of him as a romantic writer of wholesome and elegant fiction, suitable for family reading, an image of Stevenson that soon led those who were anxious to debunk Victorian pieties to attack his literary reputation and do their best to consign him to the nursery as only a writer for children. Stevenson's early association with the late Victorian men of letters came back to haunt him in the twentieth century, not least because it fell to Sidney Colvin (d. 1927) to edit his works and his letters, under Fanny's censorious eye. The disquieting side of Stevenson which is discernible in *The Amateur Emigrant* (and not absent from *Travels with a Donkey*) – his interest in the virtues of ordinary people in unromantic circumstances, his independent ideas about authority and its exercise, his reflections on how we are shaped by culture and geography, his mistrust of dogmatism and his doubts about the wholeness of the self – might have been more readily noticed in his work if 'From the Clyde to Sandy Hook' had been available earlier in its original form.

So too would have been the development of Stevenson as a writer, and the importance of the years 1878 and 1879 in that development. Not that these years represent a sudden and complete conversion: after the Cévennes, the Atlantic and the Plains Stevenson was undoubtedly a changed man, but he was still capable of the kind of writing he had done before – essays, travelogue and minor fiction. It would take some years for some of the lessons he had learned to bear fruit, in, for example, the vivid descriptions of the hardships of travel in *Kidnapped* (1886) and the sense there of a countryside where historic deeds have happened, with a young man blundering across it into their aftermath; or in the fractures of personality in *The Strange Case of Dr Jekyll and Mr Hyde* (1886) and *The Master of Ballantrae* (1889). These works are of course fiction, but perhaps in them Stevenson was just disguising what in his factual narratives Fanny and Colvin found so unsuitable; or perhaps for Stevenson there is really no difference and, just as his writings about the South Seas form the fertile ground for his magnificent late stories, so the experiences recorded in *Travels with a Donkey* and *The Amateur Emigrant* feed into the novels that were to make his reputation less than a decade later.

NOTES

1. Although Stevenson's second name was spelled 'Lewis' at his birth, from his early childhood the family spelled it 'Louis', and that became the accepted way.

2. David Daiches, *Robert Louis Stevenson* (Glasgow: William Maclellan, 1947), p. 17.

3. Richard Holmes, *Footsteps* (London: Hodder & Stoughton, 1985), p. 38.

4. Gordon Golding (ed.), *The Cévennes Journal* (Edinburgh: Mainstream Publishing, 1978), p. 38.

5. ibid., p. 91.

6. Holmes, *Footsteps*, p. 56.

7. Bradford A. Booth and Ernest Mehew (eds), *The Letters of Robert Louis Stevenson* (New Haven: Yale University Press, 1994–5), vol. 2, letter to Bob Stevenson, April 1879, p. 313.

8. The heroine of *Pippa Passes* (1841) by Robert Browning (1812–89).

9. In an essay on Stevenson's travel writings James Wilson claims

that travel writing allowed Stevenson to 'reveal himself ... The travel books and the letters allowed him his nearest approach to autobiography, to a full-length self-portrait' ('Landscape with Figures', in Andrew Noble (ed.), *Robert Louis Stevenson* (London and Totowa, NJ: Vision and Barnes & Noble, 1983), p. 90) but in fact the figure of the narrator in *Travels with a Donkey*, and later in *The Amateur Emigrant*, is surely much more elusive than that.

10. Golding (ed.), *Cévennes Journal*, pp. 68–9.
11. Holmes, *Footsteps*, p. 33.
12. Golding (ed.), *Cévennes Journal*, p. 112.
13. ibid., p. 157.
14. Ian Bell, *Dreams of Exile* (Edinburgh: Mainstream Publishing, 1992), p. 141.
15. Holmes, *Footsteps*, p. 65.
16. See Paul Maixner (ed.), *Robert Louis Stevenson: The Critical Heritage* (London: Routledge & Kegan Paul, 1981), pp. 62–74.
17. See Andrew Noble's introduction to *From the Clyde to California: Robert Louis Stevenson's Emigrant Journey* (Aberdeen: Aberdeen University Press, 1985 (Noble's edition of *The Amateur Emigrant*)), pp. 3–33.
18. Noble, *From the Clyde to California*, p. 6.

Further Reading

EDITIONS OF STEVENSON'S WORKS

Edinburgh Edition, ed. Sidney Colvin (London: Chatto & Windus, 1894–8), 28 vols.

Pentland Edition, with bibliographical notes by Edmund Gosse (London: Cassell, 1906–7), 20 vols.

Swanston Edition, with an introduction by Andrew Lang (London: Chatto & Windus, 1911–12), 25 vols.

Vailima Edition, ed. Lloyd Osbourne and Fanny Van de Grift Stevenson (London: Heinemann, 1922–3), 26 vols.

Tusitala Edition, with prefaces and introductions by Lloyd Osbourne and Fanny Van de Grift Stevenson (London: Heinemann, 1923–4), 35 vols.

Waverley Edition (London: Waverley Book Company, 1924–5), 26 vols.

BOOKS AND ARTICLES ON STEVENSON

Bell, Ian, *Robert Louis Stevenson: Dreams of Exile* (Edinburgh: Mainstream Publishing, 1992). A well-written recent biography.

Booth, Bradford A., and Ernest Mehew (eds), *The Letters of Robert Louis Stevenson* (New Haven: Yale University Press, 1994–5). The standard edition of Stevenson's letters, in 8 volumes. Vols. 2 and 3 cover the periods of *Travels with a Donkey* and *The Amateur Emigrant*, although there are few letters from the latter, since Stevenson was concealing his plans from most of his family and friends, and at odds with them once he reached America.

Castle, Alan, *The Robert Louis Stevenson Trail* (Milnthorpe: Cicerone Press, 1992). A modern guide to Stevenson's route through the Cévennes, with details of accommodation, restaurants, tourist offices, things to see and distances between places. Fully illustrated with maps and photographs.

Daiches, David, *Robert Louis Stevenson* (Glasgow: William Maclellan, 1947). An early study of Stevenson which still has interesting things to say about his travel writing.

Furnas, J. C., *Voyage to Windward* (London: Faber & Faber, 1952). Usually regarded as the standard biography of Stevenson. Full of detail, and presents a balanced view of its subject.

Golding, Gordon (ed.), *The Cévennes Journal: Notes on a Journey through the French Highlands* (Edinburgh: Mainstream Publishing, 1978; New York: Taplinger Publishing, 1979). The first publication of the journal upon which *Travels with a Donkey* is based, this book has a wealth of notes and other information about Stevenson and the Cévennes, much of it from the French point of view.

Hart, James D. (ed.), *From Scotland to Silverado* (Cambridge, Mass.: Belknap Press of Harvard University Press, 1966). An edition of *The Amateur Emigrant* and other of Stevenson's American travel writings with a full introduction and useful notes.

Holmes, Richard, *Footsteps* (London: Hodder & Stoughton, 1985). Chapter 1, '1964: Travels', is an account of a journey retracing Stevenson's path through the Cévennes and speculating on the motives for his travels (see the Introduction to the present edition).

Mackay, Margaret, *The Violent Friend: The Story of Mrs Robert Louis Stevenson, 1840–1914* (New York: Doubleday, 1968; abridged edition, London: Dent, 1969). A biography of Fanny Osbourne, Stevenson's wife.

Maixner, Paul (ed.), *Robert Louis Stevenson: The Critical Heritage* (London: Routledge & Kegan Paul, 1981). Reprints the earliest reviews of all Stevenson's works, along

with discussion of his career and selected comments from
Stevenson himself.

Noble, Andrew, *From the Clyde to California: Robert Louis
Stevenson's Emigrant Journey* (Aberdeen: Aberdeen University
Press, 1985). Another edition of *The Amateur Emigrant*,
with a long and challenging introduction, notes and some
excellent illustrations.

Wilson, James, 'Landscape with Figures', in Andrew Noble
(ed.), *Robert Louis Stevenson* (London and Totowa, NJ:
Vision and Barnes & Noble, 1983), pp. 73–95. An essay
on Stevenson's travel writing which includes comment on
Travels with a Donkey and *The Amateur Emigrant*.

ONLINE RESOURCES

The Robert Louis Stevenson Website
  http://wwwesterni.unibg.it/siti_esterni/rls/rls.htm
  A gateway to information about Stevenson on the Web, with
  illustrations and biographical details.

Robert Louis Stevenson Trail
  http://users.skynet.be/sky42224/RLS-Trail.html
  A thoroughly illustrated description of Stevenson's route
  through the Cévennes as it is today, in French but with an
  introductory page in English.

Association 'Sur le Chemin de Robert Louis Stevenson'
  http://www.chemin-stevenson.org
  The website of a group of tourism professionals interested in
  developing the Stevenson trail through the Cévennes. The site
  has an English version and is richly illustrated with photographs and other images.

Robert Louis Stevenson GR70
  http://www.gr70-stevenson.com
  A site offering links to tourist information about places in
  the Cévennes connected with Stevenson's journey, including
  walks along his route. Text mainly in French, but with many
  illustrations.

Camisards.net
> http://www.camisards.net
> Camisard history, biography, documents, bibliography and much else, in French, with some English translations.

The Ships List
> http://www.theshipslist.com/index.html
> A site with detailed information about nineteenth-century transatlantic and other emigrant ships.

1895 US Atlas
> http://www.livgenmi.com/1895/
> An atlas showing railroad routes, and searchable for individual place-names, of the USA not long after Stevenson crossed the country.

Central Pacific Railroad Photographic History Museum
> http://www.cprr.org/Museum
> A webpage that includes maps and other images of the Central Pacific Railroad at the end of the nineteenth century.

A Note on the Texts

The published text of *Travels with a Donkey in the Cévennes* (1879) is based on the journal Stevenson kept on his journey through the Cévennes. This lacks the first and last two sections of the published *Travels* and there are a number of other differences, many stylistic. The published version is more polished, and some of the differences are substantial. In his 1978 edition of the journal Gordon Golding lists thirteen passages which were omitted from *Travels with a Donkey*, although many are short and none more than a few pages. For the published edition, on the other hand, Stevenson added most of the material on the Camisards in the later chapters and extensively revised some earlier episodes, notably the ending of 'The Monks' and the climax of 'A Night among the Pines'.

It is indisputable that the published version of *Travels with a Donkey* represents Stevenson's preferred version of the text, and as well as being the one familiar to readers it is also fuller than the Cévennes journal. The text used here is therefore *Travels with a Donkey in the Cévennes*, from volume XV of the Waverley Edition (London: The Waverley Book Company, 1925), while the notes to the present edition indicate some of the more significant variations and omissions from the journal. These are taken from *The Cévennes Journal: Notes on a Journey through the French Highlands*, edited by Gordon Golding (Edinburgh: Mainstream Publishing; New York: Taplinger Publishing, 1979). I am grateful for permission to quote from the text of this edition, and occasionally to quote from its very interesting notes.

*

The case of *The Amateur Emigrant* is almost the reverse. Whereas the *Travels* might be said to represent an expansion of the original journal upon which it is based, the versions of *The Amateur Emigrant* published partly during and just after Stevenson's lifetime are seriously truncated forms of what he originally intended to publish. The second section, 'Across the Plains', appeared in *Longman's Magazine* in July and August 1883 and then with other essays in book form in 1892, but with substantial cuts to the text. The first section, 'From the Clyde to Sandy Hook', only appeared after the author's death in an edition of *The Amateur Emigrant* published in 1895 as the third volume of the Edinburgh Edition of Stevenson's works edited by his friend Sidney Colvin. Since Colvin had been one of those who opposed Stevenson's plans to publish *The Amateur Emigrant* as written, it is not surprising that his 1895 text retains the cuts made earlier to 'Across the Plains' and prints a similarly edited version of 'From the Clyde to Sandy Hook'.

Who was responsible for these cuts is not very clear; in his later years, working in America and then in Samoa, Stevenson relied on collaborators in England, Colvin in particular, to see his writings through the press. There is some evidence that Stevenson agreed to alter his original text for publication, but the published book seems to be largely the result of Colvin's editing. Although some of his cuts do improve the text, many are evident bowdlerizing and some are simply puzzling. The chief omissions are some of Stevenson's more trenchant remarks on the treatment of emigrants aboard ship and on social issues concerning the United States. These remarks were presumably suppressed by Colvin to avoid giving offence, a real enough danger in view of Stevenson's criticisms of the White Star Line and the US railroad companies, that are close to being libellous.

The manuscript on which the published version of *The Amateur Emigrant* is based is now in the Beinecke Rare Book and Manuscript Library at Yale University and has been published a number of times, notably by James D. Hart in *From Scotland to Silverado* (1966) and by Roger G. Swearingen in *The Amateur Emigrant with some First Impressions of America* (Ashland, Oregon: L. Osborne) (1976–7). I am grateful to the Beinecke

Rare Book and Manuscript Library for permission to quote extracts from this manuscript, as well as to James D. Hart and the Belknap Press of Harvard University Press for permission to quote from Hart's edition. Since it was clearly Stevenson's intention that the full version of his book should be published, and since in any case the additional passages contain much of great value – not only for Stevenson studies but for anyone interested in nineteenth-century emigration and in America in the 1870s – the text of *The Amateur Emigrant* given here, based primarily on that of the Tusitala Edition (London: Heinemann, 1924, volume XVIII), restores about ten thousand words, taken from Hart's edition and set in angle brackets, that are missing from the usual published versions.

Both published editions are reproduced here as they originally appeared – including Stevenson's spellings – save for the removal of full points after terms of address such as 'Mr' and 'Dr', the correction of obvious typographical errors, and the replacement of em-dashes with spaced en-dashes and of double quotation marks with single. The extracts from the manuscript of *The Amateur Emigrant* are exactly as they appear in Hart's edition.

Map 1. The Cévennes (Stevenson's spellings)

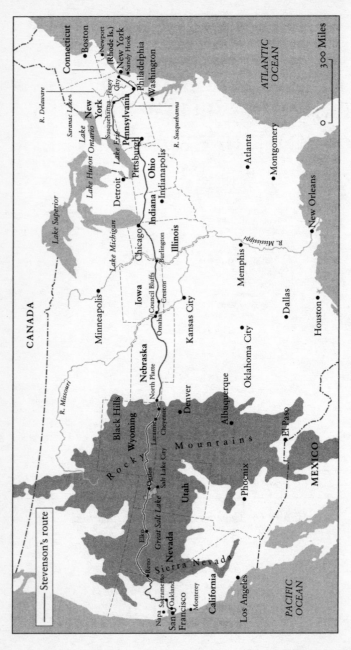

Map 2. Travelling across the USA

TRAVELS WITH A DONKEY IN THE CÉVENNES

Contents

THE COUNTRY OF THE CAMISARDS

DEDICATION

My dear Sidney Colvin,[1]

The journey which this little book is to describe was very agreeable and fortunate for me. After an uncouth beginning, I had the best of luck to the end. But we are all travellers in what John Bunyan[2] *calls the wilderness of this world – all, too, travellers with a donkey; and the best that we find in our travels is an honest friend. He is a fortunate voyager who finds many. We travel, indeed, to find them. They are the end and the reward of life. They keep us worthy of ourselves; and, when we are alone, we are only nearer to the absent.*

Every book is, in an intimate sense, a circular letter to the friends of him who writes it. They alone take his meaning; they find private messages, assurances of love, and expressions of gratitude dropped for them in every corner. The public is but a generous patron who defrays the postage. Yet though the letter is directed to all, we have an old and kindly custom of addressing it on the outside to one. Of what shall a man be proud, if he is not proud of his friends? And so, my dear Sidney Colvin, it is with pride that I sign myself

Affectionately yours,

R.L.S.

VELAY[1]

'Many are the mighty things, and naught is more mighty than
man . . . He masters by his devices the tenant of the fields.'
Sophocles.[2]

'Who hath loosed the bands of the wild ass?'
Job.[3]

The Donkey, the Pack, and the Pack-Saddle

In a little place called Le Monastier, in a pleasant highland valley
fifteen miles from Le Puy, I spent about a month of fine days.
Monastier is notable for the making of lace, for drunkenness, for
freedom of language, and for unparalleled political dissension.
There are adherents of each of the four French parties – Legitimists, Orleanists, Imperialists, and Republicans[4] – in this little
mountain-town; and they all hate, loathe, decry, and calumniate
each other. Except for business purposes, or to give each other
the lie in a tavern brawl, they have laid aside even the civility of
speech. 'Tis a mere mountain Poland. In the midst of this Babylon[5] I found myself a rallying-point; every one was anxious to
be kind and helpful to the stranger. This was not merely from
the natural hospitality of mountain people, nor even from the
surprise with which I was regarded as a man living of his own
free will in Le Monastier, when he might just as well have lived
anywhere else in this big world; it arose a good deal from
my projected excursion southward through the Cévennes. A
traveller of my sort was a thing hitherto unheard-of in that
district. I was looked upon with contempt, like a man who
should project a journey to the moon, but yet with a respectful
interest, like one setting forth for the inclement Pole. All were
ready to help in my preparations; a crowd of sympathisers

supported me at the critical moment of a bargain; not a step was taken but was heralded by glasses round and celebrated by a dinner or a breakfast.

It was already hard upon October before I was ready to set forth, and at the high altitudes over which my road lay there was no Indian summer to be looked for. I was determined, if not to camp out, at least to have the means of camping out in my possession; for there is nothing more harassing to an easy mind than the necessity of reaching shelter by dusk, and the hospitality of a village inn is not always to be reckoned sure by those who trudge on foot. A tent, above all for a solitary travel-ler, is troublesome to pitch, and troublesome to strike again; and even on the march it forms a conspicuous feature in your baggage. A sleeping-sack, on the other hand, is always ready – you have only to get into it; it serves a double purpose – a bed by night, a portmanteau by day; and it does not advertise your intention of camping out to every curious passer-by. This is a huge point. If the camp is not secret, it is but a troubled resting-place; you become a public character; the convivial rustic visits your bedside after an early supper; and you must sleep with one eye open, and be up before the day. I decided on a sleeping-sack; and after repeated visits to Le Puy, and a deal of high living for myself and my advisers, a sleeping-sack was designed, constructed, and triumphantly brought home.

This child of my invention was nearly six feet square, exclusive of two triangular flaps to serve as a pillow by night and as the top and bottom of the sack by day. I call it 'the sack,' but it was never a sack by more than courtesy: only a sort of long roll or sausage, green waterproof cart cloth without and blue sheep's fur within. It was commodious as a valise, warm and dry for a bed. There was luxurious turning room for one; and at a pinch the thing might serve for two. I could bury myself in it up to the neck; for my head I trusted to a fur cap, with a hood to fold down over my ears and a band to pass under my nose like a respirator; and in case of heavy rain I proposed to make myself a little tent, or tentlet, with my waterproof coat, three stones, and a bent branch.

It will readily be conceived that I could not carry this huge package on my own, merely human, shoulders. It remained to choose a beast of burden. Now, a horse is a fine lady among animals, flighty, timid, delicate in eating, of tender health; he is too valuable and too restive to be left alone, so that you are chained to your brute as to a fellow galley-slave; a dangerous road puts him out of his wits; in short, he's an uncertain and exacting ally, and adds thirty-fold to the troubles of the voyager. What I required was something cheap and small and hardy, and of a stolid and peaceful temper; and all these requisites pointed to a donkey.

There dwelt an old man in Monastier, of rather unsound intellect according to some, much followed by street-boys, and known to fame as Father Adam.[6] Father Adam had a cart, and to draw the cart a diminutive she-ass, not much bigger than a dog, the colour of a mouse, with a kindly eye and a determined under-jaw. There was something neat and high-bred, a quakerish elegance, about the rogue that hit my fancy on the spot. Our first interview was in Monastier market-place. To prove her good temper, one child after another was set upon her back to ride, and one after another went head over heels into the air; until a want of confidence began to reign in youthful bosoms, and the experiment was discontinued from a dearth of subjects. I was already backed by a deputation of my friends; but as if this were not enough, all the buyers and sellers came round and helped me in the bargain; and the ass and I and Father Adam were the centre of a hubbub for near half an hour. At length she passed into my service for the consideration of sixty-five francs and a glass of brandy. The sack had already cost eighty francs and two glasses of beer; so that Modestine, as I instantly baptised her, was upon all accounts the cheaper article. Indeed, that was as it should be; for she was only an appurtenance of my mattress, or self-acting bedstead on four castors.

I had a last interview with Father Adam in a billiard-room at the witching hour of dawn, when I administered the brandy. He professed himself greatly touched by the separation, and declared he had often bought white bread for the donkey when he had been content with black bread for himself; but this, according to the best authorities, must have been a flight of fancy. He had a name in the village for brutally misusing the ass; yet it is certain that he shed a tear, and the tear made a clean mark down one cheek.

By the advice of a fallacious local saddler, a leather pad was made for me with rings to fasten on my bundle; and I thoughtfully completed my kit and arranged my toilette. By way of armoury and utensils, I took a revolver, a little spirit-lamp and pan, a lantern and some halfpenny candles, a jack-knife and a large leather flask. The main cargo consisted of two entire changes of warm clothing – besides my travelling wear of country velveteen, pilot-coat, and knitted spencer[7] – some books, and my railway-rug, which, being also in the form of a bag, made me a double castle for cold nights. The permanent larder was represented by cakes of chocolate and tins of Bologna sausage.[8] All this, except what I carried about my person, was easily stowed into the sheepskin bag; and by good fortune I threw in my empty knapsack, rather for convenience of carriage than from any thought that I should want it on my journey. For more immediate needs, I took a leg of cold mutton, a bottle of Beaujolais, an empty bottle to carry milk, an egg-beater, and a considerable quantity of black bread and white, like Father Adam, for myself and donkey, only in my scheme of things the destinations were reversed.

Monastrians, of all shades of thought in politics, had agreed in threatening me with many ludicrous misadventures, and with sudden death in many surprising forms. Cold, wolves, robbers, above all the nocturnal practical joker, were daily and eloquently forced on my attention. Yet in these vaticinations, the true, patent danger was left out. Like Christian,[9] it was from my pack I suffered by the way. Before telling my own mishaps, let me, in two words, relate the lesson of my experience. If the pack is well strapped at the ends, and hung at full length – not doubled, for your life – across the pack-saddle, the traveller is safe. The saddle will certainly not fit, such is the imperfection of our transitory life; it will assuredly topple and tend to overset; but there are stones on every roadside, and a man soon learns the art of correcting any tendency to overbalance with a well-adjusted stone.

On the day of my departure I was up a little after five; by six, we began to load the donkey; and ten minutes after, my hopes were in the dust. The pad would not stay on Modestine's back for half a moment. I returned it to its maker, with whom I had so contumelious a passage that the street outside was crowded from wall to wall with gossips looking on and listening. The pad changed hands with much vivacity; perhaps it would be more descriptive to say that we threw it at each other's heads; and, any rate, we were very warm and unfriendly, and spoke with a deal of freedom.

I had a common donkey pack-saddle – a *barde*, as they call it – fitted upon Modestine; and once more loaded her with my effects. The doubled sack, my pilot-coat (for it was warm, and I was to walk in my waistcoat), a great bar of black bread, and an open basket containing the white bread, the mutton, and the bottles, were all corded together in a very elaborate system of knots, and I looked on the result with fatuous content. In such a monstrous deck-cargo, all poised above the donkey's shoulders, with nothing below to balance, on a brand-new pack-saddle that had not yet been worn to fit the animal, and fastened with brand-new girths that might be expected to stretch and slacken by the way, even a very careless traveller should have seen disaster brewing. That elaborate system of knots, again, was the work of too many sympathisers to be very artfully designed. It is true they tightened the cords with a will; as many as three at a time would have a foot against Modestine's quarters, and be hauling with clenched teeth; but I learned afterwards that one thoughtful person, without any exercise of force, can make a more solid job than half a dozen heated and enthusiastic grooms. I was then but a novice; even after the misadventure of the pad nothing could disturb my security, and I went forth from the stable-door as an ox goeth to the slaughter.[10]

The Green Donkey-Driver

The bell of Monastier was just striking nine as I got quit of these preliminary troubles and descended the hill through the common.[11] As long as I was within sight of the windows, a secret shame and the fear of some laughable defeat withheld me from tampering with Modestine. She tripped along upon her four small hoofs with a sober daintiness of gait; from time to time she shook her ears or her tail; and she looked so small under the bundle that my mind misgave me. We got across the ford without difficulty – there was no doubt about the matter, she was docility itself – and once on the other bank, where the road begins to mount through pine-woods, I took in my right hand the unhallowed staff, and with a quaking spirit applied it to the donkey. Modestine brisked up her pace for perhaps three steps, and then relapsed into her former minuet. Another application had the same effect, and so with the third. I am worthy the name of an Englishman,[12] and it goes against my conscience to lay my hand rudely on a female. I desisted, and looked her all over from head to foot; the poor brute's knees were trembling and her breathing was distressed; it was plain that she could go no faster on a hill. God forbid, thought I, that I should brutalise this innocent creature; let her go at her own pace, and let me patiently follow.

What that pace was, there is no word mean enough to describe; it was something as much slower than a walk as a walk is slower than a run; it kept me hanging on each foot for an incredible length of time; in five minutes it exhausted the spirit and set up a fever in all the muscles of the leg. And yet I had to keep close at hand and measure my advance exactly upon hers; for if I dropped a few yards into the rear, or went on a few yards ahead, Modestine came instantly to a halt and began to browse. The thought that this was to last from here to Alais[13] nearly broke my heart. Of all conceivable journeys, this promised to be the most tedious. I tried to tell myself it was a lovely day; I tried to charm my foreboding spirit with tobacco; but I had a vision ever present to me of the long, long roads, up hill and down dale, and a pair of figures ever infinitesimally moving, foot by foot, a yard to the minute, and, like things enchanted in a nightmare, approaching no nearer to the goal.

In the meantime there came up behind us a tall peasant, perhaps forty years of age, of an ironical snuffy countenance, and arrayed in the green tail-coat of the country. He overtook us hand over hand, and stopped to consider our pitiful advance.

'Your donkey,' says he, 'is very old?'

I told him, I believed not.

Then, he supposed, we had come far.

I told him, we had but newly left Monastier.

'*Et vous marchez comme ça!*'[14] cried he; and, throwing back his head, he laughed long and heartily. I watched him, half prepared to feel offended, until he had satisfied his mirth; and then, 'You must have no pity on these animals,' said he; and, plucking a switch out of a thicket, he began to lace Modestine about the stern-works, uttering a cry. The rogue pricked up her ears and broke into a good round pace, which she kept up without flagging, and without exhibiting the least symptom of distress, as long as the peasant kept beside us. Her former panting and shaking had been, I regret to say, a piece of comedy.

My *deus ex machinâ*,[15] before he left me, supplied some excellent, if inhumane, advice; presented me with the switch, which he declared she would feel more tenderly than my cane; and finally taught me the true cry or masonic word of donkey-drivers, 'Proot!'[16] All the time, he regarded me with a comical, incredulous air, which was embarrassing to confront; and smiled over my donkey-driving, as I might have smiled over his orthography, or his green tail-coat. But it was not my turn for the moment.

I was proud of my new lore, and thought I had learned the art to perfection. And certainly Modestine did wonders for the rest of the forenoon, and I had a breathing space to look about me. It was Sabbath; the mountain-fields were all vacant in the sunshine; and as we came down through St Martin de Frugères, the church was crowded to the door, there were people kneeling without upon the steps, and the sound of the priest's chanting came forth out of the dim interior. It gave me a home feeling on the spot; for I am a countryman of the Sabbath, so to speak, and all Sabbath observances, like a Scottish accent, strike in me mixed feelings, grateful and the reverse. It is only a traveller, hurrying by like a person from another planet, who can rightly enjoy the peace and beauty of the great ascetic feast. The sight of the resting country does his spirit good. There is something better than music in the wide unusual silence; and it disposes him to amiable thoughts, like the sound of a little river or the warmth of sunlight.[17]

In this pleasant humour I came down the hill to where Goudet stands in the green end of a valley, with Château Beaufort opposite upon a rocky steep, and the stream, as clear as crystal, lying in a deep pool between them. Above and below, you may hear it wimpling over the stones, an amiable stripling of a river, which it seems absurd to call the Loire. On all sides, Goudet is shut in by mountains; rocky footpaths, practicable at best for donkeys, join it to the outer world of France; and the men and women drink and swear, in their green corner, or look up at the snow-clad peaks in winter from the threshold of their homes, in an isolation, you would think, like that of Homer's Cyclops.[18] But it is not so; the postman reaches Goudet with the letter-bag; the aspiring youth of Goudet are within a day's walk of the railway at Le Puy; and here in the inn you may find an engraved portrait of the host's nephew, Régis Senac,[19] 'Professor of Fencing and Champion of the two Americas,' a distinction gained by him, along with the sum of five hundred dollars, at Tammany Hall, New York, on the 10th April, 1876.

I hurried over my midday meal, and was early forth again. But, alas, as we climbed the interminable hill upon the other side, 'Proot!' seemed to have lost its virtue. I prooted like a lion, I prooted mellifluously like a sucking-dove;[20] but Modestine would be neither softened nor intimidated. She held doggedly to her pace; nothing but a blow would move her, and that only for a second. I must follow at her heels, incessantly belabouring. A moment's pause in this ignoble toil, and she relapsed into her own private gait. I think I never heard of anyone in as mean a situation. I must reach the lake of Bouchet, where I meant to camp, before sundown, and, to have even a hope of this, I must instantly maltreat this uncomplaining animal. The sound of my own blows sickened me. Once, when I looked at her, she had a faint resemblance to a lady of my acquaintance who formerly loaded me with kindness; and this increased my horror of my cruelty.

To make matters worse, we encountered another donkey, ranging at will upon the roadside; and this other donkey chanced to be a gentleman. He and Modestine met nickering for joy, and I had to separate the pair and beat down their young romance with a renewed and feverish bastinado.[21] If the other donkey had had the heart of a male under his hide, he would have fallen upon me tooth and hoof; and this was a kind of consolation – he was plainly unworthy of Modestine's affection. But the incident saddened me, as did everything that spoke of my donkey's sex.

It was blazing hot up the valley, windless, with vehement sun upon my shoulders; and I had to labour so consistently with my stick that the sweat ran into my eyes. Every five minutes, too, the pack, the basket, and the pilot-coat would take an ugly slew to one side or the other; and I had to stop Modestine, just when I had got her to a tolerable pace of about two miles an hour, to tug, push, shoulder, and readjust the load. And at last, in the village of Ussel, saddle and all, the whole hypothec,[22] turned round and grovelled in the dust below the donkey's belly. She, none better pleased, incontinently drew up and seemed to smile; and a party of one man, two women, and two children came up, and, standing round me in a half-circle, encouraged her by their example.

I had the devil's own trouble to get the thing righted; and the instant I had done so, without hesitation, it toppled and fell down upon the other side. Judge if I was hot! And yet not a hand was offered to assist me. The man, indeed, told me I ought to have a package of a different shape. I suggested, if he knew nothing better to the point in my predicament, he might hold his tongue. And the good-natured dog agreed with me smilingly. It was the most despicable fix.[23] I must plainly content myself with the pack for Modestine, and take the following items for my own share of the portage: a cane, a quart flask, a pilot-jacket heavily weighted in the pockets, two pounds of black bread, and an open basket full of meats and bottles. I believe I may say I am not devoid of greatness of soul; for I did not recoil from this infamous burden. I disposed it, Heaven knows how, so as to be mildly portable, and then proceeded to steer Modestine through the village.[24] She tried, as was indeed her invariable habit, to enter every house and every courtyard in the whole length; and, encumbered as I was, without a hand to help myself, no words can render an idea of my difficulties. A priest, with six or seven others, was examining a church in process of repair, and he and his acolytes laughed loudly as they saw my plight. I remembered having laughed myself when I had seen good men struggling with adversity in the person of a jackass, and the recollection filled me with penitence. That was in my old light days, before this trouble came upon me. God knows at least that I shall never laugh again, thought I. But oh, what a cruel thing is a farce to those engaged in it!

A little out of the village, Modestine, filled with the demon, set her heart upon a by-road, and positively refused to leave it. I dropped all my bundles, and, I am ashamed to say, struck the poor sinner twice across the face. It was pitiful to see her lift up her head with shut eyes, as if waiting for another blow. I came very near crying; but I did a wiser thing than that, and sat squarely down by the roadside to consider my situation under the cheerful influence of tobacco and a nip of brandy. Modestine, in the meanwhile, munched some black bread with a contrite, hypocritical air. It was plain that I must make a sacrifice to the gods of shipwreck. I threw away the empty bottle destined to carry milk; I threw away my own white bread, and, disdaining to act by general average,[25] kept the black bread for Modestine; lastly, I threw away the cold leg of mutton and the egg-whisk, although this last was dear to my heart.[26] Thus I found room for everything in the basket, and even stowed the boating-coat on the top. By means of an end of cord I slung it under one arm; and although the cord cut my shoulder, and the jacket hung almost to the ground, it was with a heart greatly lightened that I set forth again.

I had now an arm free to thrash Modestine, and cruelly I chastised her.[27] If I were to reach the lakeside before dark she must bestir her little shanks to some tune. Already the sun had gone down into a windy-looking mist; and although there were still a few streaks of gold far off to the east on the hills and the black fir-woods, all was cold and grey about our onward path. An infinity of little country by-roads led hither and thither among the fields. It was the most pointless labyrinth. I could see my destination overhead, or rather the peak that dominates it, but choose as I pleased, the roads always ended by turning away from it, and sneaking back towards the valley, or northward along the margin of the hills. The failing light, the waning colour, the naked, unhomely, stony country through which I was travelling, threw me into some despondency. I promise you, the stick was not idle; I think every decent step that Modestine took must have cost me at least two emphatic blows. There was not another sound in the neighbourhood but that of my unwearying bastinado.[28]

Suddenly, in the midst of my toils, the load once more bit the dust, and, as by enchantment, all the cords were simultaneously loosened, and the road scattered with my dear possessions. The packing was to begin again from the beginning; and as I had to invent a new and better system, I do not doubt but I lost half an hour. It began to be dusk in earnest as I reached a wilderness of turf and stones. It had the air of being a road which should lead everywhere at the same time; and I was falling into something not unlike despair when I saw two figures stalking towards me over the stones. They walked one behind the other like tramps, but their pace was remarkable. The son led the way, a tall, ill-made, sombre, Scottish-looking man; the mother followed, all in her Sunday's best, with an elegantly embroidered ribbon to her cap, and a new felt hat atop, and proffering, as she strode along with kilted petticoats, a string of obscene and blasphemous oaths.

I hailed the son and asked him my direction. He pointed loosely west and north-west, muttered an inaudible comment, and, without slackening his pace for an instant, stalked on, as he was going, right athwart my path. The mother followed without so much as raising her head. I shouted and shouted after them, but they continued to scale the hillside, and turned a deaf ear to my outcries. At last, leaving Modestine by herself, I was constrained to run after them, hailing the while. They stopped as I drew near, the mother still cursing;[29] and I could see she was a handsome, motherly, respectable-looking woman. The son once more answered me roughly and inaudibly, and was for setting out again. But this time I simply collared the mother, who was nearest me, and, apologising for my violence, declared that I could not let them go until they had put me on my road. They were neither of them offended – rather mollified than otherwise; told me I had only to follow them; and then the mother asked me what I wanted by the lake at such an hour. I replied, in the Scottish manner, by inquiring if she had far to go herself. She told me, with another oath, that she had an hour and a half's road before her. And then, without salutation, the pair strode forward again up the hillside in the gathering dusk.

I returned for Modestine, pushed her briskly forward, and, after a sharp ascent of twenty minutes, reached the edge of a plateau. The view, looking back on my day's journey, was both wild and sad. Mount Mézenc[30] and the peaks beyond St Julien stood out in trenchant gloom against a cold glitter in the east; and the intervening field of hills had fallen together into one broad wash of shadow, except here and there the outline of a wooded sugar-loaf in black, here and there a white irregular patch to represent a cultivated farm, and here and there a blot where the Loire, the Gazeille, or the Laussonne wandered in a gorge.[31]

Soon we were on a high-road, and surprise seized on my mind as I beheld a village of some magnitude close at hand; for I had been told that the neighbourhood of the lake was uninhabited except by trout. The road smoked in the twilight with children driving home cattle from the fields; and a pair of mounted stride-legged women, hat and cap and all, dashed past me at a hammering trot from the canton where they had been to church and market. I asked one of the children where I was. At Bouchet St Nicolas, he told me. Thither, about a mile south of my destination, and on the other side of a respectable summit, had these confused roads and treacherous peasantry conducted me. My shoulder was cut, so that it hurt sharply; my arm ached like toothache from perpetual beating; I gave up the lake and my design to camp, and asked for the *auberge*.[32]

I Have a Goad

The *auberge* of Bouchet St Nicolas was among the least pretentious I have ever visited; but I saw many more of the like upon my journey. Indeed, it was typical of these French highlands. Imagine a cottage of two stories, with a bench before the door; the stable and kitchen in a suite, so that Modestine and I could hear each other dining; furniture of the plainest, earthen floors, a single bed-chamber for travellers, and that without any convenience but beds. In the kitchen cooking and eating go forward side by side, and the family sleep at night. Anyone who has a fancy to wash must do so in public at the common table. The food is sometimes spare; hard fish and omelette have been my portion more than once; the wine is of the smallest, the brandy abominable to man; and the visit of a fat sow, grouting[33] under the table and rubbing against your legs, is no impossible accompaniment to dinner.

But the people of the inn, in nine cases out of ten, show themselves friendly and considerate. As soon as you cross the doors you cease to be a stranger; and although this peasantry are rude and forbidding on the highway, they show a tincture of kind breeding when you share their hearth. At Bouchet, for instance, I uncorked my bottle of Beaujolais, and asked the host to join me. He would take but little.

'I am an amateur[34] of such wine, do you see?' he said, 'and I am capable of leaving you not enough.'

In these hedge-inns the traveller is expected to eat with his own knife; unless he ask, no other will be supplied: with a glass, a whang[35] of bread, and an iron fork, the table is completely laid. My knife was cordially admired by the landlord of Bouchet, and the spring filled him with wonder.

'I should never have guessed that,' he said. 'I would bet,' he added, weighing it in his hand, 'that this cost you not less than five francs.'

When I told him it had cost me twenty, his jaw dropped.

He was a mild, handsome, sensible, friendly old man, astonishingly ignorant. His wife, who was not so pleasant in her manners, knew how to read, although I do not suppose she ever did so. She had a share of brains and spoke with a cutting emphasis, like one who ruled the roast.

'My man knows nothing,' she said, with an angry nod; 'he is like the beasts.'

And the old gentleman signified acquiescence with his head. There was no contempt on her part, and no shame on his; the facts were accepted loyally, and no more about the matter.

I was tightly cross-examined about my journey; and the lady understood in a moment, and sketched out what I should put into my book when I got home. 'Whether people harvest or not in such or such a place; if there were forests; studies of manners; what, for example, I and the master of the house say to you; the beauties of Nature, and all that.' And she interrogated me with a look.

'It is just that,' said I.

'You see,' she added to her husband, 'I understood that.'

They were both much interested by the story of my misadventures.

'In the morning,' said the husband, 'I will make you something better than your cane. Such a beast as that feels nothing; it is in the proverb – *dur comme un âne*;[36] you might beat her insensible with a cudgel, and yet you would arrive nowhere.'

Something better! I little knew what he was offering.[37]

The sleeping-room was furnished with two beds, I had one; and I will own I was a little abashed to find a young man and his wife and child in the act of mounting into the other. This was my first experience of the sort; and if I am always to feel equally silly and extraneous, I pray God it be my last as well. I kept my eyes to myself, and know nothing of the woman except that she had beautiful arms,[38] and seemed no whit abashed by my appearance. As a matter of fact, the situation was more trying to me than to the pair. A pair keep each other in countenance; it is the single gentleman who has to blush. But I could not help attributing my sentiments to the husband, and sought to conciliate his tolerance with a cup of brandy from my flask. He told me that he was a cooper of Alais travelling to St Etienne in search of work, and that in his spare moments he followed the fatal calling of a maker of matches.[39] Me he readily enough divined to be a brandy merchant.

I was up first in the morning (Monday, September 23rd), and hastened my toilette guiltily, so as to leave a clear field for madam, the cooper's wife. I drank a bowl of milk, and set off to explore the neighbourhood of Bouchet. It was perishing cold, a grey, windy, wintry morning; misty clouds flew fast and low; the wind piped over the naked platform; and the only speck of colour was away behind Mount Mézenc and the eastern hills, where the sky still wore the orange of the dawn.

It was five in the morning, and four thousand feet above the sea; and I had to bury my hands in my pockets and trot. People were trooping out to the labours of the field by twos and threes, and all turned round to stare upon the stranger. I had seen them coming back last night, I saw them going afield again; and there was the life of Bouchet in a nutshell.

When I came back to the inn for a bit of breakfast, the landlady was in the kitchen, combing out her daughter's hair; and I made her my compliments upon its beauty.

'Oh, no,' said the mother; 'it is not so beautiful as it ought to be. Look, it is too fine.'

Thus does a wise peasantry console itself under adverse physical circumstances, and, by a startling democratic process, the defects of the majority decide the type of beauty.

'And where,' said I, 'is monsieur?'

'The master of the house is upstairs,' she answered, 'making you a goad.'

Blessed be the man who invented goads! Blessed the innkeeper of Bouchet St Nicolas, who introduced me to their use! This plain wand, with an eighth of an inch of pin, was indeed a sceptre when he put it in my hands. Thenceforward Modestine was my slave. A prick, and she passed the most inviting stable-door. A prick, and she broke forth into a gallant little trotlet that devoured the miles. It was not a remarkable speed, when all was said; and we took four hours to cover ten miles at the best of it. But what a heavenly change since yesterday! No more wielding of the ugly cudgel; no more flailing with an aching arm; no more broadsword exercise, but a discreet and gentlemanly fence. And what although now and then a drop of blood should appear on Modestine's mouse-coloured wedge-like rump? I should have preferred it otherwise, indeed; but yesterday's exploits had purged my heart of all humanity. The perverse little devil, since she would not be taken with kindness, must even go with pricking.

It was bleak and bitter cold, and, except a cavalcade of stride-legged ladies and a pair of post-runners, the road was dead solitary all the way to Pradelles. I scarce remember an incident but one. A handsome foal with a bell about his neck came charging up to us upon a stretch of common, sniffed the air martially as one about to do great deeds, and, suddenly thinking otherwise in his green young heart, put about and galloped off as he had come, the bell tinkling in the wind. For a long while afterwards I saw his noble attitude as he drew up, and heard the note of his bell; and when I struck the high-road, the song of the telegraph-wires seemed to continue the same music.

Pradelles stands on a hillside, high above the Allier, surrounded by rich meadows. They were cutting aftermath[40] on all sides, which gave the neighbourhood, this gusty autumn morning, an untimely smell of hay. On the opposite bank of the Allier the land kept mounting for miles to the horizon: a tanned and sallow autumn landscape, with black blots of fir-wood and white roads wandering through the hills. Over all this the clouds shed a uniform and purplish shadow, sad and somewhat menacing, exaggerating height and distance, and throwing into still higher relief the twisted ribbons of the highway. It was a cheerless prospect, but one stimulating to a traveller. For I was now upon the limit of Velay, and all that I beheld lay in another country – wild Gévaudan,[41] mountainous, uncultivated, and but recently disforested from terror of the wolves.

Wolves, alas! like bandits, seem to flee the traveller's advance; and you may trudge through all our comfortable Europe, and not meet with an adventure worth the name. But here, if any-where, a man was on the frontiers of hope. For this was the land of the ever-memorable BEAST, the Napoleon Bonaparte of wolves. What a career was his! He lived ten months at free quarters in Gévaudan and Vivarais;[42] he ate women and children and 'shepherdesses celebrated for their beauty'; he pursued armed horsemen; he has been seen at broad noonday chasing a post-chaise and outrider along the king's high-road, and chaise and outrider fleeing before him at the gallop. He was placarded like a political offender, and ten thousand francs were offered for his head. And yet, when he was shot and sent to Versailles,[43] behold! a common wolf, and even small for that. 'Though I could reach from pole to pole,' sang Alexander Pope; the Little Corporal shook Europe; and if all wolves had been as this wolf, they would have changed the history of man. M. Élic Berthet[44] has made him the hero of a novel, which I have read, and do not wish to read again.

I hurried over my lunch, and was proof against the landlady's desire that I should visit our Lady of Pradelles, 'who performed many miracles, although she was of wood'; and before three-quarters of an hour I was goading Modestine down the steep descent that leads to Langogne on the Allier. On both sides of the road, in big dusty fields, farmers were preparing for next spring. Every fifty yards a yoke of great-necked stolid oxen were patiently haling at the plough. I saw one of these mild, formidable servants of the glebe, who took a sudden interest in Modestine and me. The furrow down which he was journeying lay at an angle to the road, and his head was solidly fixed to the yoke like those of caryatides below a ponderous cornice; but he screwed round his big honest eyes and followed us with a ruminating look, until his master bade him turn the plough and proceed to reascend the field. From all these furrowing ploughshares, from the feet of oxen, from a labourer here and there who was breaking the dry clods with a hoe,[45] the wind carried away a thin dust like so much smoke. It was a fine, busy, breathing, rustic landscape; and as I continued to descend, the highlands of Gévaudan kept mounting in front of me against the sky.

I had crossed the Loire the day before; now I was to cross the Allier; so near are these two confluents in their youth. Just at the bridge of Langogne, as the long-promised rain was beginning to fall, a lassie of some seven or eight addressed me in the sacramental phrase, '*D'où'st-ce-que vous venez?*'[46] She did it with so high an air that she set me laughing, and this cut her to the quick. She was evidently one who reckoned on respect, and stood looking after me in silent dudgeon, as I crossed the bridge and entered the county of Gévaudan.

UPPER GÉVAUDAN

'The way also here was very wearisome through dirt and slabbiness; nor was there on all this ground so much as one inn or victualling-house wherein to refresh the feebler sort.'
Pilgrim's Progress.[1]

A Camp in the Dark

The next day (Tuesday, September 24th), it was two o'clock in the afternoon before I got my journal written up and my knapsack repaired, for I was determined to carry my knapsack in the future and have no more ado with baskets; and half an hour afterwards I set out for Le Cheylard l'Évêque, a place on the borders of the forest of Mercoire. A man, I was told, should walk there in an hour and a half; and I thought it scarce too ambitious to suppose that a man encumbered with a donkey might cover the same distance in four hours.

All the way up the long hill from Langogne it rained and hailed alternately; the wind kept freshening steadily, although slowly; plentiful hurrying clouds – some dragging veils of straight rain-shower, others massed and luminous, as though promising snow – careered out of the north and followed me along my way. I was soon out of the cultivated basin of the Allier, and away from the ploughing oxen, and such-like sights of the country. Moor, heathery marsh, tracts of rock and pines, woods of birch all jewelled with the autumn yellow, here and there a few naked cottages and bleak fields – these were the characters of the country. Hill and valley followed valley and hill; the little green and stony cattle-tracks wandered in and out of one another, split into three or four, died away in marshy hollows, and began again sporadically on hillsides or at the borders of a wood.

There was no direct road to Cheylard, and it was no easy

affair to make a passage in this uneven country and through this intermittent labyrinth of tracks. It must have been about four when I struck Sagnerousse, and went on my way rejoicing in a sure point of departure. Two hours afterwards, the dusk rapidly falling, in a lull of the wind, I issued from a fir-wood where I had long been wandering, and found, not the looked-for village, but another marish[2] bottom among rough-and-tumble hills. For some time past I had heard the ringing of cattle-bells ahead; and now, as I came out of the skirts of the wood, I saw near upon a dozen cows and perhaps as many more black figures, which I conjectured to be children, although the mist had almost unrecognisably exaggerated their forms. These were all silently following each other round and round in a circle, now taking hands, now breaking up with chains and reverences. A dance of children appeals to very innocent and lively thoughts; but, at nightfall on the marshes, the thing was eerie and fantastic to behold. Even I, who am well enough read in Herbert Spencer,[3] felt a sort of silence fall for an instant on my mind. The next, I was pricking Modestine forward, and guiding her like an unruly ship through the open. In a path, she went doggedly ahead of her own accord, as before a fair wind; but once on the turf or among heather, and the brute became demented. The tendency of lost travellers to go round in a circle was developed in her to the degree of passion, and it took all the steering I had in me to keep even a decently straight course through a single field.

While I was thus desperately tacking through the bog, children and cattle began to disperse, until only a pair of girls remained behind. From these I sought direction on my path. The peasantry in general were but little disposed to counsel a wayfarer. One old devil simply retired into his house, and barricaded the door on my approach; and I might beat and shout myself hoarse, he turned a deaf ear. Another, having given me a direction which, as I found afterwards, I had misunderstood, complacently watched me going wrong without adding a sign. He did not care a stalk of parsley if I wandered all night upon the hills! As for these two girls, they were a pair of impudent sly sluts, with not a thought but mischief. One put out her tongue at me, the other bade me follow the cows; and they both giggled and jogged each other's elbows. The Beast of Gévaudan ate about a hundred children of this district; I began to think of him with sympathy.

Leaving the girls, I pushed on through the bog, and got into another wood and upon a well-marked road. It grew darker and darker. Modestine, suddenly beginning to smell mischief, bettered the pace of her own accord, and from that time forward gave me no trouble. It was the first sign of intelligence I had occasion to remark in her. At the same time, the wind freshened into half a gale, and another heavy discharge of rain came flying up out of the north. At the other side of the wood I sighted some red windows in the dusk. This was the hamlet of Fouzilhic; three houses on a hillside, near a wood of birches. Here I found a delightful old man, who came a little way with me in the rain to put me safely on the road for Cheylard. He would hear of no reward; but shook his hands above his head almost as if in menace, and refused volubly and shrilly, in unmitigated *patois*.[4]

All seemed right at last. My thoughts began to turn upon dinner and a fireside, and my heart was agreeably softened in my bosom. Alas, and I was on the brink of new and greater miseries! Suddenly, at a single swoop, the night fell. I have been abroad in many a black night, but never in a blacker. A glimmer of rocks, a glimmer of the track where it was well beaten, a certain fleecy density, or night within night, for a tree – this was all that I could discriminate. The sky was simply darkness overhead; even the flying clouds pursued their way invisibly to human eyesight. I could not distinguish my hand at arm's length from the track, nor my goad, at the same distance, from the meadows or the sky.

Soon the road that I was following split, after the fashion of the country, into three or four in a piece of rocky meadow. Since Modestine had shown such a fancy for beaten roads, I tried her instinct in this predicament. But the instinct of an ass is what might be expected from the name; in half a minute she was clambering round and round among some boulders, as lost a donkey as you would wish to see. I should have camped long before had I been properly provided; but as this was to be so short a stage, I had brought no wine, no bread for myself, and little over a pound for my lady-friend. Add to this, that I and

Modestine were both handsomely wetted by the showers. But now, if I could have found some water, I should have camped at once in spite of all. Water, however, being entirely absent, except in the form of rain, I determined to return to Fouzilhic, and ask a guide a little farther on my way – 'a little farther lend thy guiding hand.'[5]

The thing was easy to decide, hard to accomplish. In this sensible[6] roaring blackness I was sure of nothing but the direction of the wind. To this I set my face; the road had disappeared, and I went across country, now in marshy opens, now baffled by walls unscalable to Modestine, until I came once more in sight of some red windows. This time they were differently disposed. It was not Fouzilhic, but Fouzilhac, a hamlet little distant from the other in space, but worlds away in the spirit of its inhabitants. I tied Modestine to a gate, and groped forward, stumbling among rocks, plunging mid-leg in bog, until I gained the entrance of the village. In the first lighted house there was a woman who would not open to me. She could do nothing, she cried to me through the door, being alone and lame; but if I would apply at the next house, there was a man who could help me if he had a mind.

They came to the next door in force, a man, two women, and a girl, and brought a pair of lanterns to examine the wayfarer. The man was not ill-looking, but had a shifty smile. He leaned against the door-post, and heard me state my case. All I asked was a guide as far as Cheylard.

'C'est que, voyez-vous, il fait noir,' said he.

I told him that was just my reason for requiring help.

'I understand that,' said he, looking uncomfortable; 'mais – c'est – de la peine.'

I was willing to pay, I said. He shook his head. I rose as high as ten francs; but he continued to shake his head. 'Name your own price, then,' said I.

'Ce n'est pas ça,' he said at length, and with evident difficulty; 'but I am not going to cross the door – mais je ne sortirai pas de la porte.'

I grew a little warm, and asked him what he proposed that I should do.

'Where are you going beyond Cheylard?' he asked by way of answer.

'That is no affair of yours,' I returned, for I was not going to indulge his bestial curiosity; 'it changes nothing in my present predicament.'

'*C'est vrai, ça,*' he acknowledged, with a laugh; '*oui, c'est vrai. Et d'où venez-vous?*'

A better man than I might have felt nettled.

'Oh,' said I, 'I am not going to answer any of your questions, so you may spare yourself the trouble of putting them. I am late enough already; I want help. If you will not guide me yourself, at least help me to find someone else who will.'

'Hold on,' he cried suddenly. 'Was it not you who passed in the meadow while it was still day?'

'Yes, yes,' said the girl, whom I had not hitherto recognised; 'it was monsieur; I told him to follow the cow.'

'As for you, mademoiselle,' said I, 'you are a *farceuse*.'[7]

'And,' added the man, 'what the devil have you done to be still here?'

What the devil, indeed! But there I was.

'The great thing,' said I, 'is to make an end of it'; and once more proposed that he should help me to find a guide.

'*C'est que,*' he said again, '*c'est que – il fait noir.*'

'Very well,' said I; 'take one of your lanterns.'

'No,' he cried, drawing a thought backward, and again intrenching himself behind one of his former phrases; 'I will not cross the door.'

I looked at him. I saw unaffected terror struggling on his face with unaffected shame; he was smiling pitifully and wetting his lip with his tongue, like a detected schoolboy. I drew a brief picture of my state, and asked him what I was to do.

'I don't know,' he said; 'I will not cross the door.'

Here was the Beast of Gévaudan, and no mistake.

'Sir,' said I, with my most commanding manners, 'you are a coward.'

And with that I turned my back upon the family party, who hastened to retire within their fortifications; and the famous door was closed again, but not till I had overheard the sound of laughter. *Filia barbara pater barbarior.*[8] Let me say it in the plural: the Beasts of Gévaudan.

The lanterns had somewhat dazzled me, and I ploughed distressfully among stones and rubbish-heaps. All the other houses in the village were both dark and silent; and though I knocked at here and there a door, my knocking was unanswered. It was a bad business; I gave up Fouzilhac with my curses. The rain had stopped, and the wind, which still kept rising, began to dry my coat and trousers. 'Very well,' thought I, 'water or no water, I must camp.' But the first thing was to return to Modestine. I am pretty sure I was twenty minutes groping for my lady in the dark; and if it had not been for the unkindly services of the bog, into which I once more stumbled, I might have still been groping for her at the dawn. My next business was to gain the shelter of a wood, for the wind was cold as well as boisterous. How, in this well-wooded district, I should have been so long in finding one, is another of the insoluble mysteries of this day's adventures; but I will take my oath that I put near an hour to the discovery.

At last black trees began to show upon my left, and, suddenly crossing the road, made a cave of unmitigated blackness right in front. I call it a cave without exaggeration; to pass below that arch of leaves was like entering a dungeon. I felt about until my hand encountered a stout branch, and to this I tied Modestine, a haggard, drenched, desponding donkey. Then I lowered my pack, laid it along the wall on the margin of the road, and unbuckled the straps. I knew well enough where the lantern was; but where were the candles? I groped and groped among the tumbled articles, and, while I was thus groping, suddenly I touched the spirit-lamp. Salvation! This would serve my turn as well. The wind roared unwearyingly among the trees; I could hear the boughs tossing and the leaves churning through half a mile of forest; yet the scene of my encampment was not only as black as the pit, but admirably sheltered. At the second match the wick caught flame. The light was both livid and shifting; but it cut me off from the universe, and doubled the darkness of the surrounding night.

I tied Modestine more conveniently for herself, and broke up half the black bread for her supper, reserving the other half against the morning. Then I gathered what I should want within reach, took off my wet boots and gaiters, which I wrapped in my waterproof, arranged my knapsack for a pillow under the flap of my sleeping-bag, insinuated my limbs into the interior, and buckled myself in like a *bambino*.[9] I opened a tin of Bologna sausage and broke a cake of chocolate, and that was all I had to eat. It may sound offensive, but I ate them together, bite by bite, by way of bread and meat. All I had to wash down this revolting mixture was neat brandy: a revolting beverage in itself. But I was rare and hungry; ate well, and smoked one of the best cigarettes in my experience. Then I put a stone in my straw hat, pulled the flap of my fur cap over my neck and eyes, put my revolver ready to my hand, and snuggled well down among the sheepskins.

I questioned at first if I were sleepy, for I felt my heart beating faster than usual, as if with an agreeable excitement to which my mind remained a stranger. But as soon as my eyelids touched, that subtle glue leaped between them, and they would no more come separate.

The wind among the trees was my lullaby. Sometimes it sounded for minutes together with a steady even rush, not rising nor abating; and again it would swell and burst like a great crashing breaker, and the trees would patter me all over with big drops from the rain of the afternoon. Night after night, in my own bedroom in the country, I have given ear to this perturbing concert of the wind among the woods; but whether it was a difference in the trees, or the lie of the ground, or because I was myself outside and in the midst of it, the fact remains that the wind sang to a different tune among these woods of Gévaudan. I hearkened and hearkened; and meanwhile sleep took gradual possession of my body and subdued my thoughts and senses; but still my last waking effort was to listen and distinguish, and my last conscious state was one of wonder at the foreign clamour in my ears.

Twice in the course of the dark hours – once when a stone galled me underneath the sack, and again when the poor patient Modestine, growing angry, pawed and stamped upon the road – I was recalled for a brief while to consciousness, and saw a star or two overhead, and the lace-like edge of the foliage against the sky. When I awoke for the third time (Wednesday, September 25th), the world was flooded with a blue light, the mother of the dawn. I saw the leaves labouring in the wind and the ribbon of the road; and, on turning my head, there was Modestine tied to a beech, and standing half across the path in an attitude of inimitable patience. I closed my eyes again, and set to thinking over the experience of the night. I was surprised to find how easy and pleasant it had been, even in this tempestuous weather. The stone which annoyed me would not have been there, had I not been forced to camp blindfold in the opaque night; and I had felt no other inconvenience, except when my feet encountered the lantern or the second volume of Peyrat's *Pastors of the Desert* [10] among the mixed contents of my sleeping-bag; nay, more, I had felt not a touch of cold, and awakened with unusually lightsome and clear sensations.

With that, I shook myself, got once more into my boots and gaiters, and, breaking up the rest of the bread for Modestine, strolled about to see in what part of the world I had awakened. Ulysses, left on Ithaca, [11] and with a mind unsettled by the goddess, was not more pleasantly astray. I have been after an adventure all my life, a pure dispassionate adventure, such as befell early and heroic voyagers; and thus to be found by morning in a random woodside nook in Gévaudan – not knowing north from south, as strange to my surroundings as the first man upon the earth, an inland castaway – was to find a fraction of my day-dreams realised. I was on the skirts of a little wood of birch, sprinkled with a few beeches; behind, it adjoined another wood of fir; and in front, it broke up and went down in open order into a shallow and meadowy dale. All around there were bare hill-tops, some near, some far away, as the perspective closed or opened, but none apparently much higher than the rest. The wind huddled the trees. The golden specks of autumn in the birches tossed shiveringly. Overhead the sky was full of strings and shreds of vapour, flying, vanishing, reappearing, and turning about an axis like tumblers, as the wind hounded them through heaven. It was wild weather and famishing cold. I ate some chocolate, swallowed a mouthful of brandy, and smoked a cigarette before the cold should have time to disable my fingers. And by the time I had got all this done, and had made my pack and bound it on the pack-saddle, the day was tiptoe on the threshold of the east. We had not gone many steps along the lane, before the sun, still invisible to me, sent a glow of gold over some cloud mountains that lay ranged along the eastern sky.

The wind had us on the stern, and hurried us bitingly forward. I buttoned myself into my coat, and walked on in a pleasant frame of mind with all men, when suddenly, at a corner, there was Fouzilhic once more in front of me. Nor only that, but there was the old gentleman who had escorted me so far the night before, running out of his house at sight of me, with hands upraised in horror.

'My poor boy!' he cried, 'what does this mean?'

I told him what had happened. He beat his old hands like clappers in a mill, to think how lightly he had let me go; but when he heard of the man of Fouzilhac, anger and depression seized upon his mind.

'This time, at least,' said he, 'there shall be no mistake.'

And he limped along, for he was very rheumatic, for about half a mile, and until I was almost within sight of Cheylard, the destination I had hunted for so long.

Cheylard and Luc

Candidly, it seemed little worthy of all this searching. A few broken ends of village, with no particular street, but a succession of open places heaped with logs and fagots; a couple of tilted crosses, a shrine to Our Lady of all Graces on the summit of a little hill; and all this, upon a rattling highland river, in the corner of a naked valley. What went ye out for to see?[12] thought I to myself. But the place had a life of its own. I found a board commemorating the liberalities of Cheylard for the past year, hung up, like a banner, in the diminutive and tottering church. In 1877, it appeared, the inhabitants subscribed forty-eight

francs ten centimes for the 'Work of the Propagation of the
Faith.' Some of this, I could not help hoping, would be applied
to my native land. Cheylard scrapes together halfpence for the
darkened souls in Edinburgh; while Balquhidder and Dunrossness[13] bemoan the ignorance of Rome. Thus, to the high entertainment of the angels, do we pelt each other with evangelists,
like schoolboys bickering in the snow.

The inn was again singularly unpretentious. The whole furniture of a not ill-to-do family was in the kitchen: the beds,
the cradle, the clothes, the plate-rack, the meal-chest, and the
photograph of the parish priest. There were five children, one
of whom was set to its morning prayers at the stair-foot soon
after my arrival, and a sixth would ere long be forthcoming. I
was kindly received by these good folk. They were much interested in my misadventure. The wood in which I had slept
belonged to them, the man of Fouzilhac they thought a monster
of iniquity, and counselled me warmly to summon him at law –
'because I might have died.' The good wife was horror-stricken
to see me drink over a pint of uncreamed milk.

'You will do yourself an evil,' she said. 'Permit me to boil it
for you.'

After I had begun the morning on this delightful liquor, she
having an infinity of things to arrange, I was permitted, nay
requested, to make a bowl of chocolate for myself. My boots
and gaiters were hung up to dry, and, seeing me trying to write
my journal on my knee, the eldest daughter let down a hinged
table in the chimney-corner for my convenience. Here I wrote,
drank my chocolate, and finally ate an omelette before I left.
The table was thick with dust; for, as they explained, it was not
used except in winter weather. I had a clear look up the vent,
through brown agglomerations of soot and blue vapour, to the
sky; and whenever a handful of twigs was thrown on to the fire,
my legs were scorched by the blaze.

The husband had begun life as a muleteer, and when I came
to charge Modestine showed himself full of the prudence of his
art. 'You will have to change this package,' said he; 'it ought to
be in two parts, and then you might have double the weight.'

I explained that I wanted no more weight; and for no donkey hitherto created would I cut my sleeping-bag in two.

'It fatigues her, however,' said the innkeeper; 'it fatigues her greatly on the march. Look.'

Alas, there were her two forelegs no better than raw beef on the inside, and blood was running from under her tail. They told me when I started, and I was ready to believe it, that before a few days I should come to love Modestine like a dog. Three days had passed, we had shared some misadventures, and my heart was still as cold as a potato towards my beast of burden. She was pretty enough to look at; but then she had given proof of dead stupidity, redeemed indeed by patience, but aggravated by flashes of sorry and ill-judged light-heartedness.[14] And I own this new discovery seemed another point against her. What the devil was the good of a she-ass if she could not carry a sleeping-bag and a few necessaries? I saw the end of the fable rapidly approaching, when I should have to carry Modestine. Æsop was the man to know the world! I assure you I set out with heavy thoughts upon my short day's march.[15]

It was not only heavy thoughts about Modestine that weighted me upon the way; it was a leaden business altogether. For first, the wind blew so rudely that I had to hold on the pack with one hand from Cheylard to Luc; and second, my road lay through one of the most beggarly countries in the world. It was like the worst of the Scottish Highlands, only worse; cold, naked, and ignoble, scant of wood, scant of heather, scant of life. A road and some fences broke the unvarying waste, and the line of the road was marked by upright pillars, to serve in time of snow.

Why anyone should desire to visit either Luc or Cheylard is more than my much-inventing spirit can suppose. For my part, I travel not to go anywhere, but to go. I travel for travel's sake.[16] The great affair is to move; to feel the needs and hitches of our life more nearly; to come down off this feather-bed of civilisation, and find the globe granite underfoot and strewn with cutting flints. Alas, as we get up in life, and are more preoccupied with our affairs, even a holiday is a thing that must be worked for. To hold a pack upon a pack-saddle against a gale out of the freezing north is no high industry, but it is one that serves to occupy and compose the mind. And when the present is so exacting, who can annoy himself about the future?

I came out at length above the Allier. A more unsightly prospect at this season of the year it would be hard to fancy. Shelving hills rose round it on all sides, here dabbled with wood and fields, there rising to peaks alternately naked and hairy with pines. The colour throughout was black or ashen, and came to a point in the ruins of the castle of Luc, which pricked up impudently from below my feet, carrying on a pinnacle a tall white statue of Our Lady, which, I heard with interest, weighed fifty quintals, and was to be dedicated on the 6th of October. Through this sorry landscape trickled the Allier and a tributary of nearly equal size, which came down to join it through a broad nude valley in Vivarais. The weather had somewhat lightened, and the clouds massed in squadron; but the fierce wind still hunted them through heaven, and cast great ungainly splashes of shadow and sunlight over the scene.

Luc itself was a straggling double file of houses wedged between hill and river. It had no beauty, nor was there any notable feature, save the old castle overhead with its fifty quintals of brand-new Madonna. But the inn was clean and large. The kitchen, with its two box-beds hung with clean check curtains, with its wide stone chimney, its chimney-shelf four yards long and garnished with lanterns and religious statuettes, its array of chests and pair of ticking clocks, was the very model of what a kitchen ought to be; a melodrama kitchen, suitable for bandits or noblemen in disguise. Nor was the scene disgraced by the landlady, a handsome, silent, dark old woman, clothed and hooded in black like a nun. Even the public bedroom had a character of its own, with the long deal tables and benches, where fifty might have dined,[17] set out as for a harvest-home, and the three box-beds along the wall. In one of these, lying on straw and covered with a pair of table-napkins, did I do penance all night long in goose-flesh and chattering teeth, and sigh from time to time as I awakened for my sheepskin sack and the lee of some great wood.

OUR LADY OF THE SNOWS[1]

'I behold
The House, the Brotherhood austere –
And what am I, that I am here?'
            Matthew Arnold.[2]

Father Apollinaris

Next morning (Thursday, 26th September) I took the road in a new order. The sack was no longer doubled, but hung at full length across the saddle, a green sausage six feet long with a tuft of blue wool hanging out of either end. It was more picturesque, it spared the donkey, and, as I began to see, it would insure stability, blow high, blow low. But it was not without a pang that I had so decided. For although I had purchased a new cord, and made all as fast as I was able, I was yet jealously uneasy lest the flaps should tumble out and scatter my effects along the line of march.[3]

My way lay up the bald valley of the river, along the march of Vivarais and Gévaudan. The hills of Gévaudan on the right were a little more naked, if anything, than those of Vivarais upon the left, and the former had a monopoly of a low dotty underwood that grew thickly in the gorges and died out in solitary burrs upon the shoulders and the summits. Black bricks of fir-wood were plastered here and there upon both sides, and here and there were cultivated fields. A railway ran beside the river; the only bit of railway in Gévaudan, although there are many proposals afoot and surveys being made, and even, as they tell me, a station standing ready-built in Mende.[4] A year or two hence and this may be another world. The desert is beleaguered. Now may some Languedocian Wordsworth turn the sonnet into *patois*: 'Mountains and vales and floods, heard YE that whistle?'[5]

At a place called La Bastide I was directed to leave the river, and follow a road that mounted on the left among the hills of Vivarais, the modern Ardèche; for I was now come within a little way of my strange destination, the Trappist[6] monastery of Our Lady of the Snows. The sun came out as I left the shelter of a pine wood, and I beheld suddenly a fine wild landscape to the south. High rocky hills, as blue as sapphire, closed the view, and between these lay ridge upon ridge, heathery, craggy, the sun glittering on veins of rock, the underwood clambering in the hollows, as rude as God made them at the first. There was not a sign of man's hand in all the prospect; and indeed not a trace of his passage, save where generation after generation had walked in twisted footpaths, in and out among the beeches, and up and down upon the channelled slopes. The mists, which had hitherto beset me, were now broken into clouds, and fled swiftly and shone brightly in the sun. I drew a long breath. It was grateful to come, after so long, upon a scene of some attraction for the human heart. I own I like definite form in what my eyes are to rest upon; and if landscapes were sold, like the sheets of characters of my boyhood, one penny plain and twopence coloured,[7] I should go the length of twopence every day of my life.

But if things had grown better to the south, it was still desolate and inclement near at hand. A spidery cross on every hill-top marked the neighbourhood of a religious house; and a quarter of a mile beyond, the outlook southward opening out and growing bolder with every step, a white statue of the Virgin at the corner of a young plantation directed the traveller to Our Lady of the Snows. Here, then, I struck leftward, and pursued my way, driving my secular donkey before me, and creaking in my secular boots and gaiters, towards the asylum of silence.

I had not gone very far ere the wind brought to me the clanging of a bell, and somehow, I can scarce tell why, my heart sank within me at the sound. I have rarely approached anything with more unaffected terror than the monastery of Our Lady of the Snows. This it is to have had a Protestant education. And suddenly, on turning a corner, fear took hold on me from head to foot – slavish, superstitious fear; and though I did not stop in my advance, yet I went on slowly, like a man who should have passed a bourne[8] unnoticed, and strayed into the country of the dead. For there upon the narrow new-made road, between the stripling pines, was a mediæval friar, fighting with a barrowful of turfs. Every Sunday of my childhood I used to study the *Hermits* of Marco Sadeler[9] – enchanting prints, full of wood and field and mediæval landscapes, as large as a county, for the imagination to go a-travelling in; and here, sure enough, was one of Marco Sadeler's heroes. He was robed in white like any spectre, and the hood falling back, in the instancy of his contention with the barrow, disclosed a pate as bald and yellow as a skull. He might have been buried any time these thousand years, and all the lively parts of him resolved into earth and broken up with the farmer's harrow.

I was troubled besides in my mind as to etiquette. Durst I address a person who was under a vow of silence? Clearly not. But drawing near, I doffed my cap to him with a far-away super-stitious reverence. He nodded back, and cheerfully addressed me. Was I going to the monastery? Who was I? An Englishman? Ah, an Irishman, then?

'No,' I said, 'a Scotsman.'[10]

A Scotsman? Ah, he had never seen a Scotsman before. And he looked me all over, his good, honest, brawny countenance shining with interest, as a boy might look upon a lion or an alligator. From him I learned with disgust that I could not be received at Our Lady of the Snows; I might get a meal, perhaps, but that was all. And then, as our talk ran on, and it turned out that I was not a pedlar, but a literary man, who drew land-scapes[11] and was going to write a book, he changed his manner of thinking as to my reception (for I fear they respect persons even in a Trappist monastery), and told me I must be sure to ask for the Father Prior, and state my case to him in full. On second thoughts he determined to go down with me himself; he thought he could manage for me better. Might he say that I was a geographer?

No; I thought, in the interests of truth, he positively might not.

'Very well, then' (with disappointment), 'an author.'

It appeared he had been in a seminary with six young Irishmen, all priests, long since, who had received newspapers and kept him informed of the state of ecclesiastical affairs in England. And he asked me eagerly after Dr Pusey, for whose conversion the good man had continued ever since to pray night and morning.

'I thought he was very near the truth,' he said; 'and he will reach it yet; there is so much virtue in prayer.'[12]

He must be a stiff, ungodly Protestant who can take anything but pleasure in this kind and hopeful story. While he was thus near the subject, the good father asked me if I were a Christian; and when he found I was not, or not after his way, he glossed it over with great goodwill.

The road which we were following, and which this stalwart father had made with his own two hands within the space of a year, came to a corner, and showed us some white buildings, a little farther on beyond the wood. At the same time, the bell once more sounded abroad. We were hard upon the monastery. Father Apollinaris[13] (for that was my companion's name) stopped me.

'I must not speak to you down there,' he said. 'Ask for the Brother Porter, and all will be well. But try to see me as you go out again through the wood, where I may speak to you. I am charmed to have made your acquaintance.'

And then suddenly raising his arms, flapping his fingers, and crying out twice, 'I must not speak! I must not speak!' he ran away in front of me, and disappeared into the monastery door.

I own this somewhat ghastly eccentricity went a good way to revive my terrors. But where one was so good and simple, why should not all be alike? I took heart of grace, and went forward to the gate as fast as Modestine, who seemed to have a disaffection for monasteries, would permit. It was the first door, in my acquaintance of her, which she had not shown an indecent haste to enter. I summoned the place in form, though with a quaking heart. Father Michael,[14] the Father Hospitaller, and a pair of brown-robed brothers came to the gate and spoke with me a while. I think my sack was the great attraction; it had already beguiled the heart of poor Apollinaris, who had charged me on my life to show it to the Father Prior. But whether it was my address, or the sack, or the idea speedily published among that part of the brotherhood who attend on strangers that I was not a pedlar after all, I found no difficulty as to my reception. Modestine was led away by a layman to the stables, and I and my pack were received into Our Lady of the Snows.

The Monks

Father Michael, a pleasant, fresh-faced, smiling man, perhaps of thirty-five, took me to the pantry, and gave me a glass of liqueur to stay me until dinner. We had some talk, or rather I should say he listened to my prattle indulgently enough, but with an abstracted air, like a spirit with a thing of clay. And truly, when I remember that I descanted principally on my appetite, and that it must have been by that time more than eighteen hours since Father Michael had so much as broken bread, I can well understand that he would find an earthly savour in my conversation. But his manner, though superior, was exquisitely gracious; and I find I have a lurking curiosity as to Father Michael's past.

The whet administered, I was left alone for a little in the monastery garden. This is no more than the main court, laid out in sandy paths and beds of parti-coloured dahlias, and with a fountain and a black statue of the Virgin in the centre. The buildings stand around it four-square, bleak, as yet unseasoned by the years and weather, and with no other features than a belfry and a pair of slated gables. Brothers in white, brothers in brown, passed silently along the sanded alleys; and when I first came out, three hooded monks were kneeling on the terrace at their prayers. A naked hill commands the monastery upon one side, and the wood commands it on the other. It lies exposed to wind; the snow falls off and on from October to May, and sometimes lies six weeks on end; but if they stood in Eden, with a climate like heaven's, the buildings themselves would offer the same wintry and cheerless aspect; and for my part, on this wild September day, before I was called to dinner, I felt chilly in and out.

When I had eaten well and heartily, Brother Ambrose,[15] a hearty conversable Frenchman (for all those who wait on strangers have the liberty to speak), led me to a little room in that part of the building which is set apart for *MM. les retraitants*.[16] It was clean and whitewashed, and furnished with strict necessaries, a crucifix, a bust of the late Pope, the *Imitation*[17] in French, a book of religious meditations, and the *Life of Elizabeth Seton*[18] – evangelist, it would appear, of North America and of New England in particular. As far as my experience goes, there is a fair field for some more evangelisation in these quarters; but think of Cotton Mather![19] I should like to give him a reading of this little work in heaven, where I hope he dwells; but perhaps he knows all that already, and much more; and perhaps he and Mrs Seton are the dearest friends, and gladly unite their voices in the everlasting psalm. Over the table, to conclude the inventory of the room, hung a set of regulations for *MM. les retraitants*: what services they should attend, when they were to tell their beads or meditate, and when they were to rise and go to rest. At the foot was a notable N.B.: '*Le temps libre est employé à l'examen de conscience, à la confession, à faire de bonnes résolutions*,'[20] etc. To make good resolutions, indeed! You might talk as fruitfully of making the hair grow on your head.

I had scarce explored my niche when Brother Ambrose returned. An English boarder, it appeared, would like to speak with me. I professed my willingness, and the friar ushered in a fresh, young, little Irishman of fifty,[21] a deacon of the Church, arrayed in strict canonicals, and wearing on his head what, in default of knowledge, I can only call the ecclesiastical shako. He had lived seven years in retreat at a convent of nuns in Belgium, and now five at Our Lady of the Snows; he never saw an English newspaper; he spoke French imperfectly, and had he spoken it like a native, there was not much chance of conversation where he dwelt. With this, he was a man eminently sociable, greedy of news, and simple-minded like a child. If I was pleased to have a guide about the monastery, he was no less delighted to see an English face and hear an English tongue.

He showed me his own room, where he passed his time among breviaries, Hebrew Bibles, and the Waverley Novels.[22] Thence he led me to the cloisters, into the chapter-house, through the vestry, where the brothers' gowns and broad straw hats were hanging up, each with his religious name upon a board – names full of legendary suavity and interest, such as Basil, Hilarion, Raphael, or Pacifique; into the library, where were all the works of Veuillot and Chateaubriand, and the *Odes et Ballades*, if you please, and even Molière,[23] to say nothing of innumerable fathers and a great variety of local and general historians. Thence my good Irishman took me round the workshops, where brothers bake bread, and make cartwheels, and take photographs; where one superintends a collection of curiosities, and another a gallery of rabbits. For in a Trappist monastery each monk has an occupation of his own choice, apart from his religious duties and the general labours of the house. Each must sing in the choir, if he has a voice and ear, and join in the haymaking if he has a hand to stir; but in his private hours, although he must be occupied, he may be occupied on what he likes. Thus I was told that one brother was engaged with literature; while Father Apollinaris busies himself in making roads, and the Abbot employs himself in binding books. It is not so long since this Abbot was consecrated, by the way; and on that occasion, by a special grace, his mother was permitted to enter the chapel and witness the ceremony of consecration. A proud day for her to have a son a mitred abbot; it makes you glad to think they let her in.[24]

In all these journeyings to and fro, many silent fathers and brethren fell in our way. Usually they paid no more regard to our passage than if we had been a cloud; but sometimes the good deacon had a permission to ask of them, and it was granted by a peculiar movement of the hands, almost like that of a dog's paws in swimming, or refused by the usual negative signs, and in either case with lowered eyelids and a certain air of contrition, as of a man who was steering very close to evil.

The monks, by special grace of their Abbot, were still taking two meals a day; but it was already time for their grand fast, which begins somewhere in September and lasts till Easter, and during which they eat but once in the twenty-four hours, and that at two in the afternoon, twelve hours after they have begun the toil and vigil of the day. Their meals are scanty, but even of these they eat sparingly; and though each is allowed a small carafe of wine, many refrain from this indulgence. Without doubt, the most of mankind grossly over-eat themselves; our meals serve not only for support, but as a hearty and natural diversion from the labour of life. Although excess may be hurtful, I should have thought this Trappist regimen defective. And I am astonished, as I look back, at the freshness of face and cheerfulness of manner of all whom I beheld. A happier nor a healthier company I should scarce suppose that I have ever seen. As a matter of fact, on this bleak upland, and with the incessant occupation of the monks, life is of an uncertain tenure, and death no infrequent visitor, at Our Lady of the Snows. This, at least, was what was told me. But if they die easily, they must live healthily in the meantime, for they seemed all firm of flesh and high in colour; and the only morbid sign that I could observe, an unusual brilliancy of eye, was one that served rather to increase the general impression of vivacity and strength.

Those with whom I spoke were singularly sweet-tempered, with what I can only call a holy cheerfulness in air and conversation. There is a note, in the direction to visitors, telling them not to be offended at the curt speech of those who wait upon them, since it is proper to monks to speak little. The note might have been spared; to a man the hospitallers were all brimming with innocent talk, and, in my experience of the monastery, it was easier to begin than to break off a conversation. With the exception of Father Michael, who was a man of the world, they showed themselves full of kind and healthy interest in all sorts of subjects – in politics, in voyages, in my sleeping-sack – and not without a certain pleasure in the sound of their own voices.

As for those who are restricted to silence, I can only wonder how they bear their solemn and cheerless isolation. And yet, apart from any view of mortification, I can see a certain policy, not only in the exclusion of women, but in this vow of silence.

I have had some experience of lay phalansteries,[25] of an artistic, not to say a bacchanalian, character; and seen more than one association easily formed and yet more easily dispersed. With a Cistercian rule, perhaps they might have lasted longer. In the neighbourhood of women it is but a touch-and-go association that can be formed among defenceless men; the stronger electricity is sure to triumph; the dreams of boyhood, the schemes of youth, are abandoned after an interview of ten minutes, and the arts and sciences, and professional male jollity, deserted at once for two sweet eyes and a caressing accent. And next after this, the tongue is the great divider.

I am almost ashamed to pursue this worldly criticism of a religious rule;[26] but there is yet another point in which the Trappist order appeals to me as a model of wisdom. By two in the morning the clapper goes upon the bell, and so on, hour by hour, and sometimes quarter by quarter, till eight, the hour of rest; so infinitesimally is the day divided among different occupations. The man who keeps rabbits, for example, hurries from his hutches to the chapel, the chapter-room, or the refectory, all day long: every hour he has an office to sing, a duty to perform; from two, when he rises in the dark, till eight, when he returns to receive the comfortable gift of sleep, he is upon his feet and occupied with manifold and changing business. I know many persons, worth several thousands in the year, who are not so fortunate in the disposal of their lives. Into how many houses would not the note of the monastery bell, dividing the day into manageable portions, bring peace of mind and healthful activity of body? We speak of hardships, but the true hardship is to be a dull fool, and permitted to mismanage life in our own dull and foolish manner.

From this point of view, we may perhaps better understand the monk's existence. A long novitiate, and every proof of constancy of mind and strength of body is required before admission to the order; but I could not find that many were discouraged. In the photographer's studio, which figures so strangely among the outbuildings, my eye was attracted by the portrait of a young fellow in the uniform of a private of foot. This was one of the novices, who came of age for service, and marched and drilled and mounted guard for the proper time among the garrison of Algiers.[27] Here was a man who had surely seen both sides of life before deciding; yet as soon as he was set free from service he returned to finish his novitiate.

This austere rule entitles a man to heaven as by right. When the Trappist sickens, he quits not his habit; he lies in the bed of death as he has prayed and laboured in his frugal and silent existence; and when the Liberator comes, at the very moment, even before they have carried him in his robe to lie his little last in the chapel among continual chantings, joy-bells break forth, as if for a marriage, from the slated belfry, and proclaim throughout the neighbourhood that another soul has gone to God.

At night, under the conduct of my kind Irishman, I took my place in the gallery to hear compline and *Salve Regina*,[28] with which the Cistercians bring every day to a conclusion. There were none of those circumstances which strike the Protestant as childish or as tawdry in the public offices of Rome. A stern simplicity, heightened by the romance of the surroundings, spoke directly to the heart. I recall the whitewashed chapel, the hooded figures in the choir, the lights alternately occluded and revealed, the strong manly singing, the silence that ensued, the sight of cowled heads bowed in prayer, and then the clear trenchant beating of the bell, breaking in to show that the last office was over and the hour of sleep had come; and when I remember, I am not surprised that I made my escape into the court with somewhat whirling fancies, and stood like a man bewildered in the windy starry night.

But I was weary; and when I had quieted my spirits with Elizabeth Seton's memoirs – a dull work – the cold and the raving of the wind among the pines (for my room was on that side of the monastery which adjoins the woods) disposed me readily to slumber. I was wakened at black midnight, as it seemed, though it was really two in the morning, by the first stroke upon the bell. All the brothers were then hurrying to the chapel; the dead in life, at this untimely hour, were already beginning the uncomforted labours of their day. The dead in life – there was a chill reflection. And the words of a French song came back into my memory, telling of the best of our mixed existence:

> 'Que t'as de belles filles,
>   Giroflé!
>   Girofla!
> Que t'as de belles filles,
> *L'Amour les comptera!*'

And I blessed God that I was free to wander, free to hope, and free to love.[29]

The Boarders

But there was another side to my residence at Our Lady of the Snows. At this late season there were not many boarders; and yet I was not alone in the public part of the monastery. This itself is hard by the gate, with a small dining-room on the ground-floor, and a whole corridor of cells similar to mine upstairs. I have stupidly forgotten the board for a regular *retrait-ant*; but it was somewhere between three and five francs a day, and I think most probably the first. Chance visitors like myself might give what they chose as a free-will offering, but nothing was demanded. I may mention that when I was going away Father Michael refused twenty francs as excessive. I explained the reasoning which led me to offer him so much; but even then, from a curious point of honour, he would not accept it with his own hand. 'I have no right to refuse for the monastery,' he explained, 'but I should prefer if you would give it to one of the brothers.'

I had dined alone, because I arrived late; but at supper I found two other guests. One was a country parish priest, who had walked over that morning from the seat of his cure near Mende to enjoy four days of solitude and prayer. He was a grenadier in person, with the hale colour and circular wrinkles of a peasant; and as he complained much of how he had been impeded by his skirts upon the march, I have a vivid fancy portrait of him, striding along, upright, big-boned, with kilted cassock, through the bleak hills of Gévaudan. The other was a short, grizzling, thick-set man, from forty-five to fifty, dressed in tweed with a knitted spencer, and the red ribbon[30] of a decoration in his button-hole. This last was a hard person to classify. He was an old soldier, who had seen service and risen to the rank of commandant; and he retained some of the brisk decisive manners of the camp. On the other hand, as soon as his resignation was accepted, he had come to Our Lady of the Snows as a boarder, and after a brief experience of its ways, had decided to remain as a novice. Already the new life was beginning to modify his appearance; already he had acquired somewhat of the quiet and smiling air of the brethren; and he was yet neither an officer nor a Trappist, but partook of the character of each. And certainly here was a man in an interesting nick of life. Out of the noise of cannon and trumpets, he was in the act of passing into this still country bordering on the grave, where men sleep nightly in their grave-clothes, and, like phantoms, communicate by signs.

At supper we talked politics. I make it my business, when I am in France, to preach political goodwill and moderation, and to dwell on the example of Poland, much as some alarmists in England dwell on the example of Carthage.[31] The priest and the commandant assured me of their sympathy with all I said, and made a heavy sighing over the bitterness of contemporary feeling.

'Why, you cannot say anything to a man with which he does not absolutely agree,' said I, 'but he flies up at you in a temper.'

They both declared that such a state of things was anti-christian.

While we were thus agreeing, what should my tongue stumble upon but a word in praise of Gambetta's moderation?[32] The old soldier's countenance was instantly suffused with blood; with the palms of his hands he beat the table like a naughty child.

'*Comment, monsieur?*'[33] he shouted. '*Comment?* Gambetta moderate? Will you dare to justify these words?'

But the priest had not forgotten the tenor of our talk. And

suddenly, in the height of his fury, the old soldier found a warning look directed on his face: the absurdity of his behaviour was brought home to him in a flash; and the storm came to an abrupt end, without another word.

It was only in the morning, over our coffee (Friday, September 27th), that this couple found out I was a heretic. I suppose I had misled them by some admiring expressions as to the monastic life around us; and it was only by a point-blank question that the truth came out. I had been tolerantly used, both by simple Father Apollinaris and astute Father Michael; and the good Irish deacon, when he heard of my religious weakness, had only patted me upon the shoulder and said, 'You must be a Catholic and come to heaven.' But I was now among a different sect of orthodox. These two men were bitter and upright and narrow, like the worst of Scotsmen, and indeed, upon my heart, I fancy they were worse. The priest snorted aloud like a battle-horse.

'*Et vous prétendez mourir dans cette espèce de croyance?*'[34] he demanded; and there is no type used by mortal printers large enough to qualify his accent.

I humbly indicated that I had no design of changing.

But he could not away with such a monstrous attitude. 'No, no,' he cried, 'you must change. You have come here, God has led you here, and you must embrace the opportunity.'

I made a slip in policy; I appealed to the family affections, though I was speaking to a priest and a soldier, two classes of men circumstantially divorced from the kind and homely ties of life.

'Your father and mother?' cried the priest. 'Very well; you will convert them in their turn when you go home.'

I think I see my father's face! I would rather tackle the Gætulian lion[35] in his den than embark on such an enterprise against the family theologian.

But now the hunt was up; priest and soldier were in full cry for my conversion; and the Work of the Propagation of the Faith, for which the people of Cheylard subscribed forty-eight francs ten centimes during 1877, was being gallantly pursued against myself. It was an odd but most effective proselytising. They never sought to convince me in argument, where I might have attempted some defence, but took it for granted that I was both ashamed and terrified at my position, and urged me solely on the point of time. Now, they said, when God had led me to Our Lady of the Snows, now was the appointed hour.

'Do not be withheld by false shame,' observed the priest, for my encouragement.

For one who feels very similarly to all sects of religion, and who has never been able, even for a moment, to weigh seriously the merit of this or that creed on the eternal side of things, however much he may see to praise or blame upon the secular and temporal side, the situation thus created was both unfair and painful. I committed my second fault in tact, and tried to plead that it was all the same thing in the end, and we were all drawing near by different sides to the same kind and undiscriminating Friend and Father. That, as it seems to lay spirits, would be the only gospel worthy of the name. But different men think differently; and this revolutionary aspiration brought down the priest with all the terrors of the law. He launched into harrowing details of hell. The damned, he said – on the authority of a little book which he had read not a week before, and which, to add conviction to conviction, he had fully intended to bring along with him in his pocket – were to occupy the same attitude through all eternity in the midst of dismal tortures. And as he thus expatiated, he grew in nobility of aspect with his enthusiasm.

As a result the pair concluded that I should seek out the Prior, since the Abbot was from home, and lay my case immediately before him.

'C'est mon conseil comme ancien militaire,' observed the commandant; 'et celui de monsieur comme prêtre.'[36]

'Oui,' added the curé, sententiously nodding; 'comme ancien militaire – et comme prêtre.'

At this moment, whilst I was somewhat embarrassed how to answer, in came one of the monks, a little brown fellow, as lively as a grig,[37] and with an Italian accent, who threw himself at once into the contention, but in a milder and more persuasive vein, as befitted one of these pleasant brethren. Look at him, he said. The rule was very hard; he would have dearly liked to stay in his own country, Italy – it was well known how beautiful it was, the beautiful Italy; but then there were no Trappists in Italy; and he had a soul to save; and here he was.

I am afraid I must be at bottom, what a cheerful Indian critic has dubbed me, 'a faddling hedonist';[38] for this description of the brother's motives gave me somewhat of a shock. I should have preferred to think he had chosen the life for its own sake, and not for ulterior purposes; and this shows how profoundly I was out of sympathy with these good Trappists, even when I was doing my best to sympathise. But to the *curé* the argument seemed decisive.

'Hear that!' he cried. 'And I have seen a marquis here, a marquis, a marquis' – he repeated the holy word three times over – 'and other persons high in society; and generals. And here, at your side, is this gentleman, who has been so many years in armies – decorated, an old warrior. And here he is, ready to dedicate himself to God.'

I was by this time so thoroughly embarrassed that I pleaded cold feet, and made my escape from the apartment. It was a furious windy morning, with a sky much cleared, and long and potent intervals of sunshine; and I wandered until dinner in the wild country towards the east, sorely staggered and beaten upon by the gale, but rewarded with some striking views.

At dinner the Work of the Propagation of the Faith was recommenced, and on this occasion still more distastefully to me. The priest asked me many questions as to the contemptible faith of my fathers, and received my replies with a kind of ecclesiastical titter.

'Your sect,' he said once; 'for I think you will admit it would be doing it too much honour to call it a religion.'

'As you please, monsieur,' said I. '*La parole est à vous*.'[39]

At length I grew annoyed beyond endurance; and although he was on his own ground, and, what is more to the purpose, an old man, and so holding a claim upon my toleration, I could not avoid a protest against this uncivil usage. He was sadly discountenanced.

'I assure you,' he said, 'I have no inclination to laugh in my heart. I have no other feeling but interest in your soul.'

And there ended my conversion. Honest man! he was no dangerous deceiver; but a country parson, full of zeal and faith. Long may he tread Gévaudan with his kilted skirts – a man strong to walk and strong to comfort his parishioners in death! I dare say he would beat bravely through a snowstorm where his duty called him; and it is not always the most faithful believer who makes the cunningest apostle.

UPPER GÉVAUDAN

(continued)

'The bed was made, the room was fit,
By punctual eve the stars were lit:
The air was sweet, the water ran;
No need was there for maid or man,
When we put up, my ass and I,
At God's green caravanserai.'
  Old Play[1]

Across the Goulet

The wind fell during dinner, and the sky remained clear; so it was under better auspices that I loaded Modestine before the monastery gate. My Irish friend accompanied me so far on the way. As we came through the wood, there was Père Apollinaire hauling his barrow; and he too quitted his labours to go with me for perhaps a hundred yards, holding my hand between both of his in front of him.[2] I parted first from one and then from the other with unfeigned regret, but yet with the glee of the traveller who shakes off the dust of one stage before hurrying forth upon another. Then Modestine and I mounted the course of the Allier, which here led us back into Gévaudan towards its sources in the forest of Mercoire. It was but an inconsiderable burn before we left its guidance. Thence, over a hill, our way lay through a naked plateau, until we reached Chasseradès at sundown.

The company in the inn kitchen that night were all men employed in survey for one of the projected railways. They were intelligent and conversable, and we decided the future of France over hot wine, until the state of the clock frightened us to rest. There were four beds in the little upstairs room; and we slept six. But I had a bed to myself, and persuaded them to leave the window open.

'*Hé, bourgeois; il est cinq heures!*'[3] was the cry that wakened me in the morning (Saturday, September 28th). The room was full of a transparent darkness, which dimly showed me the other three beds and the five different nightcaps on the pillows. But out of the window the dawn was growing ruddy in a long belt over the hill-tops, and day was about to flood the plateau. The hour was inspiriting; and there seemed a promise of calm weather, which was perfectly fulfilled. I was soon under way with Modestine. The road lay for a while over the plateau, and then descended through a precipitous village into the valley of the Chassezac. This stream ran among green meadows, well hidden from the world by its steep banks; the broom was in flower, and here and there was a hamlet sending up its smoke.

At last the path crossed the Chassezac upon a bridge, and, forsaking this deep hollow, set itself to cross the mountain of La Goulet. It wound up through Lestampes by upland fields and woods of beech and birch, and with every corner brought me into an acquaintance with some new interest. Even in the gully of the Chassezac my ear had been struck by a noise like that of a great bass bell ringing at the distance of many miles; but this, as I continued to mount and draw nearer to it, seemed to change in character, and I found at length that it came from someone leading flocks afield to the note of a rural horn. The narrow street of Lestampes stood full of sheep, from wall to wall – black sheep and white, bleating like the birds in spring, and each one accompanying himself upon the sheep-bell round his neck. It made a pathetic concert, all in treble. A little higher, and I passed a pair of men in a tree with pruning-hooks, and one of them was singing the music of a *bourrée*.[4] Still further, and when I was already threading the birches, the crowing of cocks came cheerfully up to my ears, and along with that the voice of a flute discoursing a deliberate and plaintive air from one of the upland villages. I pictured to myself some grizzled, apple-cheeked, country schoolmaster fluting in his bit of a garden in the clear autumn sunshine. All these beautiful and interesting sounds filled my heart with an unwonted expectation; and it appeared to me that, once past this range which I was mounting, I should descend into the garden of the world. Nor was I deceived, for I was now done with rains and winds and a bleak country. The first part of my journey ended here; and this was like an induction of sweet sounds into the other and more beautiful.

There are other degrees of *feyness*,[5] as of punishment, besides the capital; and I was now led by my good spirits into an adventure which I relate in the interest of future donkey-drivers. The road zigzagged so widely on the hillside that I chose a short-cut by map and compass, and struck through the dwarf woods to catch the road again upon a higher level. It was my one serious conflict with Modestine. She would none of my short-cut; she turned in my face, she backed, she reared; she, whom I had hitherto imagined to be dumb, actually brayed with a loud hoarse flourish, like a cock crowing for the dawn. I plied the goad with one hand; with the other, so steep was the ascent, I had to hold on the pack-saddle. Half a dozen times she was nearly over backwards on the top of me; half a dozen times, from sheer weariness of spirit, I was nearly giving it up, and leading her down again to follow the road. But I took the thing as a wager, and fought it through. I was surprised, as I went on my way again, by what appeared to be chill raindrops falling on my hand, and more than once looked up in wonder at the cloudless sky. But it was only sweat which came dropping from my brow.

Over the summit of the Goulet there was no marked road – only upright stones posted from space to space to guide the drovers. The turf underfoot was springy and well scented. I had no company but a lark or two, and met but one bullock-cart between Lestampes and Bleymard. In front of me I saw a shallow valley, and beyond that the range of the Lozère, sparsely wooded and well enough modelled in the flanks, but straight and dull in outline. There was scarce a sign of culture; only about Bleymard, the white high-road from Villefort to Mende traversed a range of meadows, set with spiry poplars, and sounding from side to side with the bells of flocks and herds.

A Night among the Pines

From Bleymard after dinner, although it was already late, I set out to scale a portion of the Lozère. An ill-marked stony drove-road guided me forward; and I met nearly half a dozen bullock-carts descending from the woods, each laden with a whole pine-tree for the winter's firing.[6] At the top of the woods, which do not climb very high upon this cold ridge, I struck leftward by a path among the pines, until I hit on a dell of green turf, where a streamlet made a little spout over some stones to serve me for a water-tap. 'In a more sacred or sequestered bower – nor nymph nor faunus haunted.'[7] The trees were not old, but they grew thickly round the glade: there was no outlook, except north-eastward upon distant hill-tops, or straight upward to the sky; and the encampment felt secure and private like a room. By the time I had made my arrangements and fed Modestine, the day was already beginning to decline. I buckled myself to the knees into my sack and made a hearty meal;[8] and as soon as the sun went down, I pulled my cap over my eyes and fell asleep.

Night is a dead monotonous period under a roof; but in the open world it passes lightly, with its stars and dews and perfumes, and the hours are marked by changes in the face of Nature. What seems a kind of temporal death to people choked between walls and curtains, is only a light and living slumber to the man who sleeps afield. All night long he can hear Nature breathing deeply and freely; even as she takes her rest she turns and smiles; and there is one stirring hour unknown to those who dwell in houses, when a wakeful influence goes abroad over the sleeping hemisphere, and all the outdoor world are on their feet. It is then that the cock first crows, not this time to announce the dawn, but like a cheerful watchman speeding the course of night. Cattle awake on the meadows; sheep break their fast on dewy hillsides, and change to a new lair among the ferns; and houseless men, who have lain down with the fowls, open their dim eyes and behold the beauty of the night.

At what inaudible summons, at what gentle touch of Nature, are all these sleepers thus recalled in the same hour to life? Do the stars rain down an influence, or do we share some thrill of mother earth below our resting bodies? Even shepherds and old country-folk, who are the deepest read in these arcana, have not a guess as to the means or purpose of this nightly resurrection. Towards two in the morning they declare the thing takes place; and neither know nor inquire further. And at least it is a pleasant incident. We are disturbed in our slumber, only, like the luxurious Montaigne,[9] 'that we may the better and more sensibly relish it.' We have a moment to look upon the stars, and there is a special pleasure for some minds in the reflection that we share the impulse with all outdoor creatures in our neighbourhood, that we have escaped out of the Bastille[10] of civilisation, and are become, for the time being, a mere kindly animal and a sheep of Nature's flock.

When that hour came to me among the pines, I wakened thirsty. My tin was standing by me half full of water. I emptied it at a draught; and feeling broad awake after this internal cold aspersion, sat upright to make a cigarette. The stars were clear, coloured, and jewel-like, but not frosty. A faint silvery vapour stood for the Milky Way. All around me the black fir-points stood upright and stock-still. By the whiteness of the pack-saddle, I could see Modestine walking round and round at the length of her tether; I could hear her steadily munching at the sward; but there was not another sound, save the indescribable quiet talk of the runnel over the stones. I lay lazily smoking and studying the colour of the sky, as we call the void of space, from where it showed a reddish grey behind the pines to where it showed a glossy blue-black between the stars.[11] As if to be more like a pedlar, I wear a silver ring. This I could see faintly shining as I raised or lowered the cigarette; and at each whiff the inside of my hand was illuminated, and became for a second the highest light in the landscape.

A faint wind, more like a moving coolness than a stream of air, passed down the glade from time to time; so that even in my great chamber the air was being renewed all night long. I thought with horror of the inn at Chasseradès and the congregated nightcaps; with horror of the nocturnal prowesses of clerks and students, of hot theatres and pass-keys and close rooms. I have not often enjoyed a more serene possession of myself, nor felt more independent of material aids. The outer world, from which we cower into our houses, seemed after all a gentle habitable place; and night after night a man's bed, it seemed, was laid and waiting for him in the fields, where God keeps an open house. I thought I had rediscovered one of those truths which are revealed to savages and hid from political economists: at the least, I had discovered a new pleasure for myself. And yet even while I was exulting in my solitude I became aware of a strange lack. I wished a companion to lie near me in the starlight, silent and not moving, but ever within touch. For there is a fellowship more quiet even than solitude, and which, rightly understood, is solitude made perfect. And to live out of doors with the woman a man loves is of all lives the most complete and free.[12]

As I thus lay, between content and longing, a faint noise stole towards me through the pines. I thought, at first, it was the crowing of cocks or the barking of dogs at some very distant farm; but steadily and gradually it took articulate shape in my ears, until I became aware that a passenger was going by upon the high-road in the valley, and singing loudly as he went. There was more of goodwill than grace in his performance; but he trolled with ample lungs; and the sound of his voice took hold upon the hillside and set the air shaking in the leafy glens. I have heard people passing by night in sleeping cities; some of them sang; one, I remember, played loudly on the bagpipes. I have heard the rattle of a cart or carriage spring up suddenly after hours of stillness, and pass, for some minutes, within the range of my hearing as I lay abed. There is a romance about all who are abroad in the black hours, and with something of a thrill we try to guess their business. But here the romance was double: first, this glad passenger, lit internally with wine, who sent up his voice in music through the night; and then I, on the other hand, buckled into my sack, and smoking alone in the pine-woods between four and five thousand feet towards the stars.

When I awoke again (Sunday, 29th September), many of the stars had disappeared; only the stronger companions of the night still burned visibly overhead; and away towards the east I

saw a faint haze of light upon the horizon, such as had been the
Milky Way when I was last awake. Day was at hand. I lit my
lantern, and by its glow-worm light put on my boots and gaiters;
then I broke up some bread for Modestine, filled my can at the
water-tap, and lit my spirit-lamp to boil myself some chocolate.
The blue darkness lay long in the glade where I had so sweetly
slumbered; but soon there was a broad streak of orange melting
into gold along the mountain-tops of Vivarais. A solemn glee
possessed my mind at this gradual and lovely coming in of day.
I heard the runnel with delight; I looked round me for something
beautiful and unexpected; but the still black pine-trees, the
hollow glade, the munching ass, remained unchanged in figure.
Nothing had altered but the light, and that, indeed, shed over
all a spirit of life and of breathing peace, and moved me to a
strange exhilaration.

I drank my water-chocolate, which was hot if it was not rich,
and strolled here and there, and up and down about the glade.
While I was thus delaying, a gush of steady wind, as long as a
heavy sigh, poured direct out of the quarter of the morning. It
was cold, and set me sneezing. The trees near at hand tossed
their black plumes in its passage; and I could see the thin distant
spires of pine along the edge of the hill rock slightly to and fro
against the golden east. Ten minutes after, the sunlight spread
at a gallop along the hillside, scattering shadows and sparkles,
and the day had come completely.

I hastened to prepare my pack, and tackle the steep ascent
that lay before me; but I had something on my mind. It was only
a fancy; yet a fancy will sometimes be importunate. I had been
most hospitably received and punctually served in my green
caravanserai. The room was airy, the water excellent, and the
dawn had called me to a moment. I say nothing of the tapestries
or the inimitable ceiling, nor yet of the view which I commanded
from the windows; but I felt I was in someone's debt for all this
liberal entertainment. And so it pleased me, in a half-laughing
way, to leave pieces of money on the turf as I went along, until
I had left enough for my night's lodging. I trust they did not fall
to some rich and churlish drover.

THE COUNTRY OF
THE CAMISARDS[1]

'We travelled in the print of olden wars;
   Yet all the land was green;
   And love we found, and peace,
   Where fire and war had been.
They pass and smile, the children of the sword –
   No more the sword they wield:
   And O, how deep the corn
   Along the battlefield!'
W. P. Bannatyne.

Across the Lozère

The track that I had followed in the evening soon died out, and I continued to follow over a bald turf ascent a row of stone pillars,[2] such as had conducted me across the Goulet. It was already warm. I tied my jacket on the pack, and walked in my knitted waistcoat. Modestine herself was in high spirits, and broke of her own accord, for the first time in my experience, into a jolting trot that sent the oats swashing in the pocket of my coat. The view, back upon the northern Gévaudan, extended with every step; scarce a tree, scarce a house, appeared upon the fields of wild hill that ran north, east, and west, all blue and gold in the haze and sunlight of the morning. A multitude of little birds kept sweeping and twittering about my path; they perched on the stone pillars, they pecked and strutted on the turf, and I saw them circle in volleys in the blue air, and show, from time to time, translucent flickering wings between the sun and me.

Almost from the first moment of my march a faint large noise,

like a distant surf, had filled my ears. Sometimes I was tempted
to think it the voice of a neighbouring waterfall, and sometimes
a subjective result of the utter stillness of the hill. But as I
continued to advance, the noise increased and became like the
hissing of an enormous tea-urn, and at the same time breaths of
cool air began to reach me from the direction of the summit. At
length I understood. It was blowing stiffly from the south upon
the other slope of the Lozère, and every step that I took I was
drawing nearer to the wind.

Although it had been long desired, it was quite unexpectedly
at last that my eyes rose above the summit. A step that seemed
no way more decisive than many other steps that had preceded
it – and, 'like stout Cortez when, with eagle eyes, he stared at
the Pacific,'[3] I took possession, in my own name, of a new
quarter of the world. For behold, instead of the gross turf
rampart I had been mounting for so long, a view into the hazy
air of heaven, and a land of intricate blue hills below my feet.

The Lozère lies nearly east and west, cutting Gévaudan into
two unequal parts; its highest point, this Pic de Finiels, on which
I was then standing, rises upwards of five thousand six hundred
feet above the sea, and in clear weather commands a view over
all lower Languedoc to the Mediterranean Sea. I have spoken
with people who either pretended or believed that they had seen,
from the Pic de Finiels, white ships sailing by Montpellier and
Cette.[4] Behind was the upland northern country through which
my way had lain, peopled by a dull race, without wood, without
much grandeur of hill-form, and famous in the past for little
besides wolves. But in front of me, half-veiled in sunny haze,
lay a new Gévaudan, rich, picturesque, illustrious for stirring
events. Speaking largely, I was in the Cévennes at Monastier,
and during all my journey; but there is a strict and local sense
in which only this confused and shaggy country at my feet has
any title to the name, and in this sense the peasantry employ the
word. These are the Cévennes with an emphasis; the Cévennes
of the Cévennes. In that undecipherable labyrinth of hills, a war
of bandits, a war of wild beasts, raged for two years between
the Grand Monarch[5] with all his troops and marshals on the
one hand, and a few thousand Protestant mountaineers upon

the other. A hundred and eighty years ago, the Camisards held a station even on the Lozère, where I stood; they had an organisation, arsenals, a military and religious hierarchy; their affairs were 'the discourse of every coffee-house' in London; England sent fleets in their support; their leaders prophesied and murdered; with colours and drums, and the singing of old French psalms, their bands sometimes affronted daylight, marched before walled cities, and dispersed the generals of the king; and sometimes at night, or in masquerade, possessed themselves of strong castles, and avenged treachery upon their allies and cruelty upon their foes. There, a hundred and eighty years ago, was the chivalrous Roland, 'Count and Lord Roland, generalissimo of the Protestants in France,' grave, silent, imperious, pock-marked ex-dragoon, whom a lady followed in his wanderings out of love. There was Cavalier, a baker's apprentice with a genius for war, elected brigadier of Camisards at seventeen, to die at fifty-five the English Governor of Jersey. There again was Castanet,[6] a partisan leader in a voluminous peruke and with a taste for controversial divinity. Strange generals, who moved apart to take counsel with the God of Hosts, and fled or offered battle, set sentinels or slept in an unguarded camp, as the Spirit whispered to their hearts! And there, to follow these and other leaders, was the rank and file of prophets and disciples, bold, patient, indefatigable, hardy to run upon the mountains, cheering their rough life with psalms, eager to fight, eager to pray, listening devoutly to the oracles of brain-sick children, and mystically putting a grain of wheat among the pewter balls with which they charged their muskets.

I had travelled hitherto through a dull district, and in the track of nothing more notable than the child-eating Beast of Gévaudan, the Napoleon Bonaparte of wolves. But now I was to go down into the scene of a romantic chapter – or, better, a romantic foot-note – in the history of the world. What was left of all this bygone dust and heroism? I was told that Protestantism still survived in this head seat of Protestant resistance; so much the priest himself had told me in the monastery parlour. But I had yet to learn if it were a bare survival, or a lively and generous tradition. Again, if in the northern Cévennes the people are

narrow in religious judgments, and more filled with zeal than
charity, what was I to look for in this land of persecution and
reprisal – in a land where the tyranny of the Church produced
the Camisard rebellion, and the terror of the Camisards threw
the Catholic peasantry into legalised revolt upon the other side,
so that Camisard and Florentin[7] skulked for each other's lives
among the mountains?

Just on the brow of the hill, where I paused to look before
me, the series of stone pillars came abruptly to an end; and only
a little below, a sort of track appeared and began to go down a
break-neck slope, turning like a corkscrew as it went. It led into
a valley between falling hills, stubbly with rocks like a reaped
field of corn, and floored farther down with green meadows. I
followed the track with precipitation; the steepness of the slope,
the continual agile turning of the line of descent, and the old
unwearied hope of finding something new in a new country, all
conspired to lend me wings. Yet a little lower and a stream
began, collecting itself together out of many fountains, and soon
making a glad noise among the hills. Sometimes it would cross
the track in a bit of waterfall, with a pool, in which Modestine
refreshed her feet.

The whole descent is like a dream to me, so rapidly was it
accomplished. I had scarcely left the summit ere the valley had
closed round my path, and the sun beat upon me, walking in a
stagnant lowland atmosphere. The track became a road, and
went up and down in easy undulations. I passed cabin after
cabin, but all seemed deserted; and I saw not a human creature
nor heard any sound except that of the stream. I was, however,
in a different country from the day before. The stony skeleton
of the world was here vigorously displayed to sun and air. The
slopes were steep and changeful. Oak-trees clung along the hills,
well grown, wealthy in leaf, and touched by the autumn with
strong and luminous colours. Here and there another stream
would fall in from the right or the left, down a gorge of snow-
white and tumultuary boulders. The river in the bottom (for it
was rapidly growing a river, collecting on all hands as it trotted
on its way) here foamed a while in desperate rapids, and there

lay in pools of the most enchanting sea-green shot with watery browns. As far as I have gone, I have never seen a river of so changeful and delicate a hue; crystal was not more clear, the meadows were not by half so green; and at every pool I saw I felt a thrill of longing to be out of these hot, dusty, and material garments, and bathe my naked body in the mountain air and water. All the time as I went on I never forgot it was the Sabbath; the stillness was a perpetual reminder; and I heard in spirit the church-bells clamouring all over Europe, and the psalms of a thousand churches.

At length a human sound struck upon my ear – a cry strangely modulated between pathos and derision; and looking across the valley, I saw a little urchin sitting in a meadow, with his hands about his knees, and dwarfed to almost comical smallness by the distance. But the rogue had picked me out as I went down the road, from oak wood on to oak wood, driving Modestine; and he made me the compliments of the new country in this tremulous high-pitched salutation. And as all noises are lovely and natural at a sufficient distance, this also, coming through so much clean hill air and crossing all the green valley, sounded pleasant to my ear, and seemed a thing rustic, like the oaks or the river.

A little after, the stream that I was following fell into the Tarn at Pont de Montvert of bloody memory.

Pont de Montvert

One of the first things I encountered in Pont de Montvert was, if I remember rightly, the Protestant temple; but this was but the type of other novelties. A subtle atmosphere distinguishes a town in England from a town in France, or even in Scotland. At Carlisle you can see you are in one country; at Dumfries,[8] thirty miles away, you are as sure that you are in the other. I should find it difficult to tell in what particulars Pont de Montvert differed from Monastier or Langogne, or even Bleymard; but the difference existed, and spoke eloquently to the eyes. The place, with its houses, its lanes, its glaring river-bed, wore an indescribable air of the South.

All was Sunday bustle in the streets and in the public-house, as all had been Sabbath peace among the mountains. There must have been near a score of us at dinner by eleven before noon; and after I had eaten and drunken, and sat writing up my journal, I suppose as many more came dropping in one after another, or by twos and threes. In crossing the Lozère I had not only come among new natural features, but moved into the territory of a different race. These people, as they hurriedly despatched their viands in an intricate sword-play of knives, questioned and answered me with a degree of intelligence which excelled all that I had met, except among the railway folk at Chasseradès. They had open telling faces, and were lively both in speech and manner. They not only entered thoroughly into the spirit of my little trip, but more than one declared, if he were rich enough, he would like to set forth on such another.[9]

Even physically there was a pleasant change. I had not seen a pretty woman since I left Monastier, and there but one. Now of the three who sat down with me to dinner, one was certainly not beautiful – a poor timid thing of forty, quite troubled at this roaring *table-d'hôte*,[10] whom I squired and helped to wine, and pledged and tried generally to encourage, with quite a contrary effect; but the other two, both married, were both more handsome than the average of women. And Clarisse? What shall I say of Clarisse? She waited the table with a heavy placable nonchalance, like a performing cow;[11] her great grey eyes were steeped in amorous languor; her features, although fleshy, were of an original and accurate design; her mouth had a curl; her nostril spoke of dainty pride; her cheek fell into strange and interesting lines. It was a face capable of strong emotion, and, with training, it offered the promise of delicate sentiment. It seemed pitiful to see so good a model left to country admirers and a country way of thought. Beauty should at least have touched society; then, in a moment, it throws off a weight that lay upon it, it becomes conscious of itself, it puts on an elegance, learns a gait and a carriage of the head, and, in a moment, *patet dea*.[12] Before I left I assured Clarisse of my hearty admiration. She took it like milk, without embarrassment or wonder, merely looking at me steadily with her great eyes; and I own the result upon myself was some confusion. If Clarisse could read English, I should not dare to add that her figure was unworthy of her face. Hers was a case for stays; but that may perhaps grow better as she gets up in years.

Pont de Montvert, or Greenhill Bridge, as we might say at home, is a place memorable in the story of the Camisards. It was here that the war broke out; here that those southern Covenanters slew their Archbishop Sharpe.[13] The persecution on the one hand, the febrile enthusiasm on the other, are almost equally difficult to understand in these quiet modern days, and with our easy modern beliefs and disbeliefs. The Protestants were one and all beside their right minds with zeal and sorrow. They were all prophets and prophetesses. Children at the breast would exhort their parents to good works. 'A child of fifteen months at Quissac spoke from its mother's arms, agitated and sobbing, distinctly and with a loud voice.' Marshal Villars[14] has seen a town where all the women 'seemed possessed by the devil,' and had trembling fits, and uttered prophecies publicly upon the streets. A prophetess of Vivarais was hanged at Montpellier because blood flowed from her eyes and nose, and she declared that she was weeping tears of blood for the misfortunes of the Protestants. And it was not only women and children. Stalwart dangerous fellows, used to swing the sickle or to wield the forest axe, were likewise shaken with strange paroxysms, and spoke oracles with sobs and streaming tears. A persecution unsurpassed in violence had lasted near a score of years, and this was the result upon the persecuted; hanging, burning, breaking on the wheel, had been vain; the dragoons had left their hoof-marks over all the country-side; there were men rowing in the galleys, and women pining in the prisons of the Church; and not a thought was changed in the heart of any upright Protestant.

Now the head and forefront of the persecution – after Lamoignon de Bâvile – François de Langlade du Chayla[15] (pronounced Chéïla), Archpriest of the Cévennes and Inspector of Missions in the same country, had a house in which he sometimes dwelt in the town of Pont de Montvert. He was a conscientious person, who seems to have been intended by nature for a pirate, and now fifty-five, an age by which a man has learned all the moderation of which he is capable. A missionary in his youth in China, he there suffered martyrdom, was left for dead, and only succoured and brought back to life by the charity of a pariah. We must suppose the pariah devoid of second-sight, and not purposely malicious in this act. Such an experience, it might be thought, would have cured a man of the desire to persecute; but the human spirit is a thing strangely put together; and, having been a Christian martyr, Du Chayla became a Christian persecutor. The Work of the Propagation of the Faith went roundly forward in his hands. His house in Pont de Montvert served him as a prison. There he closed the hands of his prisoners upon live coal, and plucked out the hairs of their beard, to convince them that they were deceived in their opinions. And yet had not he himself tried and proved the inefficacy of these carnal arguments among the Buddhists in China?

Not only was life made intolerable in Languedoc, but flight was rigidly forbidden. One Massip, a muleteer, and well acquainted with the mountain-paths, had already guided several troops of fugitives in safety to Geneva; and on him, with another convoy, consisting mostly of women dressed as men, Du Chayla, in an evil hour for himself, laid his hands. The Sunday following, there was a conventicle[16] of Protestants in the woods of Altefage upon Mont Bougès; where there stood up one Séguier – Spirit Séguier,[17] as his companions called him – a wool-carder, tall, black-faced, and toothless, but a man full of prophecy. He declared, in the name of God, that the time for submission had gone by, and they must betake themselves to arms for the deliverance of their brethren and the destruction of the priests.

The next night, 24th July, 1702, a sound disturbed the Inspector of Missions as he sat in his prison-house at Pont de Montvert; the voices of many men upraised in psalmody drew nearer and nearer through the town. It was ten at night; he had his court about him, priests, soldiers, and servants, to the number of twelve or fifteen; and now dreading the insolence of a conventicle below his very windows, he ordered forth his soldiers to report. But the psalm-singers were already at his door, fifty strong, led by the inspired Séguier, and breathing death. To their summons, the archpriest made answer like a stout old persecutor, and bade his garrison fire upon the mob. One Camisard (for, according to some, it was in this night's work that they came by the name) fell at this discharge; his comrades burst in the door with hatchets and a beam of wood, overran the lower story of the house, set free the prisoners, and finding one of them in the *vine*, a sort of Scavenger's Daughter[18] of the place and period, redoubled in fury against Du Chayla, and sought by repeated assaults to carry the upper floors. But he, on his side, had given absolution to his men, and they bravely held the staircase.

'Children of God,' cried the prophet, 'hold your hands. Let us burn the house, with the priest and the satellites of Baal.'[19]

The fire caught readily. Out of an upper window Du Chayla and his men lowered themselves into the garden by means of knotted sheets; some escaped across the river under the bullets of the insurgents; but the archpriest himself fell, broke his thigh, and could only crawl into the hedge. What were his reflections as this second martyrdom drew near? A poor, brave, besotted, hateful man, who had done his duty resolutely according to his light both in the Cévennes and China. He found at least one telling word to say in his defence; for when the roof fell in and the upbursting flames discovered his retreat, and they came and dragged him to the public place of the town, raging and calling him damned – 'If I be damned,' said he, 'why should you also damn yourselves?'

Here was a good reason for the last; but in the course of his inspectorship he had given many stronger which all told in a contrary direction; and these he was now to hear. One by one, Séguier first, the Camisards drew near and stabbed him. 'This,' they said, 'is for my father broken on the wheel. This for my brother in the galleys. That for my mother or my sister imprisoned in your cursed convents.' Each gave his blow and his reason; and then all kneeled and sang psalms around the body till the dawn. With the dawn, still singing, they defiled away towards Fugères, farther up the Tarn, to pursue the work of vengeance,

leaving Du Chayla's prison-house in ruins, and his body pierced
with two-and-fifty wounds upon the public place.

'Tis a wild night's work, with its accompaniment of psalms;
and it seems as if a psalm must always have a sound of threatening in that town upon the Tarn. But the story does not end, even
so far as concerns Pont de Montvert, with the departure of the
Camisards. The career of Séguier was brief and bloody. Two
more priests and a whole family at Ladevèze, from the father to
the servants, fell by his hand or by his orders; and yet he was
but a day or two at large, and restrained all the time by the
presence of the soldiery. Taken at length by a famous soldier of
fortune, Captain Poul,[20] he appeared unmoved before his judges.

'Your name?' they asked.

'Pierre Séguier.'

'Why are you called Spirit?'

'Because the Spirit of the Lord is with me.'

'Your domicile?'

'Lately in the desert, and soon in heaven.'

'Have you no remorse for your crimes?'

'I have committed none. *My soul is like a garden full of shelter
and of fountains.*'[21]

At Pont de Montvert, on the 12th of August, he had his right
hand stricken from his body, and was burned alive. And his soul
was like a garden? So perhaps was the soul of Du Chayla, the
Christian martyr. And perhaps if you could read in my soul, or
I could read in yours, our own composure might seem little less
surprising.

Du Chayla's house still stands, with a new roof, beside one
of the bridges of the town; and if you are curious you may see
the terrace-garden into which he dropped.

In the Valley of the Tarn

A new road leads from Pont de Montvert to Florac by the valley
of the Tarn; a smooth sandy ledge, it runs about half-way
between the summit of the cliffs and the river in the bottom of

the valley; and I went in and out, as I followed it, from bays of shadow into promontories of afternoon sun. This was a pass like that of Killiecrankie,[22] a deep turning gully in the hills, with the Tarn making a wonderful hoarse uproar far below, and craggy summits standing in the sunshine high above. A thin fringe of ash-trees ran about the hill-tops, like ivy on a ruin; but on the lower slopes and far up every glen the Spanish chestnut-trees stood each four-square to heaven under its tented foliage. Some were planted each on its own terrace, no larger than a bed; some, trusting in their roots, found strength to grow and prosper and be straight and large upon the rapid slopes of the valley; others, where there was a margin to the river, stood marshalled in a line and mighty like cedars of Lebanon. Yet even where they grew most thickly they were not to be thought of as a wood, but as a herd of stalwart individuals; and the dome of each tree stood forth separate and large, and as it were a little hill, from among the domes of its companions. They gave forth a faint sweet perfume which pervaded the air of the afternoon; autumn had put tints of gold and tarnish in the green; and the sun so shone through and kindled the broad foliage, that each chestnut was relieved against another, not in shadow, but in light. A humble sketcher here laid down his pencil in despair.

I wish I could convey a notion of the growth of these noble trees; of how they strike out boughs like the oak, and trail sprays of drooping foliage like the willow; of how they stand on upright fluted columns like the pillars of a church; or like the olive, from the most shattered bole can put out smooth and youthful shoots, and begin a new life upon the ruins of the old. Thus they partake of the nature of many different trees; and even their prickly top-knots, seen near at hand against the sky, have a certain palm-like air that impresses the imagination. But their individuality, although compounded of so many elements, is but the richer and the more original. And to look down upon a level filled with these knolls of foliage, or to see a clan of old unconquerable chestnuts cluster 'like herded elephants' upon the spur of a mountain, is to rise to higher thoughts of the powers that are in Nature.

Between Modestine's laggard humour and the beauty of the

scene, we made little progress all that afternoon;[23] and at last
finding the sun, although still far from setting, was already
beginning to desert the narrow valley of the Tarn, I began to
cast about for a place to camp in. This was not easy to find;
the terraces were too narrow, and the ground, where it was
unterraced, was usually too steep for a man to lie upon. I should
have slipped all night, and awakened towards morning with my
feet or my head in the river.

After perhaps a mile, I saw, some sixty feet above the road, a
little plateau large enough to hold my sack, and securely para-
peted by the trunk of an aged and enormous chestnut. Thither,
with infinite trouble, I goaded and kicked the reluctant Modestine, and there I hastened to unload her. There was only room
for myself upon the plateau, and I had to go nearly as high again
before I found so much as standing room for the ass. It was on
a heap of rolling stones, on an artificial terrace, certainly not
five feet square in all. Here I tied her to a chestnut, and having
given her corn and bread and made a pile of chestnut-leaves, of
which I found her greedy, I descended once more to my own
encampment.

The position was unpleasantly exposed. One or two carts
went by upon the road; and as long as daylight lasted I concealed
myself, for all the world like a hunted Camisard,[24] behind my
fortification of vast chestnut trunk; for I was passionately afraid
of discovery and the visit of jocular persons in the night. Moreover, I saw that I must be early awake; for these chestnut gardens
had been the scene of industry no further gone than on the day
before. The slope was strewn with lopped branches, and here
and there a great package of leaves was propped against a trunk;
for even the leaves are serviceable, and the peasants use them in
winter by way of fodder for their animals. I picked a meal in
fear and trembling, half lying down to hide myself from the
road; and I daresay I was as much concerned as if I had been
a scout from Joani's band above upon the Lozère or from
Salomon's[25] across the Tarn in the old times of psalm-singing
and blood. Or, indeed, perhaps more; for the Camisards had a
remarkable confidence in God; and a tale comes back into my
memory of how the Count of Gévaudan, riding with a party of

dragoons and a notary at his saddle-bow to enforce the oath of
fidelity in all the country hamlets, entered a valley in the woods,
and found Cavalier and his men at dinner, gaily seated on the
grass, and their hats crowned with box-tree garlands, while
fifteen women washed their linen in the stream. Such was a
field festival in 1703; at that date Antony Watteau[26] would be
painting similar subjects.

This was a very different camp from that of the night before
in the cool and silent pine woods. It was warm and even stifling
in the valley. The shrill song of frogs, like the tremolo note of a
whistle with a pea in it, rang up from the riverside before the
sun was down. In the growing dusk, faint rustlings began to run
to and fro among the fallen leaves; from time to time a faint
chirping or cheeping noise would fall upon my ear; and from
time to time I thought I could see the movement of something
swift and indistinct between the chestnuts. A profusion of large
ants swarmed upon the ground;[27] bats whisked by, and mos-
quitoes droned overhead. The long boughs with their bunches of
leaves hung against the sky like garlands; and those immediately
above and around me had somewhat the air of a trellis which
should have been wrecked and half overthrown in a gale of wind.

Sleep for a long time fled my eyelids; and just as I was beginning to feel quiet stealing over my limbs, and settling densely on
my mind, a noise at my head startled me broad awake again,
and, I will frankly confess it, brought my heart into my mouth.
It was such a noise as a person would make scratching loudly
with a finger-nail; it came from under the knapsack which served
me for a pillow, and it was thrice repeated before I had time to
sit up and turn about. Nothing was to be seen, nothing more
was to be heard, but a few of these mysterious rustlings far and
near, and the ceaseless accompaniment of the river and the
frogs. I learned next day that the chestnut gardens are infested
by rats; rustling, chirping, and scraping were probably all due
to these; but the puzzle, for the moment, was insoluble, and I
had to compose myself for sleep, as best I could, in wondering
uncertainty about my neighbours.[28]

I was wakened in the grey of the morning (Monday,
30th September) by the sound of footsteps not far off upon the

stones, and, opening my eyes, I beheld a peasant going by among the chestnuts by a footpath that I had not hitherto observed. He turned his head neither to the right nor to the left, and disappeared in a few strides among the foliage. Here was an escape! But it was plainly more than time to be moving. The peasantry were abroad; scarce less terrible to me in my nondescript position than the soldiers of Captain Poul to an undaunted Camisard.[29] I fed Modestine with what haste I could; but as I was returning to my sack, I saw a man and a boy come down the hillside in a direction crossing mine. They unintelligibly hailed me, and I replied with inarticulate but cheerful sounds, and hurried forward to get into my gaiters.

The pair, who seemed to be father and son, came slowly up to the plateau, and stood close beside me for some time in silence. The bed was open, and I saw with regret my revolver lying patently disclosed on the blue wool. At last, after they had looked me all over, and the silence had grown laughably embarrassing, the man demanded in what seemed unfriendly tones:—

'You have slept here?'

'Yes,' said I. 'As you see.'

'Why?' he asked.

'My faith!' I answered lightly, 'I was tired.'

He next inquired where I was going and what I had had for dinner; and then, without the least transition, 'C'est bien,'[30] he added, 'come along.' And he and his son, without another word, turned off to the next chestnut-tree but one, which they set to pruning. The thing had passed off more simply than I hoped. He was a grave, respectable man; and his unfriendly voice did not imply that he thought he was speaking to a criminal, but merely to an inferior.

I was soon on the road, nibbling a cake of chocolate and seriously occupied with a case of conscience. Was I to pay for my night's lodging? I had slept ill, the bed was full of fleas in the shape of ants, there was no water in the room, the very dawn had neglected to call me in the morning. I might have missed a train, had there been any in the neighbourhood to catch. Clearly I was dissatisfied with my entertainment; and I decided I should not pay unless I met a beggar.

The valley looked even lovelier by morning; and soon the road descended to the level of the river. Here, in a place where many straight and prosperous chestnuts stood together, making an aisle upon a swarded terrace, I made my morning toilette in the water of the Tarn. It was marvellously clear, thrillingly[31] cool; the soapsuds disappeared as if by magic in the swift current, and the white boulders gave one a model for cleanliness. To wash in one of God's rivers in the open air seems to me a sort of cheerful solemnity or semi-pagan act of worship. To dabble among dishes in a bedroom may perhaps make clean the body; but the imagination takes no share in such a cleansing. I went on with a light and peaceful heart, and sang psalms to the spiritual ear as I advanced.

Suddenly up came an old woman, who point-blank demanded alms.

'Good!' thought I; 'here comes the waiter with the bill.'

And I paid for my night's lodgings on the spot. Take it how you please, but this was the first and the last beggar that I met with during all my tour.[32]

A step or two farther I was overtaken by an old man in a brown nightcap, clear-eyed, weather-beaten, with a faint, excited smile. A little girl followed him, driving two sheep and a goat; but she kept in our wake, while the old man walked beside me and talked about the morning and the valley. It was not much past six; and for healthy people who have slept enough, that is an hour of expansion and of open and trustful talk.

'*Connaissez-vous le Seigneur?*'[33] he said at length.

I asked him what Seigneur he meant; but he only repeated the question with more emphasis and a look in his eyes denoting hope and interest.

'Ah!' said I, pointing upwards, 'I understand you now. Yes, I know Him; He is the best of acquaintances.'

The old man said he was delighted. 'Hold,' he added, striking his bosom; 'it makes me happy here.' There were a few who knew the Lord in these valleys, he went on to tell me; not many, but a few. 'Many are called,' he quoted, 'and few chosen.'[34]

'My father,' said I, 'it is not easy to say who know the Lord; and it is none of our business. Protestants and Catholics, and even those who worship stones, may know Him and be known by Him, for He has made all.'

I did not know I was so good a preacher.

The old man assured me he thought as I did, and repeated his expressions of pleasure at meeting me. 'We are so few,' he said. 'They call us Moravians here; but down in the department of Gard, where there are also a good number, they are called Derbists,[35] after an English pastor.'

I began to understand that I was figuring, in questionable taste, as a member of some sect to me unknown; but I was more pleased with the pleasure of my companion than embarrassed by my own equivocal position. Indeed, I can see no dishonesty in not avowing a difference; and especially in these high matters, where we have all a sufficient assurance that, whoever may be in the wrong, we ourselves are not completely in the right. The truth is much talked about; but this old man in a brown nightcap showed himself so simple, sweet, and friendly that I am not unwilling to profess myself his convert. He was, as a matter of fact, a Plymouth Brother.[36] Of what that involves in the way of doctrine I have no idea nor the time to inform myself; but I know right well that we are all embarked upon a troublesome world, the children of one Father, striving in many essential points to do and to become the same. And although it was somewhat in a mistake that he shook hands with me so often and showed himself so ready to receive my words, that was a mistake of the truth-finding sort. For charity begins blindfold; and only through a series of similar misapprehensions rises at length into a settled principle of love and patience, and a firm belief in all our fellow-men. If I deceived this good old man, in the like manner I would willingly go on to deceive others. And if ever at length, out of our separate and sad ways, we should all come together into one common house, I have a hope, to which I cling dearly, that my mountain Plymouth Brother will hasten to shake hands with me again.

Thus, talking like Christian and Faithful[37] by the way, he and I came down upon a hamlet by the Tarn. It was but a humble place, called La Vernède, with less than a dozen houses, and a Protestant chapel on a knoll. Here he dwelt; and here, at the inn, I ordered my breakfast. The inn was kept by an agreeable young man, a stone-breaker on the road, and his sister, a pretty and engaging girl.[38] The village schoolmaster dropped in to speak with the stranger. And these were all Protestants – a fact which pleased me more than I should have expected; and, what pleased me still more, they seemed all upright and simple people. The Plymouth Brother hung round me with a sort of yearning interest, and returned at least thrice to make sure I was enjoying my meal. His behaviour touched me deeply at the time, and even now moves me in recollection. He feared to intrude, but he would not willingly forego one moment of my society; and he seemed never weary of shaking me by the hand.

When all the rest had drifted off to their day's work, I sat for near half an hour with the young mistress of the house, who talked pleasantly over her seam of the chestnut harvest, and the beauties of the Tarn, and old family affections, broken up when young folk go from home, yet still subsisting. Hers, I am sure, was a sweet nature, with a country plainness and much delicacy underneath; and he who takes her to his heart will doubtless be a fortunate young man.

The valley below La Vernède pleased me more and more as I went forward. Now the hills approached from either hand, naked and crumbling, and walled in the river between cliffs; and now the valley widened and became green. The road led me past the old castle of Miral[39] on a steep; past a battlemented monastery, long since broken up and turned into a church and parsonage; and past a cluster of black roofs, the village of Cocurès, sitting among vineyards and meadows and orchards thick with red apples, and where, along the highway, they were knocking down walnuts from the roadside trees, and gathering them in sacks and baskets. The hills, however much the vale might open, were still tall and bare, with cliffy battlements and here and there a pointed summit; and the Tarn still rattled through the stones with a mountain noise. I had been led by bagmen of a picturesque turn of mind, to expect a horrific country after the heart of Byron;[40] but to my Scottish eyes it seemed smiling and plentiful, as the weather still gave an impression of high summer to my Scottish body; although the chestnuts were already picked out by the autumn, and the poplars, that here began to mingle with them, had turned into pale gold against the approach of winter.[41]

There was something in this landscape, smiling although wild, that explained to me the spirit of the Southern Covenanters. Those who took to the hills for conscience' sake in Scotland had all gloomy and bedevilled thoughts; for once that they received God's comfort they would be twice engaged with Satan; but the Camisards had only bright and supporting visions. They dealt much more in blood, both given and taken; yet I find no obsession of the Evil One in their records. With a light conscience, they pursued their life in these rough times and circumstances. The soul of Séguier, let us not forget, was like a garden. They knew they were on God's side, with a knowledge that has no parallel among the Scots; for the Scots, although they might be certain of the cause, could never rest confident of the person.

'We flew,' says one old Camisard, 'when we heard the sound of psalm-singing, we flew as if with wings. We felt within us an animating ardour, a transporting desire. The feeling cannot be expressed in words. It is a thing that must have been experienced to be understood. However weary we might be, we thought no more of our weariness and grew light, so soon as the psalms fell upon our ears.'

The valley of the Tarn and the people whom I met at La Vernède not only explain to me this passage, but the twenty years of suffering which those, who were so stiff and so bloody when once they betook themselves to war, endured with the meekness of children and the constancy of saints and peasants.

Florac

On a branch of the Tarn stands Florac, the seat of a sub-prefecture, with an old castle, an alley of planes, many quaint street-corners, and a live fountain welling from the hill.[42] It is notable, besides, for handsome women, and as one of the two capitals, Alais being the other, of the country of the Camisards.

The landlord of the inn took me, after I had eaten, to an adjoining *café*, where I, or rather my journey, became the topic of the afternoon. Every one had some suggestion for my guidance; and the sub-prefectorial map[43] was fetched from the sub-prefecture itself, and much thumbed among coffee-cups and glasses of liqueur. Most of these kind advisers were Protestant, though I observed that Protestant and Catholic intermingled in a very easy manner; and it surprised me to see what a lively memory still subsisted of the religious war. Among the hills of the south-west, by Mauchline, Cumnock, or Carsphairn,[44] in isolated farms or in the manse, serious Presbyterian people still recall the days of the great persecution, and the graves of local martyrs are still piously regarded. But in towns and among the so-called better classes, I fear that these old doings have become an idle tale. If you met a mixed company in the King's Arms at Wigtown, it is not likely that the talk would run on Covenanters. Nay, at Muirkirk of Glenluce, I found the beadle's wife had not so much as heard of Prophet Peden.[45] But these Cévenols[46] were proud of their ancestors in quite another sense; the war was their chosen topic; its exploits were their own patent of nobility; and where a man or a race has had but one adventure, and that heroic, we must expect and pardon some prolixity of reference. They told me the country was still full of legends hitherto uncollected; I heard from them about Cavalier's descendants – not direct descendants, be it understood, but only cousins or nephews – who were still prosperous people in the scene of the boy-general's exploits; and one farmer had seen the bones of old combatants dug up into the air of an afternoon in the nineteenth century, in a field where the ancestors had fought, and the great-grandchildren were peaceably ditching.

Later in the day one of the Protestant pastors was so good as to visit me: a young man, intelligent and polite, with whom I passed an hour or two in talk. Florac, he told me, is part Protestant, part Catholic; and the difference in religion is usually doubled by a difference in politics. You may judge of my surprise, coming as I did from such a babbling purgatorial Poland[47] of a place as Monastier, when I learned that the population lived together on very quiet terms, and there was even an exchange of hospitalities between households thus doubly separated. Black Camisard and White Camisard, militiaman and Miquelet and dragoon, Protestant prophet and Catholic cadet of the White Cross,[48] they had all been sabreing and shooting, burning, pillaging and murdering, their hearts hot with indignant passion; and here, after a hundred and seventy years, Protestant is still Protestant, Catholic still Catholic, in mutual toleration and mild amity of life. But the race of man, like that indomitable nature whence it sprang, has medicating virtues of its own; the years and seasons bring various harvests; the sun returns after the rain; and mankind outlives secular animosities, as a single man awakens from the passions of a day. We judge our ancestors from a more divine position; and the dust being a little laid with several centuries, we can see both sides adorned with human virtues and fighting with a show of right.

I have never thought it easy to be just, and find it daily even harder than I thought. I own I met these Protestants with delight and a sense of coming home. I was accustomed to speak their language, in another and deeper sense of the word than that which distinguishes between French and English; for the true Babel is a divergence upon morals. And hence I could hold more free communication with the Protestants, and judge them more justly, than the Catholics. Father Apollinaris may pair off with my mountain Plymouth Brother as two guileless and devout old men; yet I ask myself if I had as ready a feeling for the virtues of the Trappist; or had I been a Catholic, if I should have felt so warmly to the dissenter of La Vernède. With the first I was on terms of mere forbearance; but with the other, although only on a misunderstanding and by keeping on selected points, it was still possible to hold converse and exchange some honest thoughts. In this world of imperfection we gladly welcome even partial intimacies. If we find but one to whom we can speak out of our heart freely, with whom we can walk in love and simplicity without dissimulation, we have no ground of quarrel with the world or God.

In the Valley of the Mimente

On Tuesday, 1st October, we left Florac late in the afternoon, a tired donkey and tired donkey-driver. A little way up the Tarnon, a covered bridge of wood introduced us into the valley of the Mimente.[49] Steep rocky red mountains overhung the stream; great oaks and chestnuts grew upon the slopes or in stony terraces; here and there was a red field of millet or a few apple-trees studded with red apples; and the road passed hard by two black hamlets, one with an old castle atop to please the heart of the tourist.[50]

It was difficult here again to find a spot fit for my encampment. Even under the oaks and chestnuts the ground had not only a very rapid slope, but was heaped with loose stones; and where there was no timber the hills descended to the stream in a red precipice tufted with heather. The sun had left the highest peak in front of me, and the valley was full of the lowing sound of herdsmen's horns as they recalled the flocks into the stable, when I spied a bight of meadow some way below the roadway in an angle of the river. Thither I descended, and, tying Modestine provisionally to a tree, proceeded to investigate the neighbourhood. A grey pearly evening shadow filled the glen; objects at a little distance grew indistinct and melted bafflingly into each other; and the darkness was rising steadily like an exhalation. I approached a great oak which grew in the meadow, hard by the river's brink; when to my disgust the voices of children fell upon my ear, and I beheld a house[51] round the angle on the other bank. I had half a mind to pack and be gone again, but the growing darkness moved me to remain. I had only to make no noise until the night was fairly come, and trust to the dawn to call me early in the morning. But it was hard to be annoyed by neighbours in such a great hotel.[52]

A hollow underneath the oak was my bed. Before I had fed Modestine and arranged my sack, three stars were already brightly shining, and the others were beginning dimly to appear. I slipped down to the river, which looked very black among its rocks, to fill my can; and dined with a good appetite in the dark, for I scrupled to light a lantern while so near a house. The moon, which I had seen, a pallid crescent, all afternoon, faintly illuminated the summit of the hills, but not a ray fell into the bottom of the glen where I was lying. The oak rose before me like a pillar of darkness; and overhead the heartsome stars were set in the face of the night. No one knows the stars who has not slept, as the French happily put it, *à la belle étoile*.[53] He may know all their names and distances and magnitudes, and yet be ignorant of what alone concerns mankind, their serene and gladsome influence on the mind. The greater part of poetry is about the stars; and very justly, for they are themselves the most classical of poets. These same far-away worlds, sprinkled like tapers or shaken together like a diamond dust upon the sky, had looked not otherwise to Roland or Cavalier, when, in the words of the latter, they had 'no other tent but the sky, and no other bed than my mother earth.'

All night a strong wind blew up the valley, and the acorns fell pattering over me from the oak. Yet, on this first night of October, the air was as mild as May, and I slept with the fur thrown back.

I was much disturbed by the barking of a dog, an animal that I fear more than any wolf. A dog is vastly braver, and is besides supported by the sense of duty. If you kill a wolf, you meet with encouragement and praise; but if you kill a dog, the sacred rights of property and the domestic affections come clamouring round you for redress. At the end of a fagging day, the sharp, cruel note of a dog's bark is in itself a keen annoyance; and to a tramp like myself, he represents the sedentary and respectable world in its most hostile form. There is something of the clergyman or the lawyer about this engaging animal; and if he were not amenable to stones, the boldest man would shrink from travelling afoot. I respect dogs much in the domestic circle; but on the highway, or sleeping afield, I both detest and fear them.

I was wakened next morning (Wednesday, October 2nd) by the same dog – for I knew his bark – making a charge down the bank, and then, seeing me sit up, retreating again with great alacrity.[54] The stars were not yet quite extinguished. The heaven was of that enchanting mild grey-blue of the early morn. A still clear light began to fall, and the trees on the hillside were outlined sharply against the sky. The wind had veered more to the north, and no longer reached me in the glen; but as I was going on with my preparations, it drove a white cloud very swiftly over the hill-top; and looking up, I was surprised to see the cloud dyed with gold. In these high regions of the air, the sun was already shining as at noon. If only the clouds travelled high enough, we should see the same thing all night long. For it is always daylight in the fields of space.[55]

As I began to go up the valley, a draught of wind came down it out of the seat of the sunrise, although the clouds continued to run overhead in an almost contrary direction. A few steps farther, and I saw a whole hillside gilded with the sun; and still a little beyond, between two peaks, a centre of dazzling brilliancy appeared floating in the sky, and I was once more face to face with the big bonfire that occupies the kernel of our system.

I met but one human being that forenoon, a dark military-looking wayfarer, who carried a game-bag on a baldric;[56] but he made a remark that seems worthy of record. For when I asked him if he were Protestant or Catholic—

'Oh,' said he, 'I make no shame of my religion. I am a Catholic.'

He made no shame of it! The phrase is a piece of natural statistics; for it is the language of one in a minority. I thought with a smile of Bâvile and his dragoons, and how you may ride rough-shod over a religion for a century, and leave it only the more lively for the friction. Ireland is still Catholic; the Cévennes still Protestant. It is not a basketful of lawpapers, nor the hoofs and pistol-butts of a regiment of horse, that can change one tittle of a ploughman's thoughts. Out-door rustic people have not many ideas, but such as they have are hardy plants and thrive flourishingly in persecution. One who has grown a long while in the sweat of laborious noons, and under the stars at night, a frequenter of hills and forests, an old honest country-man, has, in the end, a sense of communion with the powers of the universe, and amicable relations towards his God. Like my mountain Plymouth Brother, he knows the Lord. His religion does not repose upon a choice of logic; it is the poetry of the man's experience, the philosophy of the history of his life. God, like a great power, like a great shining sun, has appeared to this simple fellow in the course of years, and become the ground and essence of his least reflections; and you may change creeds and dogmas by authority, or proclaim a new religion with the sound of trumpets, if you will; but here is a man who has his own thoughts, and will stubbornly adhere to them in good and evil. He is a Catholic, a Protestant, or a Plymouth Brother, in the same indefeasible sense that a man is not a woman, or a woman not a man. For he could not vary from his faith, unless he could eradicate all memory of the past, and, in a strict and not a conventional meaning, change his mind.[57]

The Heart of the Country

I was now drawing near to Cassagnas, a cluster of black roofs upon the hillside, in this wild valley, among chestnut gardens, and looked upon in the clear air by many rocky peaks. The road along the Mimente is yet new, nor have the mountaineers recovered their surprise when the first cart arrived at Cassagnas. But although it lay thus apart from the current of men's business, this hamlet had already made a figure in the history of France. Hard by, in caverns of the mountain, was one of the five arsenals of the Camisards; where they laid up clothes and corn and arms against necessity, forged bayonets and sabres, and made themselves gunpowder with willow charcoal and saltpetre boiled in kettles. To the same caves, amid this multifarious industry, the sick and wounded were brought up to heal; and there they were visited by the two surgeons, Chabrier and Tavan, and secretly nursed by women of the neighbourhood.

Of the five legions into which the Camisards were divided, it was the oldest and the most obscure that had its magazines by Cassagnas. This was the band of Spirit Séguier; men who had joined their voices with his in the 68th Psalm as they marched

down by night on the archpriest of the Cévennes. Séguier, pro-
moted to heaven, was succeeded by Salomon Couderc, whom
Cavalier treats in his memoirs as chaplain-general to the whole
army of the Camisards. He was a prophet; a great reader of the
heart, who admitted people to the sacrament or refused them
by 'intentively viewing every man' between the eyes; and had
the most of the Scriptures off by rote. And this was surely
happy; since in a surprise in August, 1703, he lost his mule, his
portfolios, and his Bible. It is only strange that they were not
surprised more often and more effectually; for this legion of
Cassagnas was truly patriarchal in its theory of war, and camped
without sentries, leaving that duty to the angels of the God for
whom they fought. This is a token, not only of their faith, but
of the trackless country where they harboured. M. de Caladon,[58]
taking a stroll one fine day, walked without warning into their
midst, as he might have walked into 'a flock of sheep in a plain,'
and found some asleep and some awake and psalm-singing. A
traitor had need of no recommendation to insinuate himself
among their ranks, beyond 'his faculty of singing psalms'; and
even the prophet Salomon 'took him into a particular friendship.' Thus, among their intricate hills, the rustic troop subsisted; and history can attribute few exploits to them but
sacraments and ecstasies.

People of this tough and simple stock will not, as I have just
been saying, prove variable in religion; nor will they get nearer
to apostasy than a mere external conformity like that of Naaman
in the house of Rimmon. When Louis XVI, in the words of the
edict,[59] 'convinced by the uselessness of a century of per-
secutions, and rather from necessity than sympathy,' granted at
last a royal grace of toleration, Cassagnas was still Protestant;
and to a man, it is so to this day. There is, indeed, one family
that is not Protestant, but neither is it Catholic. It is that of a
Catholic *curé* in revolt, who has taken to his bosom a schoolmistress. And his conduct, it is worth noting, is disapproved by the
Protestant villagers.

'It is a bad idea for a man,' said one, 'to go back from his
engagements.'[60]

The villagers whom I saw seemed intelligent after a countrified fashion, and were all plain and dignified in manner. As a Protestant myself, I was well looked upon, and my acquaintance with history gained me further respect. For we had something not unlike a religious controversy at table, a gendarme[61] and a merchant with whom I dined being both strangers to the place, and Catholics. The young men of the house stood round and supported me; and the whole discussion was tolerantly conducted, and surprised a man brought up among the infinitesimal and contentious differences of Scotland. The merchant, indeed, grew a little warm, and was far less pleased than some others with my historical acquirements. But the gendarme was mighty easy over it all.

'It's a bad idea for a man to change,' said he; and the remark was generally applauded.

That was not the opinion of the priest and soldier at Our Lady of the Snows. But this is a different race; and perhaps the same great-heartedness that upheld them to resist, now enables them to differ in a kind spirit. For courage respects courage; but where a faith has been trodden out, we may look for a mean and narrow population. The true work of Bruce and Wallace[62] was the union of the nations; not that they should stand apart a while longer, skirmishing upon their borders; but that, when the time came, they might unite with self-respect.

The merchant was much interested in my journey, and thought it dangerous to sleep afield.

'There are the wolves,' said he; 'and then it is known you are an Englishman. The English have always long purses, and it might very well enter into someone's head to deal you an ill blow some night.'

I told him I was not much afraid of such accidents; and at any rate judged it unwise to dwell upon alarms or consider small perils in the arrangement of life. Life itself, I submitted, was a far too risky business as a whole to make each additional particular of danger worth regard. 'Something,' said I, 'might burst in your inside any day of the week, and there would be an end of you, if you were locked into your room with three turns of the key.'

'*Cependant*,' said he, '*coucher dehors!*'[63]

'God,' said I, 'is everywhere.'

'*Cependant, coucher dehors!*' he repeated, and his voice was eloquent of terror.

He was the only person, in all my voyage, who saw anything hardy in so simple a proceeding; although many considered it superfluous. Only one, on the other hand, professed much delight in the idea; and that was my Plymouth Brother, who cried out, when I told him I sometimes preferred sleeping under the stars to a close and noisy alehouse, 'Now I see that you know the Lord!'

The merchant asked me for one of my cards as I was leaving, for he said I should be something to talk of in the future, and desired me to make a note of his request and reason; a desire with which I have thus complied.

A little after two I struck across the Mimente and took a rugged path southward up a hillside covered with loose stones and tufts of heather.[64] At the top, as is the habit of the country, the path disappeared; and I left my she-ass munching heather, and went forward alone to seek a road.

I was now on the separation of two vast watersheds; behind me all the streams were bound for the Garonne and the Western Ocean;[65] before me was the basin of the Rhone. Hence, as from the Lozère, you can see in clear weather the shining of the Gulf of Lyons; and perhaps from here the soldiers of Salomon may have watched for the topsails of Sir Cloudesley Shovel,[66] and the long-promised aid from England. You may take this ridge as lying in the heart of the country of the Camisards: four of the five legions camped all round it and almost within view – Salomon and Joani to the north, Castanet and Roland to the south; and when Julien[67] had finished his famous work, the devastation of the High Cévennes, which lasted all through October and November, 1703, and during which four hundred and sixty villages and hamlets were, with fire and pickaxe, utterly subverted, a man standing on this eminence would have looked forth upon a silent, smokeless, and dispeopled land. Time and man's activity have now repaired these ruins; Cassagnas is once more roofed and sending up domestic smoke; and in the chestnut gardens, in low and leafy corners, many a prosperous farmer returns, when the day's work is done, to his children and bright hearth. And still it was perhaps the wildest view of all my journey. Peak upon peak, chain upon chain of hills ran surging southward, channelled and sculptured by the winter streams, feathered from head to foot with chestnuts, and here and there breaking out into a coronal of cliffs. The sun, which was still far from setting, sent a drift of misty gold across the hill-tops, but the valleys were already plunged in a profound and quiet shadow.[68]

A very old shepherd, hobbling on a pair of sticks, and wearing a black cap of liberty,[69] as if in honour of his nearness to the grave, directed me to the road for St Germain de Calberte. There was something solemn in the isolation of this infirm and ancient creature. Where he dwelt, how he got upon this high ridge, or how he proposed to get down again, were more than I could fancy. Not far off upon my right was the famous Plan de Font Morte, where Poul with his Armenian sabre slashed down the Camisards of Séguier. This, methought, might be some Rip van Winkle[70] of the war, who had lost his comrades, fleeing before Poul, and wandered ever since upon the mountains. It might be news to him that Cavalier had surrendered, or Roland had fallen fighting with his back against an olive. And while I was thus working on my fancy, I heard him hailing in broken tones, and saw him waving me to come back with one of his two sticks. I had already got some way past him; but, leaving Modestine once more, retraced my steps.

Alas, it was a very commonplace affair. The old gentleman had forgot to ask the pedlar what he sold, and wished to remedy this neglect.

I told him sternly, 'Nothing.'

'Nothing?' cried he.

I repeated 'Nothing,' and made off.

It's odd to think of, but perhaps I thus became as inexplicable to the old man as he had been to me.

The road lay under chestnuts, and though I saw a hamlet or two below me in the vale, and many lone houses of the chestnut farmers, it was a very solitary march all afternoon; and the

evening began early underneath the trees. But I heard the voice
of a woman singing some sad, old, endless ballad not far off. It
seemed to be about love and a *bel amoureux*, her handsome
sweetheart; and I wished I could have taken up the strain and
answered her, as I went on upon my invisible woodland way,
weaving, like Pippa[71] in the poem, my own thoughts with hers.
What could I have told her? Little enough; and yet all the heart
requires. How the world gives and takes away, and brings
sweethearts near, only to separate them again into distant and
strange lands; but to love is the great amulet which makes the
world a garden; and 'hope, which comes to all,'[72] outwears the
accidents of life, and reaches with tremulous hand beyond
the grave and death. Easy to say: yea, but also, by God's mercy,
both easy and grateful to believe!

We struck at last into a wide white high-road, carpeted with
noiseless dust. The night had come; the moon had been shining
for a long while upon the opposite mountain, when on turning
a corner my donkey and I issued ourselves into her light. I had
emptied out my brandy at Florac, for I could bear the stuff no
longer, and replaced it with some generous and scented Volnay,[73] and now I drank to the moon's sacred majesty upon the
road. It was but a couple of mouthfuls; yet I became thenceforth
unconscious of my limbs, and my blood flowed with luxury.
Even Modestine was inspired by this purified nocturnal sunshine, and bestirred her little hoofs as to a livelier measure.[74]
The road wound and descended swiftly among masses of chestnuts. Hot dust rose from our feet and flowed away. Our two
shadows – mine deformed with the knapsack, hers comically
bestridden by the pack – now lay before us clearly outlined on
the road, and now, as we turned a corner, went off into the
ghostly distance, and sailed along the mountain like clouds.
From time to time a warm wind rustled down the valley, and
set all the chestnuts dangling their bunches of foliage and fruit;
the ear was filled with whispering music, and the shadows
danced in tune. And next moment the breeze had gone by, and
in all the valley nothing moved except our travelling feet. On
the opposite slope, the monstrous ribs and gullies of the mountain were faintly designed in the moonshine; and high overhead,

in some lone house, there burned one lighted window, one square spark of red in the huge field of sad nocturnal colouring.

At a certain point, as I went downward, turning many acute angles, the moon disappeared behind the hill; and I pursued my way in great darkness, until another turning shot me without preparation into St Germain de Calberte. The place was asleep and silent, and buried in opaque night. Only from a single open door, some lamplight escaped upon the road to show me I was come among men's habitations. The two last gossips of the evening, still talking by a garden wall, directed me to the inn. The landlady was getting her chicks to bed; the fire was already out, and had, not without grumbling, to be rekindled; half an hour later, and I must have gone supperless to roost.

The Last Day

When I awoke (Thursday, 3rd October), and, hearing a great flourishing of cocks and chuckling of contented hens, betook me to the window of the clean and comfortable room where I had slept the night, I looked forth on a sunshiny morning in a deep vale of chestnut gardens. It was still early, and the cock-crows, and the slanting lights, and the long shadows, encouraged me to be out and look round me.

St Germain de Calberte is a great parish nine leagues round about. At the period of the wars, and immediately before the devastation, it was inhabited by two hundred and seventy-five families, of which only nine were Catholic; and it took the *curé* seventeen September days to go from house to house on horseback for a census. But the place itself, although capital of a canton, is scarce larger than a hamlet. It lies terraced across a steep slope in the midst of mighty chestnuts. The Protestant chapel stands below upon a shoulder; in the midst of the town is the quaint old Catholic church.

It was here that poor Du Chayla, the Christian martyr, kept his library and held a court of missionaries; here he had built his tomb, thinking to lie among a grateful population whom he had redeemed from error; and hither on the morrow of his death they brought the body, pierced with two-and-fifty wounds, to be interred. Clad in his priestly robes, he was laid out in state in the church. The *curé*, taking his text from Second Samuel, twentieth chapter and twelfth verse, 'And Amasa wallowed in his blood in the highway,' preached a rousing sermon, and exhorted his brethren to die each at his post, like their unhappy and illustrious superior. In the midst of this eloquence there came a breeze that Spirit Séguier was near at hand; and behold! all the assembly took to their horses' heels, some east, some west, and the *curé* himself as far as Alais.

Strange was the position of this little Catholic metropolis, a thimbleful of Rome, in such a wild and contrary neighbourhood. On the one hand, the legion of Salomon overlooked it from Cassagnas; on the other, it was cut off from assistance by the legion of Roland at Mialet. The *curé*, Louvrelenil,[75] although he took a panic at the archpriest's funeral, and so hurriedly decamped to Alais, stood well by his isolated pulpit, and thence uttered fulminations against the crimes of the Protestants. Salomon besieged the village for an hour and a half, but was beaten back. The militiamen, on guard before the *curé's* door, could be heard, in the black hours, singing Protestant psalms and holding friendly talk with the insurgents. And in the morning, although not a shot had been fired, there would not be a round of powder in their flasks. Where was it gone? All handed over to the Camisards for a consideration. Untrusty guardians for an isolated priest!

That these continual stirs were once busy in St Germain de Calberte, the imagination with difficulty receives; all is now so quiet, the pulse of human life now beats so low and still in this hamlet of the mountains. Boys followed me a great way off, like a timid sort of lion-hunters; and people turned round to have a second look, or came out of their houses, as I went by. My passage was the first event, you would have fancied, since the Camisards. There was nothing rude or forward in this observation; it was but a pleased and wondering scrutiny, like that of oxen or the human infant; yet it wearied my spirits, and soon drove me from the street.

I took refuge on the terraces, which are here greenly carpeted with sward, and tried to imitate with a pencil the inimitable attitudes of the chestnuts as they bear up their canopy of leaves. Ever and again a little wind went by, and the nuts dropped all around me, with a light and dull sound, upon the sward. The noise was as of a thin fall of great hailstones; but there went with it a cheerful human sentiment of an approaching harvest and farmers rejoicing in their gains. Looking up, I could see the brown nut peering through the husk, which was already gaping; and between the stems the eye embraced an amphitheatre of hill, sunlit and green with leaves.

I have not often enjoyed a place more deeply. I moved in an atmosphere of pleasure, and felt light and quiet and content. But perhaps it was not the place alone that so disposed my spirit. Perhaps someone was thinking of me in another country; or perhaps some thought of my own had come and gone unnoticed, and yet done me good. For some thoughts, which sure would be the most beautiful, vanish before we can rightly scan their features; as though a god, travelling by our green highways, should but ope the door, give one smiling look into the house, and go again forever. Was it Apollo, or Mercury, or Love with folded wings? Who shall say? But we go the lighter about our business, and feel peace and pleasure in our hearts.

I dined with a pair of Catholics. They agreed in the condemnation of a young man, a Catholic, who had married a Protestant girl and gone over to the religion of his wife. A Protestant born they could understand and respect; indeed, they seemed to be of the mind of an old Catholic woman who told me that same day there was no difference between the two sects, save that 'wrong was more wrong for the Catholic,' who had more light and guidance; but this of a man's desertion filled them with contempt.

'It's a bad idea for a man to change,' said one.

It may have been accidental, but you see how this phrase pursued me; and for myself, I believe it is the current philosophy in these parts. I have some difficulty in imagining a better. It's not only a great flight of confidence for a man to change his creed and go out of his family for heaven's sake; but the odds are – nay, and the hope is – that, with all this great transition in the eyes of man, he has not changed himself a hair-breadth to the eyes of God. Honour to those who do so, for the wrench is sore. But it argues something narrow, whether of strength or weakness, whether of the prophet or the fool, in those who can take a sufficient interest in such infinitesimal and human operations, or who can quit a friendship for a doubtful process of the mind. And I think I should not leave my old creed for another, changing only words for other words; but by some brave reading, embrace it in spirit and truth, and find wrong as wrong for me as for the best of other communions.

The phylloxera[76] was in the neighbourhood; and instead of wine we drank at dinner a more economical juice of the grape – La Parisienne, they call it. It is made by putting the fruit whole into a cask with water; one by one the berries ferment and burst; what is drunk during the day is supplied at night in water; so, with ever another pitcher from the well, and ever another grape exploding and giving out its strength, one cask of Parisienne may last a family till spring. It is, as the reader will anticipate, a feeble beverage, but very pleasant to the taste.

What with dinner and coffee, it was long past three before I left St Germain de Calberte. I went down beside the Gardon of Mialet, a great glaring watercourse devoid of water, and through St Etienne de Vallée Française, or Val Francesque, as they used to call it; and towards evening began to ascend the hill of St Pierre. It was a long and steep ascent. Behind me an empty carriage returning to St Jean du Gard kept hard upon my tracks, and near the summit overtook me. The driver, like the rest of the world, was sure I was a pedlar; but, unlike others, he was sure of what I had to sell. He had noticed the blue wool which hung out of my pack at either end; and from this he had decided, beyond my power to alter his decision, that I dealt in blue-wool collars, such as decorate the neck of the French draught-horse.

I had hurried to the topmost powers of Modestine, for I dearly desired to see the view upon the other side before the day had faded. But it was night when I reached the summit; the moon was riding high and clear; and only a few grey streaks of twilight lingered in the west. A yawning valley, gulfed in blackness, lay like a hole in created nature at my feet; but the outline of the hills was sharp against the sky. There was Mount Aigoal,[77] the stronghold of Castanet. And Castanet, not only as an active undertaking leader, deserves some mention among Camisards; for there is a spray of rose among his laurel; and he showed how, even in a public tragedy, love will have its way. In the high tide of war he married, in his mountain citadel, a young and pretty lass called Mariette.[78] There were great rejoicings; and the bridegroom released five-and-twenty prisoners in honour of the glad event. Seven months afterwards Mariette, the Princess of the Cévennes, as they called her in derision, fell into the hands of the authorities, where it was like to have gone hard with her. But Castanet was a man of execution, and loved his wife. He fell on Valleraugue, and got a lady there for a hostage; and for the first and last time in that war there was an exchange of prisoners. Their daughter, pledge of some starry night upon Mount Aigoal, has left descendants to this day.

Modestine and I – it was our last meal together – had a snack upon the top of St Pierre, I on a heap of stones, she standing by me in the moonlight and decorously eating bread out of my hand. The poor brute would eat more heartily in this manner; for she had a sort of affection for me, which I was soon to betray.

It was a long descent upon St Jean du Gard, and we met no one but a carter, visible afar off by the glint of the moon on his extinguished lantern.

Before ten o'clock we had got in and were at supper; fifteen miles and a stiff hill in little beyond six hours!

Farewell, Modestine!

On examination, on the morning of October 4th, Modestine was pronounced unfit for travel. She would need at least two days' repose, according to the ostler; but I was now eager to reach Alais for my letters; and, being in a civilised country of stage-coaches, I determined to sell my lady friend and be off by the diligence that afternoon. Our yesterday's march, with the testimony of the driver who had pursued us up the long hill of St Pierre, spread a favourable notion of my donkey's capabilities. Intending purchasers were aware of an unrivalled opportunity. Before ten I had an offer of twenty-five francs; and before noon, after a desperate engagement, I sold her, saddle and all, for five-and-thirty.[79] The pecuniary gain is not obvious, but I had bought freedom into the bargain.

St Jean du Gard is a large place, and largely Protestant. The maire,[80] a Protestant, asked me to help him in a small matter which is itself characteristic of the country. The young women of the Cévennes profit by the common religion and the difference of the language to go largely as governesses into England; and here was one, a native of Mialet, struggling with English circulars from two different agencies in London. I gave what help I could; and volunteered some advice, which struck me as being excellent.

One thing more I note. The phylloxera has ravaged the vineyards in this neighbourhood; and in the early morning, under some chestnuts by the river, I found a party of men working with a cider-press. I could not at first make out what they were after, and asked one fellow to explain.

'Making cider,' he said. '*Oui, c'est comme ça. Comme dans le nord!*'[81]

There was a ring of sarcasm in his voice; the country was going to the devil.

It was not until I was fairly seated by the driver, and rattling through a rocky valley with dwarf olives, that I became aware of my bereavement. I had lost Modestine. Up to that moment I had thought I hated her; but now she was gone,

'And, Oh,
The difference to me!'[82]

For twelve days we had been fast companions; we had travelled upwards of a hundred and twenty miles, crossed several respectable ridges, and jogged along with our six legs by many a rocky and many a boggy by-road. After the first day, although sometimes I was hurt and distant in manner, I still kept my patience; and as for her, poor soul! she had come to regard me as a god. She loved to eat out of my hand. She was patient, elegant in form, the colour of an ideal mouse, and inimitably small. Her faults were those of her race and sex; her virtues were her own. Farewell, and if for ever——

Father Adam wept when he sold her to me; after I had sold her in my turn, I was tempted to follow his example; and being alone with a stage-driver and four or five agreeable young men, I did not hesitate to yield to my emotion.

THE AMATEUR EMIGRANT

Contents

I. FROM THE CLYDE TO SANDY HOOK

II. ACROSS THE PLAINS

*Leaves from the Notebook of an Emigrant
between New York and San Francisco*

DEDICATION
TO
ROBERT ALAN MOWBRAY STEVENSON[1]

Our friendship was not only founded before we were born by a community of blood, but is in itself near as old as my life. It began with our early ages, and, like a history, has been continued to the present time. Although we may not be old in the world, we are old to each other, having so long been intimates. We are now widely separated, a great sea and continent intervening; but memory, like care, mounts into iron ships and rides post behind the horseman. Neither time nor space nor enmity can conquer old affection; and as I dedicate these sketches, it is not to you only, but to all in the old country, that I send the greeting of my heart.

R. L. S.
1879

I
FROM THE CLYDE TO SANDY HOOK[1]

The Second Cabin

I first encountered my fellow-passengers on the Broomielaw[2] in Glasgow. Thence we descended the Clyde in no familiar spirit, but looking askance on each other as on possible enemies. A few Scandinavians, who had already grown acquainted on the North Sea, were friendly and voluble over their long pipes; but among English speakers distance and suspicion reigned supreme. The sun was soon overclouded, the wind freshened and grew sharp as we continued to descend the widening estuary; and with the falling temperature the gloom among the passengers increased. Two of the women wept. Any one who had come aboard might have supposed we were all absconding from the law. There was scarce a word interchanged, and no common sentiment but that of cold united us, until at length, having touched at Greenock, a pointing arm and a rush to the starboard now announced that our ocean steamer was in sight. There she lay in mid-river, at the tail of the Bank,[3] her sea-signal flying: a wall of bulwark, a street of white deck-houses, an aspiring forest of spars, larger than a church, and soon to be as populous as many an incorporated town in the land to which she was to bear us.

I was not, in truth, a steerage passenger. Although anxious to see the worst of emigrant life, I had some work to finish on the voyage, and was advised to go by the second cabin, where at least I should have a table at command. The advice was excellent; but to understand the choice, and what I gained, some outline of the internal disposition of the ship will first be necessary. In her very nose is Steerage No. 1, down two pair of stairs. A little abaft, another companion, labelled Steerage No. 2 and 3, gives admission to three galleries, two running forward towards Steerage No. 1, and the third aft towards the engines. The starboard forward gallery is the second cabin. Away abaft the engines and below the officers' cabins, to complete our survey of the vessel, there is yet a third nest of steerages, labelled 4 and 5. The second cabin, to return, is thus a modified oasis in the very heart of the steerages. Through the thin partition you can hear the steerage passengers being sick, the rattle of tin dishes as they sit at meals, the varied accents in which they converse, the crying of their children terrified by this new experience, or the clean flat smack of the parental hand in chastisement.

There are, however, many advantages for the inhabitant of this strip. He does not require to bring his own bedding or dishes, but finds berths and a table completely if somewhat roughly furnished. He enjoys a distinct superiority in diet; but this, strange to say, differs not only on different ships, but on the same ship according as her head is to the east or west. In my own experience, the principal difference between our table and that of the true steerage passenger was the table itself, and the crockery plates from which we ate. But lest I should show myself ungrateful, let me recapitulate every advantage. At breakfast, we had a choice between tea and coffee for beverage; a choice not easy to make, the two were so surprisingly alike. I found that I could sleep after the coffee and lay awake after the tea, which is proof conclusive of some chemical disparity; and even by the palate I could distinguish a smack of snuff in the former from a flavour of boiling and dish-cloths in the second. As a matter of fact, I have seen passengers, after many sips, still doubting which had been supplied them. In the way of eatables at the same meal we were gloriously favoured; for in addition to porridge, which was common to all, we had Irish stew, sometimes a bit of fish, and sometimes rissoles. The dinner of soup, roast fresh beef, boiled salt junk, and potatoes, was, I believe, exactly common to the steerage and the second cabin; only I have heard it rumoured that our potatoes were of a

superior brand; and twice a week, on pudding-days, instead of
duff, we had a saddlebag filled with currants under the name of
a plum-pudding. At tea we were served with some broken meat[4]
from the saloon; sometimes in the comparatively elegant form
of spare patties or rissoles; but as a general thing, mere chicken-
bones and flakes of fish, neither hot nor cold. If these were not
the scrapings of plates their looks belied them sorely; yet we
were all too hungry to be proud, and fell to these leavings
greedily. These, the bread, which was excellent, and the soup
and porridge, which were both good, formed my whole diet
throughout the voyage; so that except for the broken meat and
the convenience of a table I might as well have been in the
steerage outright. Had they given me porridge again in the
evening, I should have been perfectly contented with the fare.
As it was, with a few biscuits and some whisky and water before
turning in, I kept my body going and my spirits up to the mark.

The last particular in which the second-cabin passenger
remarkably stands ahead of his brother of the steerage is one
altogether of sentiment. In the steerage there are males and
females; in the second cabin ladies and gentlemen. For some
time after I came aboard I thought I was only a male; but in the
course of a voyage of discovery between decks, I came on a
brass plate, and learned that I was still a gentleman. Nobody
knew it, of course. I was lost in the crowd of males and females,
and rigorously confined to the same quarter of the deck. Who
could tell whether I housed on the port or starboard side of
Steerage No. 2 and 3? And it was only there that my superiority
became practical; everywhere else I was incognito, moving
among my inferiors with simplicity, not so much as a swagger
to indicate that I was a gentleman after all, and had broken meat
to tea. Still, I was like one with a patent of nobility in a drawer
at home; and when I felt out of spirits I could go down and
refresh myself with a look of that brass plate.

For all these advantages I paid but two guineas. Six guineas
is the steerage fare; eight that by the second cabin;[5] and when
you remember that the steerage passenger must supply bedding
and dishes, and, in five cases out of ten, either brings some

dainties with him, or privately pays the steward for extra rations, the difference in price becomes almost nominal. Air comparatively fit to breathe, food comparatively varied, and the satisfaction of being still privately a gentleman, may thus be had almost for the asking. Two of my fellow-passengers in the second cabin had already made the passage by the cheaper fare, and declared it was an experiment not to be repeated. As I go on to tell about my steerage friends, the reader will perceive that they were not alone in their opinion. Out of ten with whom I was more or less intimate, I am sure not fewer than five vowed, if they returned, to travel second cabin; and all who had left their wives behind them assured me they would go without the comfort of their presence until they could afford to bring them by saloon.

Our party in the second cabin was not perhaps the most interesting on board. Perhaps even in the saloon there was as much goodwill and character. Yet it had some elements of curiosity. There was a mixed group of Swedes, Danes, and Norsemen, one of whom, generally known by the name of 'Johnny,' in spite of his own protests, greatly diverted us by his clever, cross-country efforts to speak English, and became on the strength of that an universal favourite – it takes so little in this world of shipboard to create a popularity. There was, besides, a Scots mason, known from his favourite dish as 'Irish Stew,' three or four nondescript Scots, a fine young Irishman, O'Reilly, and a pair of young men who deserve a special word of condemnation. One of them was Scots; the other claimed to be American; admitted, after some fencing, that he was born in England; and ultimately proved to be an Irishman born and nurtured, but ashamed to own his country. He had a sister on board, whom he faithfully neglected throughout the voyage, though she was not only sick, but much his senior, and had nursed and cared for him in childhood. In appearance he was like an imbecile Henry the Third of France.[6] The Scotsman, though perhaps as big an ass, was not so dead of heart; and I have only bracketed them together because they were fast friends, and disgraced themselves equally by their conduct at the table.

Next, to turn to topics more agreeable, we had a newly married couple, devoted to each other, with a pleasant story of how they had first seen each other years ago at a preparatory school, and that very afternoon he had carried her books home for her. I do not know if this story will be plain to Southern readers;[7] but to me it recalls many a school idyll, with wrathful swains of eight and nine confronting each other stride-legs, flushed with jealousy; for to carry home a young lady's books was both a delicate attention and a privilege.

Then there was an old lady, or indeed I am not sure that she was as much old as antiquated and strangely out of place, who had left her husband, and was travelling all the way to Kansas by herself. We had to take her own word that she was married; for it was sorely contradicted by the testimony of her appearance. Nature seemed to have sanctified her for the single state; even the colour of her hair was incompatible with matrimony, and her husband, I thought, should be a man of saintly spirit and phantasmal bodily presence. She was ill, poor thing; her soul turned from the viands; the dirty tablecloth shocked her like an impropriety; and the whole strength of her endeavour was bent upon keeping her watch true to Glasgow time till she should reach New York. They had heard reports, her husband and she, of some unwarrantable disparity of hours between these two cities; and with a spirit commendably scientific, had seized on this occasion to put them to the proof. It was a good thing for the old lady; for she passed much leisure time in studying the watch. Once, when prostrated by sickness, she let it run down. It was inscribed on her harmless mind in letters of adamant that the hands of a watch must never be turned backwards; and so it behoved her to lie in wait for the exact moment ere she started it again. When she imagined this was about due, she sought out one of the young second-cabin Scotsmen, who was embarked on the same experiment as herself and had hitherto been less neglectful. She was in quest of two o'clock; and when she learned it was already seven on the shores of Clyde, she lifted up her voice and cried 'Gravy!' I had not heard this innocent expletive since I was a young child; and I suppose it must have been the same with the other Scotsmen present, for we all laughed our fill.

Last but not least, I come to my excellent friend Mr Jones. It

would be difficult to say whether I was his right-hand man or
he mine, during the voyage. Thus at table I carved, while he
only scooped gravy; but at our concerts, of which more anon,
he was the president who called up performers to sing, and I but
his messenger who ran his errands and pleaded privately with
the over-modest. I knew I liked Mr Jones from the moment I
saw him. I thought him by his face to be Scottish; nor could his
accent undeceive me. For as there is a *lingua franca* of many
tongues on the moles and in the feluccas[8] of the Mediterranean,
so there is a free or common accent among English-speaking
men who follow the sea. They catch a twang in a New England
port; from a cockney skipper, even a Scotsman sometimes learns
to drop an *h*; a word of a dialect is picked up from another hand
in the forecastle; until often the result is undecipherable, and
you have to ask for the man's place of birth. So it was with Mr
Jones. I thought him a Scotsman who had been long to sea; and
yet he was from Wales, and had been most of his life a blacksmith
at an inland forge; a few years in America and half a score of
ocean voyages having sufficed to modify his speech into the
common pattern. By his own account he was both strong and
skilful in his trade. A few years back, he had been married and
after a fashion a rich man; now the wife was dead and the money
gone. But his was the nature that looks forward, and goes on
from one year to another and through all the extremities of
fortune undismayed; and if the sky were to fall to-morrow,
I should look to see Jones, the day following, perched on a
step-ladder and getting things to rights. He was always hovering
round inventions like a bee over a flower, and lived in a dream
of patents. He had with him a patent medicine, for instance, the
composition of which he had bought years ago for five dollars
from an American pedlar, and sold the other day for a hundred
pounds (I think it was) to an English apothecary. It was called
Golden Oil; cured all maladies without exception; and I am
bound to say that I partook of it myself with good results. It is
a character of the man that he was not only perpetually dosing
himself with Golden Oil, but wherever there was a head aching
or a finger cut, there would be Jones with his bottle.

If he had one taste more strongly than another, it was to study character. Many an hour have we two walked upon the deck dissecting our neighbours in a spirit that was too purely scientific to be called unkind; whenever a quaint or human trait slipped out in conversation, you might have seen Jones and me exchanging glances; and we could hardly go to bed in comfort till we had exchanged notes and discussed the day's experience. We were then like a couple of anglers comparing a day's kill. But the fish we angled for were of a metaphysical species, and we angled as often as not in one another's baskets. Once, in the midst of a serious talk, each found there was a scrutinising eye upon himself; I own I paused in embarrassment at this double detection; but Jones, with a better civility, broke into a peal of unaffected laughter, and declared, what was the truth, that there was a pair of us indeed.

Early Impressions

We steamed out of the Clyde on Thursday night, and early on the Friday afternoon we took in our last batch of emigrants at Lough Foyle,[9] in Ireland, and said farewell to Europe. The company was now complete, and began to draw together, by inscrutable magnetisms, upon the decks. There were Scots and Irish in plenty, a few English, a few Americans, a good handful of Scandinavians, a German or two, and one Russian; all now belonging for ten days to one small iron country on the deep.

As I walked the deck and looked round upon my fellow-passengers, thus curiously assorted from all northern Europe, I began for the first time to understand the nature of emigration. Day by day throughout the passage, and thenceforward across all the States, and on to the shores of the Pacific, this knowledge grew more clear and melancholy. Emigration, from a word of the most cheerful import, came to sound most dismally in my ear. There is nothing more agreeable to picture and nothing more pathetic to behold. The abstract idea, as conceived at home, is hopeful and adventurous. A young man, you fancy, scorning restraints and helpers, issues forth into life, that great

battle, to fight for his own hand. The most pleasant stories of
ambition, of difficulties overcome, and of ultimate success, are
but as episodes to this great epic of self-help. The epic is
composed of individual heroisms; it stands to them as the victorious war which subdued an empire stands to the personal act
of bravery which spiked a single cannon and was adequately
rewarded with a medal. For in emigration the young men enter
direct and by the shipload on their heritage of work; empty
continents swarm, as at the bo's'un's whistle, with industrious
hands, and whole new empires are domesticated to the service
of man.

This is the closet picture, and is found, on trial, to consist
mostly of embellishments. The more I saw of my fellow-
passengers, the less I was tempted to the lyric note. Comparatively few of the men were below thirty; many were married,
and encumbered with families; not a few were already up in
years; and this itself was out of tune with my imaginations, for
the ideal emigrant should certainly be young. Again, I thought
he should offer to the eye some bold type of humanity, with
bluff or hawk-like features, and the stamp of an eager and
pushing disposition. Now those around me were for the most
part quiet, orderly, obedient citizens, family men broken by
adversity, elderly youths who had failed to place themselves in
life, and people who had seen better days. Mildness was the
prevailing character; mild mirth and mild endurance. In a word,
I was not taking part in an impetuous and conquering sally,
such as swept over Mexico or Siberia, but found myself, like
Marmion,[10] 'in the lost battle, borne down by the flying.'

Labouring mankind had in the last years, and throughout
Great Britain, sustained a prolonged and crushing series of
defeats. I had heard vaguely of these reverses; of whole streets
of houses standing deserted by the Tyne,[11] the cellar-doors
broken and removed for firewood; of homeless men loitering at
the street-corners of Glasgow with their chests beside them; of
closed factories, useless strikes, and starving girls. But I had
never taken them home to me or represented these distresses
livingly to my imagination. A turn of the market may be a
calamity as disastrous as the French retreat from Moscow;[12] but

it hardly lends itself to lively treatment, and makes a trifling figure in the morning papers. We may struggle as we please, we are not born economists. The individual is more affecting than the mass. It is by the scenic accidents, and the appeal to the carnal eye, that for the most part we grasp the significance of tragedies. Thus it was only now, when I found myself involved in the rout, that I began to appreciate how sharp had been the battle. We were a company of the rejected; the drunken, the incompetent, the weak, the prodigal, all who had been unable to prevail against circumstances in the one land, were now fleeing pitifully to another; and though one or two might still succeed, all had already failed. We were a shipful of failures, the broken men of England.[13] Yet it must not be supposed that these people exhibited depression. The scene, on the contrary, was cheerful. Not a tear was shed on board the vessel. All were full of hope for the future, and showed an inclination to innocent gaiety. Some were heard to sing, and all began to scrape acquaintance with small jests and ready laughter.

The children found each other out like dogs, and ran about the decks scraping acquaintance after their fashion also. 'What do you call your mither?' I heard one ask. 'Mawmaw,'[14] was the reply, indicating, I fancy, a shade of difference in the social scale. When people pass each other on the high seas of life at so early an age, the contact is but slight, and the relation more like what we may imagine to be the friendship of flies than that of men; it is so quickly joined, so easily dissolved, so open in its communications and so devoid of deeper human qualities. The children, I observed, were all in a band, and as thick as thieves at a fair, while their elders were still ceremoniously manœuvring on the outskirts of acquaintance. The sea, the ship, and the seamen were soon as familiar as home to these half-conscious little ones. It was odd to hear them, throughout the voyage, employ shore words to designate portions of the vessel. 'Co' 'way doon to yon dyke,'[15] I heard one say, probably meaning the bulwark. I often had my heart in my mouth, watching them climb into the shrouds or on the rails, while the ship went swinging through the waves; and I admired and envied the courage of their mothers, who sat by in the sun and looked on with composure at these perilous feats. 'He'll maybe be a sailor,' I heard one remark; 'now's the time to learn.' I had been on the point of running forward to interfere, but stood back at that, reproved. Very few in the more delicate classes have the nerve to look upon the peril of one dear to them; but the life of poorer folk, where necessity is so much more immediate and imperious, braces even a mother to this extreme of endurance. And perhaps, after all, it is better that the lad should break his neck than that you should break his spirit.

And since I am here on the chapter of the children, I must mention one little fellow, whose family belonged to Steerage No. 4 and 5, and who, wherever he went, was like a strain of music round the ship. He was an ugly, merry, unbreeched child of three, his lint-white hair in a tangle, his face smeared with suet and treacle; but he ran to and fro with so natural a step, and fell and picked himself up again with such grace and good-humour, that he might fairly be called beautiful when he was in motion. To meet him, crowing with laughter and beating an accompaniment to his own mirth with a tin spoon upon a tin cup, was to meet a little triumph of the human species. Even when his mother and the rest of his family lay sick and prostrate around him, he sat upright in their midst and sang aloud in the pleasant heartlessness of infancy.

Throughout the Friday, intimacy among us men made but a few advances. We discussed the probable duration of the voyage, we exchanged pieces of information, naming our trades,[16] what we hoped to find in the new world, or what we were fleeing from in the old; and, above all, we condoled together over the food and the vileness of the steerage. One or two had been so near famine that you may say they had run into the ship with the devil at their heels; and to these all seemed for the best in the best of possible steamers. But the majority were hugely discontented. Coming as they did from a country in so low a state as Great Britain, many of them from Glasgow, which commercially speaking was as good as dead, and many having long been out of work, I was surprised to find them so dainty in their notions. I myself lived almost exclusively on bread, porridge, and soup, precisely as it was supplied to them, and found it, if not luxurious, at least sufficient. But these working men were loud in their outcries. It was not 'food for human beings,' it was 'only fit for pigs,' it was 'a disgrace.' Many of them lived almost entirely upon biscuit, others on their own private supplies, and some paid extra for better rations from the ship. This marvellously changed my notion of the degree of luxury habitual to the artisan. I was prepared to hear him grumble, for grumbling is the traveller's pastime; but I was not prepared to find him turn away from a diet which was palatable to myself. Words I should have disregarded, or taken with a liberal allowance; but when a man prefers dry biscuit there can be no question of the sincerity of his disgust.

With one of their complaints I could most heartily sympathise. A single night of the steerage had filled them with horror. I had myself suffered, even in my decent second-cabin berth, from the lack of air; and as the night promised to be fine and quiet, I determined to sleep on deck, and advised all who complained of their quarters to follow my example. I daresay a dozen of others agreed to do so, and I thought we should have been quite a party. Yet, when I brought up my rug about seven bells, there was no one to be seen but the watch. That chimerical terror of good night-air, which makes men close their windows, list[17] their doors, and seal themselves up with their own poisonous exhalations, had sent all these healthy workmen down below. One would think we had been brought up in a fever country; yet in England the most malarious districts are in the bed-chambers.

I felt saddened at this defection, and yet half-pleased to have the night so quietly to myself. The wind had hauled a little ahead on the starboard bow, and was dry but chilly. I found a shelter near the fire-hole, and made myself snug for the night. The ship moved over the uneven sea with a gentle and cradling movement. The ponderous, organic labours of the engine in her bowels occupied the mind, and prepared it for slumber. From time to time a heavier lurch would disturb me as I lay, and recall me to the obscure borders of consciousness; or I heard, as it were through a veil, the clear note of the clapper on the brass and the beautiful sea-cry, 'All's well!' I know nothing, whether for poetry or music, that can surpass the effect of these two syllables in the darkness of a night at sea.

The day dawned fairly enough, and during the early part we had some pleasant hours to improve acquaintance in the open air; but towards nightfall the wind freshened, the rain began to fall, and the sea rose so high that it was difficult to keep one's footing on the deck. I have spoken of our concerts. We were indeed a musical ship's company, and cheered our way into exile with the fiddle, the accordion, and the songs of all nations. (Night after night we gathered at the aftermost limit of our domain, where it bordered on that of the saloon. Performers were called up with acclamation, some shame-faced and hanging the head, others willing and as bold as brass.) Good, bad, or indifferent – Scottish, English, Irish, Russian, German, or Norse – the songs were received with generous applause. Once or twice, a recitation, very spiritedly rendered in a powerful Scottish accent, varied the proceedings; and once we sought in vain to dance a quadrille, eight men of us together, to the music of the violin. The performers were all humorous, frisky fellows, who loved to cut capers in private life; but as soon as they were arranged for the dance, they conducted themselves like so many mutes at a funeral. I have never seen decorum pushed so far; and as this was not expected, the quadrille was soon whistled down, and the dancers departed under a cloud. Eight Frenchmen, even eight Englishmen from another rank of society, would have dared to make some fun for themselves and the spectators; but the working man, when sober, takes an extreme and even melancholy view of personal deportment. A fifth-form schoolboy is not more careful of dignity. He dares not be comical; his fun must escape from him unprepared, and above all, it must be unaccompanied by any physical demonstration. I like his society under most circumstances, but let me never again join with him in public gambols.

But the impulse to sing was strong, and triumphed over modesty and even the inclemencies of sea and sky. On this rough Saturday night, we got together by the main deck-house, in a place sheltered from the wind and rain. Some clinging to a ladder which led to the hurricane deck,[18] and the rest knitting arms or taking hands, we made a ring to support the women in the violent lurching of the ship; and when we were thus disposed, sang to our heart's content. Some of the songs were appropriate to the scene; others strikingly the reverse. Bastard doggrel of the music-hall, such as, 'Around her splendid form, I weaved the magic circle,' sounded bald, bleak, and pitifully silly. 'We don't want to fight, but, by Jingo, if we do,'[19] was in some measure saved by the vigour and unanimity with which the chorus was thrown forth into the night. I observed a Platt-Deutsch[20] mason, entirely innocent of English, adding heartily to the general effect. And perhaps the German mason is but a fair example of the sincerity with which the song was rendered; for nearly all with whom I conversed upon the subject were bitterly opposed to war, and attributed their own misfortunes, and frequently their own taste for whisky, to the campaigns in Zululand and Afghanistan.[21]

Every now and again, however, some song that touched the pathos of our situation was given forth; and you could hear by the voices that took up the burden how the sentiment came home to each. 'The Anchor's Weighed' was true for us. We were indeed 'Rocked on the bosom of the stormy deep.' How many of us could say with the singer, 'I'm lonely to-night, love, without you,' or 'Go, some one, and tell them from me, to write me a letter from home!' And when was there a more appropriate moment for 'Auld Lang Syne'[22] than now, when the land, the friends, and the affections of that mingled but beloved time were fading and fleeing behind us in the vessel's wake? It pointed forward to the hour when these labours should be overpast, to the return voyage, and to many a meeting in the sanded inn, when those who had parted in the spring of youth should again drink a cup of kindness in their age. Had not Burns contemplated emigration, I scarce believe he would have found that note.

⟨This was the first fusion of our little nationality together. The wind sang shrill in the rigging; the rain fell small and thick; the whole group, linked together as it was, was shaken and swung to and fro as the swift steamer shore into the waves. It was a general embrace, both friendly and helpful, like what one imagines of old Christian Agapes.[23] I turned many times to look behind me on the moving desert of seas, now cloud-canopied and lit with but a low nocturnal glimmer along the line of the horizon. It hemmed us in and cut us off on our swift-travelling oasis. And yet this waste was part a playground for the stormy petrel; and on the least tooth of reef, outcropping in a thousand miles of unfathomable ocean, the gull makes its home and dwells in a busy polity. And small as was our iron world, it made yet a large and habitable place in the Atlantic, compared with our globe upon the seas of space.⟩

All Sunday the weather remained wild and cloudy; many were prostrated by sickness; only five sat down to tea in the second cabin, and two of these departed abruptly ere the meal was at an end. The Sabbath was observed strictly by the majority of the emigrants. I heard an old woman express her surprise that 'the ship didna gae doon,'[24] as she saw some one pass her with a chess-board on the holy day. Some sang Scottish psalms. Many went to service, and in true Scottish fashion came back ill pleased with their divine. 'I didna think he was an experienced preacher,' said one girl to me.

It was a bleak, uncomfortable day; but at night, by six bells, although the wind had not yet moderated, the clouds were all wrecked and blown away behind the rim of the horizon, and the stars came out thickly overhead. I saw Venus burning as steadily and sweetly across this hurly-burly of the winds and waters as ever at home upon the summer woods. The engine pounded, the screw tossed out of the water with a roar, and shook the ship from end to end; the bows battled with loud reports against the billows: and as I stood in the lee-scuppers and looked up to where the funnel leaned out, over my head, vomiting smoke, and the black and monstrous topsails blotted, at each lurch, a different crop of stars, it seemed as if all this trouble were a thing of small account, and that just above the mast reigned peace unbroken and eternal.

Steerage Scenes

Our companion[25] (Steerage No. 2 and 3) was a favourite resort. Down one flight of stairs there was a comparatively large open space, the centre occupied by a hatchway, which made a convenient seat for about twenty persons, while barrels, coils of rope, and the carpenter's bench afforded perches for perhaps as many more. The canteen, or steerage bar, was on one side of the stair; on the other, a no less attractive spot, the cabin of the indefatigable interpreter. I have seen people packed into this space like herrings in a barrel, and many merry evenings prolonged there until five bells, when the lights were ruthlessly extinguished and all must go to roost.

It had been rumoured since Friday that there was a fiddler aboard, who lay sick and unmelodious in Steerage No. 1; and on the Monday forenoon, as I came down the companion, I was saluted by something in Strathspey time. A white-faced Orpheus[26] was cheerily playing to an audience of white-faced women. It was as much as he could do to play, and some of his hearers were scarce able to sit; yet they had crawled from their bunks at the first experimental flourish, and found better than medicine in the music. Some of the heaviest heads began to nod in time, and a degree of animation looked from some of the palest eyes. Humanly speaking, it is a more important matter to play the fiddle, even badly, than to write huge works upon recondite subjects. What could Mr Darwin[27] have done for these sick women? But this fellow scraped away; and the world was positively a better place for all who heard him. We have yet to understand the economical value of these mere accomplishments. I told the fiddler he was a happy man, carrying happiness about with him in his fiddle-case, and he seemed alive to the fact.

'It is a privilege,' I said. He thought a while upon the word, turning it over in his Scots head, and then answered with conviction, 'Yes, a privilege.'

That night I was summoned by 'Merrily danced the Quaker's wife'[28] into the companion of Steerage No. 4 and 5. This was, properly speaking, but a strip across a deck-house, lit by a sickly lantern which swung to and fro with the motion of the ship. Through the open slide-door we had a glimpse of a grey night sea, with patches of phosphorescent foam flying, swift as birds, into the wake, and the horizon rising and falling as the vessel rolled to the wind. In the centre the companion ladder plunged down sheerly like an open pit. Below, on the first landing, and lighted by another lamp, lads and lasses danced, not more than three at a time for lack of space, in jigs and reels and hornpipes. Above, on either side, there was a recess railed with iron, perhaps two feet wide and four long, which stood for orchestra and seats of honour. In the one balcony, five slatternly Irish lasses sat woven in a comely group. In the other was posted Orpheus, his body, which was convulsively in motion, forming an odd contrast to his somnolent, imperturbable Scots face. His brother, a dark man with a vehement, interested countenance, who made a god of the fiddler, sat by with open mouth, drinking in the general admiration and throwing out remarks to kindle it.

'That's a bonny hornpipe now,' he would say, 'it's a great favourite with performers; they dance the sand dance to it.' And he expounded the sand dance. Then suddenly, it would be a long 'Hush!' with uplifted finger and glowing, supplicating eyes; 'he's going to play "Auld Robin Gray"[29] on one string!' And throughout this excruciating movement, – 'On one string, that's on one string!' he kept crying. I would have given something myself that it had been on none; but the hearers were much awed. I called for a tune or two, and thus introduced myself to the notice of the brother, who directed his talk to me for some little while, keeping, I need hardly mention, true to his topic, like the seamen to the star. 'He's grand of it,' he said confidentially. 'His master was a music-hall man.' Indeed the music-hall man had left his mark, for our fiddler was ignorant of many of our best old airs; 'Logie o' Buchan,'[30] for instance, he only knew as a quick, jigging figure in a set of quadrilles, and had never heard it called by name. Perhaps, after all, the brother was the more interesting performer of the two. I have spoken with him afterwards repeatedly, and found him always the same quick, fiery bit of a man, not without brains; but he never showed to such advantage as when he was thus squiring the fiddler into public note. There is nothing more becoming than a genuine admiration; and it shares this with love, that it does not become contemptible although misplaced.

The dancing was but feebly carried on. The space was almost impracticably small; and the Irish wenches combined the extreme of bashfulness about this innocent display with a surprising impudence and roughness of address. Most often, either the fiddle lifted up its voice unheeded, or only a couple of lads would be footing it and snapping fingers on the landing. And such was the eagerness of the brother to display all the acquirements of his idol, and such the sleepy indifference of the performer, that the tune would as often as not be changed, and the hornpipe expire into a ballad before the dancers had cut half a dozen shuffles.

In the meantime, however, the audience had been growing more and more numerous every moment; there was hardly standing-room round the top of the companion; and the strange instinct of the race moved some of the new-comers to close both the doors, so that the atmosphere grew insupportable. It was a good place, as the saying is, to leave.

The wind hauled ahead with a head sea. By ten at night heavy sprays were flying and drumming over the forecastle; the companion of Steerage No. 1 had to be closed, and the door of communication through the second cabin thrown open. Either from the convenience of the opportunity, or because we had already a number of acquaintances in that part of the ship, Mr Jones and I paid it a late visit. Steerage No. 1 is shaped like an isosceles triangle, the sides opposite the equal angles bulging outward with the contour of the ship. It is lined with eight pens of sixteen bunks apiece, four bunks below and four above on either side. ⟨The companion lands about the middle of the greater length, and thus cuts the open space between the pens into two unequal apartments, as a drawing room and boudoir. Each of these is furnished with a table and fixed benches; that in the forward space being shaped to a point, a triangle within a triangle, to fit the inclination of the ship's timbers.⟩ At night the place is lit with two lanterns, one to each table. As the steamer beat on her way among the rough billows, the light passed through violent phases of change, and was thrown to and fro and up and down with startling swiftness. You were tempted to wonder, as you looked, how so thin a glimmer could control and disperse such solid blackness. ⟨Even by day much of the steerage enjoyed but a groping twilight. I presume (for I never saw it) that some cleansing process was carried on each morning; but there was never light enough to be particular; and in a place so full of corners and so much broken up by fixtures and partitions, dirt might lie for years without disturbance. The pens, stalls, pews – I know not what to call them – were besides, by their very design, beyond the reach of bucket and swab. Each broad shelf with its four deep divisions, formed a fourfold asylum for all manner of uncleanness. When the pen was fully occupied, with sixteen live human animals, more or less unwashed, lying immersed together in the same close air all night, and their litter of meat, dirty dishes and rank bedding tumbled all day together in foul disorder, the merest possibilities of health or cleanliness were absent.

If it was impossible to clean the steerage, it was no less impossible to clean the steerage passenger. All ablution below was rigorously forbidden. A man might give his hands a scour at the pump beside the galley, but that was exactly all. One fellow used to strip to his waist every morning and freshen his chest and shoulders; but I need not tell you he was no true steerage passenger. To wash outside in the sharp sea air of the morning is a step entirely foreign to the frowsy, herding, over-warm traditions of the working class; and a human body must apparently have been nurtured in some luxury, before it courts these rude shocks and surprises of temperature in which many men find health and vigour. Thus, even if the majority of passengers came clean aboard at Greenock, long ere the ten days were out or the shores of America in sight, all were reduced to a common level, all, who here stewed together in their own exhalations, were uncompromisingly unclean. A writer of the school of M. Zola[31] would here find an inspiration for many pages; but without entering farther into detail, let me mention the name of sea sickness, and leave its added horrors to the imagination of the reader.

I have said that, on our voyage, the ship was a good deal below her full complement of passengers. Perhaps not half of the pens numbered their complete sixteen; and every here and there an empty bunk afforded elbow-room and something like a wardrobe to the neighbours. Steerage No. 1 was especially intended for single men; yet more than one family was here installed among the others. It was strange to note how the different nationalities had drawn apart; for all English speakers were in the foremost bunks, and Germans and Scandinavians had clustered aft into a couple of pens upon the starboard side. This separation was marked and openly recognised. I remember coming down one morning to look for the Russian, and being told that I should find him 'back there wi' the Germans'.⟩ When Jones and I entered we found a little company of our acquaintances seated together at the triangular foremost table. A more forlorn party, in more dismal circumstances, it would be hard to imagine. The motion here in the ship's nose was very violent; the uproar of the sea often overpoweringly loud. The yellow flicker of the lantern spun round and round and tossed the shadows in masses. The air was hot, but it struck a chill from its fœtor. From all round in the dark bunks, the scarcely human noises of the sick joined into a kind of farmyard chorus. In the midst, these five friends of mine were keeping up what heart they could in company. ⟨They looked white and heavy-eyed; nor was it wonderful if they were indisposed; for aside from the suggestive noises which assailed the ear, there was forced upon the mind, in this quarter of the ship, a strong and almost disquieting sense of the swiftness of her advance and the rudeness of her conflict with the sea.⟩ Singing was their refuge from discomfortable thoughts and sensations. One piped, in feeble tones, 'O why left I my hame?' which seemed a pertinent question in the circumstances. Another, from the invisible horrors of a pen where he lay dog-sick upon the upper shelf, found courage, in a blink of his sufferings, to give us several verses of the 'Death of Nelson';[32] and it was odd and eerie to hear the chorus breathe feebly from all sorts of dark corners, and 'this day has done his dooty' rise and fall and be taken up again in this dim *inferno*, to an accompaniment of plunging, hollow-sounding

bows and the rattling spray-showers overhead. ⟨It seemed to me
the singer, at least, that day had done his duty. For to sing in
such a place and in such a state of health is cheerfully heroic.
Like a modern Theseus,[33] he thus combatted bad air, disease
and darkness, and threw abroad among his fellows some pleasant and courageous thoughts.⟩

All seemed unfit for conversation; a certain dizziness had
interrupted the activity of their minds; and except to sing they
were tongue-tied. There was present, however, one tall, powerful fellow of doubtful nationality, being neither quite Scotsman
nor altogether Irish, but of surprising clearness of conviction on
the highest problems. He had gone nearly beside himself on
the Sunday, because of a general backwardness to indorse his
definition of mind as 'a living, thinking substance which cannot
be felt, heard, or seen' – nor, I presume, although he failed to
mention it, smelt. Now he came forward in a pause with another
contribution to our culture.

'Just by way of change,' said he, 'I'll ask you a Scripture
riddle. There's profit in them too,' he added ungrammatically.

This was the riddle–

> C and P
> Did agree
> To cut down C;
> But C and P
> Could not agree
> Without the leave of G.
> All the people cried to see
> The crueltie
> Of C and P.

Harsh are the words of Mercury after the songs of Apollo![34]
We were a long while over the problem, shaking our heads and
gloomily wondering how a man could be such a fool; but at
length he put us out of suspense and divulged the fact that C
and P stood for Caiaphas and Pontius Pilate.[35] ⟨The more I study
his enigma, which is given here with critical exactitude, the
more deeply am I astonished by its feebleness and historical

inaccuracy. It touches moreover, in an insidious, unsettling way, on a serious problem of faith; and is probably, take it for all in all, the work of an infidel propaganda in collaboration. Or perhaps it is a *memoria technica*[36] for some exceedingly complicated date? I advise the reader to get it off by heart, for someday, who knows? it might be useful to him. For my own part, I shall never forget either the riddle or the time and place in which I heard it; and as for its propounder, though I cannot think either philosophy or history to be his forte, he seemed a brave and a warm-hearted man, and he was good to hear when he spoke about his wife and children.)

I think it must have been the riddle that settled us; but the motion and the close air likewise hurried our departure. We had not been gone long, we heard next morning, ere two or even three out of the five fell sick. We thought it little wonder on the whole, for the sea kept contrary all night. I now made my bed upon the second-cabin floor, where, although I ran the risk of being stepped upon, I had a free current of air, more or less vitiated indeed, and running only from steerage to steerage, but at least not stagnant; and from this couch, as well as the usual sounds of a rough night at sea, the hateful coughing and retching of the sick and the sobs of children, I heard a man run wild with terror beseeching his friend for encouragement. 'The ship's going down!' he cried with a thrill of agony. 'The ship's going down!' he repeated, now in a blank whisper, now with his voice rising towards a sob; and his friend might reassure him, reason with him, joke at him – all was in vain, and the old cry came back, 'The ship's going down!' There was something panicky and catching in the emotion of his tones; and I saw in a clear flash what an involved and hideous tragedy was a disaster to an emigrant ship. If this whole parishful of people came no more to land, into how many houses would the newspaper carry woe, and what a great part of the web of our corporate human life would be rent across for ever!

The next morning when I came on deck I found a new world indeed. The wind was fair; the sun mounted into a cloudless heaven; through great dark blue seas the ship cut a swath of curded foam. The horizon was dotted all day with companionable sails, and the sun shone pleasantly on the long, heaving deck.

We had many fine-weather diversions to beguile the time. There was a single chess-board and a single pack of cards. Sometimes as many as twenty of us would be playing dominoes for love. Feats of dexterity, puzzles for the intelligence, some arithmetical, some of the same order as the old problem of the fox and goose and cabbage,[37] were always welcome; and the latter, I observed, more popular as well as more conspicuously well done than the former. ⟨A party of gentlemen (I speak in the sense of caste alone) would have excelled my workman friends at hop-step-and-jump or push-the-stick,[38] but they would scarce have displayed the same patience in these lesser exercises of the mind.⟩ We had a regular daily competition to guess the vessel's progress; and twelve o'clock, when the result was published in the wheel-house, came to be a moment of considerable interest. But the interest was unmixed. Not a bet was laid upon our guesses. From the Clyde to Sandy Hook I never heard a wager offered or taken. We had, besides, romps in plenty. Puss in the Corner,[39] which we had rebaptised, in more manly style, Devil and four Corners, was my own favourite game; but there were many who preferred another, ⟨nameless as far as I know, which was diverting enough to the onlookers, but must have developed a tendency to headache in those who played. The humour of the thing⟩ was to box a person's ears until he found out who had cuffed him. ⟨The harder the smacks, the better we were all pleased. I have watched it for half an hour at a time; nor do I think it was a sense of personal dignity alone, which moved me to refrain from joining.⟩

This Tuesday morning we were all delighted with the change of weather, and in the highest possible spirits. We got in a cluster like bees, sitting between each other's feet under lee of the deck-houses. Stories and laughter went around. The children climbed about the shrouds. White faces appeared for the first time, and began to take on colour from the wind. I was kept hard at work making cigarettes for one amateur after another, and my less than moderate skill was heartily admired. Lastly, down sat the fiddler in our midst and began to discourse his reels, and jigs, and ballads, with now and then a voice or two to take up the air and throw in the interest of human speech.

Through this merry and good-hearted scene there came three cabin passengers, a gentleman and two young ladies, picking their way with little gracious titters of indulgence, and a Lady-Bountiful air[40] about nothing, which galled me to the quick. I have little of the radical in social questions, and have always nourished an idea that one person was as good as another. But I began to be troubled by this episode. It was astonishing what insults these people managed to convey by their presence. They seemed to throw their clothes in our faces. Their eyes searched us all over for tatters and incongruities. A laugh was ready at their lips; but they were too well-mannered to indulge it in our hearing. Wait a bit, till they were all back in the saloon, and then hear how wittily they would depict the manners of the steerage. We were in truth very innocently, cheerfully, and sensibly engaged, and there was no shadow of excuse for the swaying elegant superiority with which these damsels passed among us, or for the stiff and waggish glances of their squire. Not a word was said; only when they were gone Mackay[41] sullenly damned their impudence under his breath; but we were all conscious of an icy influence and a dead break in the course of our enjoyment. ⟨We had been made to feel ourselves a sort of comical lower animal. Such a fine thing it is to have manners!

One compliment I must make to the Saloon passengers: this was the only invasion of our territory that I witnessed from beginning to end of the voyage. It was a piece of very natural and needful delicacy. We were not allowed upon their part of the ship; and so they were, and ought, to be chary of intruding upon ours. Reciprocity can alone justify such a privilege. I do not say but that a cabin passenger may once in a while slink forward under cover of night, just as some careful house-holders, when the servants are once in bed, descend to the kitchen for a cigar. We also, when night had fallen, installed ourselves along the hot water pipes with our backs to the saloon deckhouse. But except in some exceptional, anonymous or apologetic fashion, I give it as my experience, the visit of a cabin passenger, will be regarded as an intrusion in the steerage.⟩

Steerage Types

⟨The type of man in our steerage was by no means one to be despised. Some were handy, some intellectual, and almost all were pleasantly and kindly disposed. I had many long and serious talks, and many a good bout of mirth with my fellow passengers and I thought they formed, upon the whole, an agreeable and well informed society.⟩

We had a fellow on board, an Irish-American, for all the world like a beggar in a print by Callot;[42] one-eyed, with great, splay, crow's-feet round the sockets; a knotty squab nose coming down over his moustache; a miraculous hat; a shirt that had been white, ay, ages long ago; an alpaca coat in its last sleeves; and, without hyperbole, no buttons to his trousers. Even in these rags and tatters, the man twinkled all over with impudence like a piece of sham jewellery; and I have heard him offer a situation to one of his fellow-passengers with the air of a lord. Nothing could overlie such a fellow; a kind of base success was written on his brow. He was then in his ill days; but I can imagine him in Congress with his mouth full of bombast and sawder.[43] As we moved in the same circle, I was brought necessarily into his society. I do not think I ever heard him say anything that was true, kind, or interesting; but there was entertainment in the man's demeanour. You might call him a half-educated Irish Tigg.[44]

Our Russian made a remarkable contrast to this impossible fellow. Rumours and legends were current in the steerages about his antecedents. Some said he was a Nihilist[45] escaping; others set him down for a harmless spendthrift, who had squandered fifty thousand roubles, and whose father had now despatched him to America by way of penance. Either tale might flourish in security; there was no contradiction to be feared, for the hero spoke not one word of English. I got on with him lumberingly enough in broken German, and learnt from his own lips that he had been an apothecary. He carried the photograph of his betrothed in a pocket-book, and remarked that it did not do her justice. The cut of his head stood out from among the passengers with an air of startling strangeness. The first natural instinct was to take him for a desperado; but although the features, to our Western eyes, had a barbaric and unhomely cast, the eye both reassured and touched. It was large and very dark and soft, with an expression of dumb endurance, as if it had often looked on desperate circumstances and never looked on them without resolution.

He cried out when I used the word. 'No, no,' he said, 'not resolution.'

'The resolution to endure,' I explained.

And then he shrugged his shoulders, and said, '*Ach, ja*,'[46] with gusto, like a man who has been flattered in his favourite pretensions. Indeed, he was always hinting at some secret sorrow; and his life, he said, had been one of unusual trouble and anxiety; so the legends of the steerage may have represented at least some shadow of the truth. Once, and once only, he sang a song at our concerts; standing forth without embarrassment, his great stature somewhat humped, his long arms frequently extended, his Kalmuck head thrown backward. It was a suitable piece of music, as deep as a cow's bellow and wild like the White Sea.[47] He was struck and charmed by the freedom and sociality of our manners. At home, he said, no one on a journey would speak to him, but those with whom he would not care to speak; thus unconsciously involving himself in the condemnation of his countrymen. But Russia was soon to be changed; the ice of the Neva was softening under the sun of civilisation; the new ideas, '*wie ein feines Violin*,'[48] were audible among the big empty drum notes of Imperial diplomacy; and he looked to see a great revival, though with a somewhat indistinct and childish hope.

We had a father and son who made a pair of Jacks-of-all-trades. It was the son who sang the 'Death of Nelson' under such contrarious circumstances ⟨and who contributed on many other occasions to make the voyage a happy period for all⟩. He was by trade a shearer of ship plates; but he could touch the organ, had led two choirs, and played the flute and piccolo in a professional string band. His repertory of songs was, besides, inexhaustible, and ranged impartially from the very best to the very worst within his reach. Nor did he seem to make the least distinction between these extremes, but would cheerfully follow up 'Tom Bowling'[49] with 'Around her splendid form.'

The father, an old, cheery, small piece of manhood, could do everything connected with tinwork from one end of the process to the other, use almost every carpenter's tool, and make picture frames to boot. 'I sat down with silver plate every Sunday,' said he, 'and pictures on the wall. I have made enough money to be rolling in my carriage. But, sir,' looking at me unsteadily with his bright rheumy eyes, 'I was troubled with a drunken wife.' He took a hostile view of matrimony in consequence. 'It's an old saying,' he remarked: 'God made 'em, and the devil he mixed 'em.'

I think he was justified by his experience. It was a dreary story. He would bring home three pounds on Saturday, and on Monday all the clothes would be in pawn. Sick of the useless struggle, he gave up a paying contract, and contented himself with small and ill-paid jobs. 'A bad job was as good as a good job for me,' he said; 'it all went the same way.' Once the wife showed signs of amendment; she kept steady for weeks on end; it was again worth while to labour and to do one's best. The husband found a good situation some distance from home, and, to make a little upon every hand, started the wife in a cook-shop; the children were here and there, busy as mice; savings began to grow together in the bank, and the golden age of hope had returned again to that unhappy family. But one week my old acquaintance, getting earlier through with his work, came home on the Friday instead of the Saturday, and there was his wife to receive him reeling drunk. He 'took and gave her a pair o' black eyes,' for which I pardon him, nailed up the cook-shop door, gave up his situation, and resigned himself to a life of poverty, with the workhouse at the end. As the children came to their full age they fled the house, and established themselves in other countries; some did well, some not so well; but the father remained at home alone with his drunken wife, all his sound-hearted pluck and varied accomplishments depressed and negatived.

Was she dead now? or, after all these years, had he broken

the chain, and run from home like a schoolboy? I could not discover which; but here at least he was out on the adventure, and still one of the bravest and most youthful men on board.

'Now, I suppose, I must put my old bones to work again,' said he; 'but I can do a turn yet.'

And the son to whom he was going, I asked, was he not able to support him?

'Oh yes,' he replied. 'But I'm never happy without a job on hand. And I'm stout; I can eat a'most anything. You see no craze about me.'

⟨I should say, to finish this sketch, that he was usually more given to listen than to speak; he was indeed an indefatigable hearer, always on the edge of the group, pipe in hand, with his best ear upraised; and though unlettered and, I think, ignorant, loved to hear serious things discussed. It is strange that I should have permitted myself to use the word ignorant, about a man who understood and could successfully practise so great a variety of trades; and yet the word must remain, for there is no other to convey my meaning. Thus I have known people to declare both painters and musicians stupid, because their thoughts, lying out of the literary path, are not suited for display in company. Colours or sounds, chisels or vices, about whatever the mind may be occupied, it is still enlarged and invigorated; and yet it remains a question, whether these thoughts which cannot be clothed and rendered commonplace in words, may not be after all the most bracing and veracious. At least it would be ignorance itself to think my old acquaintance ignorant. Although one profession may be dully acquired betwixt sleep and waking, to change from one to another implies both activity and courage of the mind. For no inducement that I can fancy, would I set myself to learn another business; because the mind has grown slothful and dreads to grapple with a mass of fresh details.⟩

This tale of a drunken wife was paralleled on board by another of a drunken father. He was a capable man, with a good chance in life; but he had drunk up two thriving businesses like a bottle of sherry, and involved his sons along with him in ruin. Now they were on board with us, fleeing his disastrous neighbourhood.

Total abstinence, like all ascetical conclusions, is unfriendly to the most generous, cheerful, and human parts of man; but it could have adduced many instances and arguments from among our ship's company. I was one day conversing with a kind and happy Scotsman, running to fat and perspiration in the physical, but with a taste for poetry and a genial sense of fun. I had asked him his hopes in emigrating. They were like those of so many others, vague and unfounded; times were bad at home; they were said to have a turn for the better in the States; and a man could get on anywhere, he thought. That was precisely the weak point of his position; for if he could get on in America, why could he not do the same in Scotland? But I never had the courage to use that argument, though it was often on the tip of my tongue, and instead I agreed with him heartily, adding, with reckless originality, 'If the man stuck to his work, and kept away from drink.'

'Ah!' said he slowly, 'the drink! You see, that's just my trouble.'

He spoke with a simplicity that was touching, looking at me at the same time with something strange and timid in his eye, half-ashamed, half-sorry, like a good child who knows he should be beaten. You would have said he recognised a destiny to which he was born, and accepted the consequences mildly. Like the merchant Abudah,[50] he was at the same time fleeing from his destiny and carrying it along with him, the whole at an expense of six guineas.

As far as I saw, drink, idleness, and incompetency were the three great causes of emigration, and for all of them, and drink first and foremost, this trick of getting transported overseas appears to me the silliest means of cure. ⟨It is like turning in bed when you are down with a fever; you will find the new position as uneasy as the last.⟩ You cannot run away from a weakness; you must some time fight it out or perish; and if that be so, why not now, and where you stand? *Cælum non animam*. Change Glenlivet for Bourbon,[51] and it is still whisky, only not so good. A sea-voyage will not give a man the nerve to put aside cheap pleasure; emigration has to be done before we climb the vessel; an aim in life is the only fortune worth the finding; and it is not to be found in foreign lands, but in the heart itself.

Speaking generally, there is no vice of this kind more contemptible than another; for each is but a result and outward sign of a soul tragically shipwrecked. In the majority of cases, cheap pleasure is resorted to by way of anodyne. The pleasure-seeker sets forth upon life with high and difficult ambitions; he meant to be nobly good and nobly happy, though at as little pains as possible to himself; and it is because all has failed in his celestial enterprise that you now behold him rolling in the garbage. Hence the comparative success of the teetotal pledge;[52] because to a man who had nothing it sets at least a negative aim in life. Somewhat as prisoners beguile their days by taming a spider, the reformed drunkard makes an interest out of abstaining from intoxicating drinks, and may live for that negation. There is something, at least, *not to be done* each day; and a cold triumph awaits him every evening.

We had one on board with us, whom I have already referred to under the name of Mackay, who seemed to me not only a good instance of this failure in life of which we have been speaking, but a good type of the intelligence which here surrounded me. Physically he was a small Scotsman, standing a little back as though he were already carrying the elements of a corporation,[53] and his looks somewhat marred by the smallness of his eyes. Mentally, he was endowed above the average. There were but few subjects on which he could not converse with understanding and a dash of wit; ⟨and from these he had voluntarily abstracted his intelligence. His style of talking was remarkable; his words were selected with great discretion and out of a full possession of the English language, and he delivered⟩ himself slowly and with gusto, like a man who enjoyed his own sententiousness. He was a dry, quick, pertinent debater, speaking with a small voice, and swinging on his heels to launch and emphasise an argument. When he began a discussion, he could not bear to leave it off, but would pick the subject to the bone, without once relinquishing a point. An engineer by trade, Mackay believed in the unlimited perfectibility of all machines except the human machine. The latter he gave up with ridicule for a compound of carrion and perverse gases. He had an appetite for disconnected facts which I can only compare to the savage taste for beads. What is called information was indeed a passion with the man, and he not only delighted to receive it, but could pay you back in kind.

With all these capabilities, here was Mackay, already no longer young, on his way to a new country, with no prospects, no money, and but little hope. He was almost tedious in the cynical disclosures of his despair. 'The ship may go down for me,' he would say, 'now or tomorrow. I have nothing to lose and nothing to hope.' And again: 'I am sick of the whole damned performance.' He was, like the kind little man already quoted, another so-called victim of the bottle. But Mackay was miles from publishing his weakness to the world; laid the blame of his failure on corrupt masters and a corrupt State policy; and after he had been one night overtaken and had played the buffoon in his cups, sternly, though not without tact, suppressed all reference to his escapade. It was a treat to see him manage this; the various jesters withered under his gaze, and you were forced to recognise in him a certain steely force, and a gift of command which might have ruled a senate.

In truth it was not whisky that had ruined him; he was ruined long before for all good human purposes but conversation. His eyes were sealed by a cheap, school-book materialism. He could see nothing in the world but money and steam-engines. He did not know what you meant by the word happiness. He had forgotten the simple emotions of childhood, and perhaps never encountered the delights of youth. He believed in production, that useful figment of economy, as if it had been real like laughter; and production, without prejudice to liquor, was his god and guide. One day he took me to task – a novel cry to me – upon the over-payment of literature. Literary men, he said, were more highly paid than artisans; yet the artisan made threshing-machines and butter-churns, and the man of letters, except in the way of a few useful handbooks, made nothing worth the while. He produced a mere fancy article. Mackay's notion of a book was Hoppus's *Measurer*. Now in my time I have possessed and even studied that work; ⟨I found Hoppus a careful although scarce a stimulating writer; and I own he left something in my soul unsatisfied.⟩ If I were to be left to-morrow on Juan

Fernandez,[54] Hoppus's is not the book that I should choose for my companion volume.

I tried to fight the point with Mackay. I made him own that he had taken pleasure in reading books otherwise, to his view, insignificant; but he was too wary to advance a step beyond the admission. It was in vain for me to argue that here was pleasure ready-made and running from the spring, whereas his ploughs and butter-churns were but means and mechanisms to give men the necessary food and leisure before they start upon the search for pleasure; he jibbed and ran away from such conclusions. The thing was different, he declared, and nothing was serviceable but what had to do with food. 'Eat, eat, eat!' he cried; 'that's the bottom and the top.' By an odd irony of circumstance, he grew so much interested in this discussion that he let the hour slip by unnoticed and had to go without his tea. He had enough sense and humour, indeed he had no lack of either, to have chuckled over this himself in private; and even to me he referred to it with the shadow of a smile. ⟨Here, at least, was my contention in a nutshell: his sentiments were saddening to me, yet it was with interest that I listened to him as he spoke; on his side, although he forgot the staff of life[55] for the pleasure he had in continuing the dispute, he thought my views not only silly but wickedly wrong.⟩

Mackay was a hot bigot. He would not hear of religion. I have seen him waste hours of time in argument with all sort of poor human creatures who understood neither him nor themselves, and he had had the boyishness to dissect and criticise even so small a matter as the riddler's definition of mind. He snorted aloud with zealotry and the lust for intellectual battle. Anything, whatever it was, that seemed to him likely to discourage the continued passionate production of corn and steam-engines he resented like a conspiracy against the people. Thus, when I put in the plea for literature, that it was only in good books, or in the society of the good, that a man could get help in his conduct, he declared I was in a different world from him. 'Damn my conduct!' said he. 'I have given it up for a bad job. My question is, "Can I drive a nail?"' And he plainly looked upon me as one who was insidiously seeking to reduce the people's annual bellyful of corn and steam-engines. ⟨I feel there is some mistake in this alarm, and that the people could get through life perhaps with less of either. But when I hinted something of that view, and that to spend less was, after all, as good a way out of the difficulty of life as to gain more, he accused me, in almost as many words, of the sin of aristocracy and a desire to grind the masses. Perhaps there was some indelicacy on my part in presenting him with such an argument; for it is not in his class that such a movement must be inaugurated; and we must see the rich honest, before we need look hopefully to see the poor considerate.

Mackay was the very man to be reclaimed by total abstinence; and if reclaimed, would present a typical instance of those useless successes and victorious defeats which are too often the only trophies of the movement. The sort of reformation that I care about must be of a more sweeping order. I have not the least aversion to the continued poverty of many tipplers; I am far more concerned about the continued prosperity and power of many unworthy capitalists. Although I am far from cherishing unfriendly feelings towards Mackay, for the man both interested and amused me, it seems still an open question whether, for the general interests of the race, he had not better remain poor and drink himself to death. There was nothing in him worth saving but his talents, which he would be sure to misapply. He had no hope but to make money and to squander it. As he is, you have a shiftless, tippling engineer; but let him be rich, and he will be an oppressor of men. Working man and master are but John and Jack; and when Mackay bewails the hard condition of his class, he is only rejecting the legitimate course of his own philosophy. 'Damn my conduct!' is an agreeable and light hearted sentiment on a man's own lips; but it becomes practically inconvenient when it is adopted as a principle by others.⟩

It may be argued that these opinions spring from the defect of culture; that a narrow and pinching way of life not only exaggerates to a man the importance of material conditions, but indirectly, by denying him the necessary books and leisure, keeps his mind ignorant of larger thoughts; and that hence springs this overwhelming concern about diet, and hence the bald view of existence professed by Mackay. Had this been an English peasant the conclusion would be tenable. ⟨I was already a young man when I was first brought into contact with some of the heavy English labourers of Suffolk;[56] and only those who have some acquaintance with the same class in Scotland, can conceive the astonishment and disgust with which I viewed the difference. To me, they seemed scarce human, but like a very gross and melancholy sort of ape; and though I may have been unfortunate in the examples that fell under my observation, the fact of my amazement is enough to my present purpose. The feeling was the more impressed on me after my return to Scotland, by a conversation with a labourer upon the shores of Fife.[57] This man was cleaning a barge, in which I was driven to take refuge from a squall of rain; and he sat down by my side, fantastically, not to say disgustingly, bedaubed with liquid manure. But his mind was clean and vigorous and full of grave thoughts. He spoke with me of education, culture and the learned professions. 'Aye,' said he, 'that's the thing for a man to be happy. *Ye see, he has aye something ayont.*'[58] It would be hard to set forth more clearly the advantages of an intellectual life. You could not call this man uncultured; and yet his is no uncommon case among the field labourers of Scotland. A sound, sometimes even an ambitious education lays the basis; the metaphysical and sentimental turn of the race leads them, at their outdoor work, to hoard and improve on what they have learned; the *Bible* and even the *Shorter Catechism*[59] (like it or not, as you please) are works of a high scope which stimulate the mind; and many a peasant has his own heresy or holds orthodoxy on some terms of his own. As a people, they are not ignorant, not uncultured and certainly, you would say, not materialistic.⟩ But Mackay had most of the elements of a liberal education. He had skirted metaphysical and mathematical studies. He had a thoughtful hold of what he knew, which would be exceptional among bankers. He had been brought up in the midst of hothouse piety, and told, with incongruous pride, the story of his own brother's deathbed ecstasies. Yet he had somehow failed to fulfil himself, and was adrift like a dead thing among external circumstances, without hope or lively preference or shaping aim. And further, there seemed a tendency among many of his fellows to fall into the same blank and unlovely opinions. One thing, indeed, is not to be learned in Scotland, and that is the way to be happy. Yet that is the whole of culture, and perhaps two-thirds of morality. Can it be that the Puritan school, by divorcing a man from nature, by thinning out his instincts, and setting a stamp of its disapproval on whole fields of human activity and interest, leads at last directly to material greed? (Not in Scotland alone, but in New England also, there are features that might justify the suspicion.)

Nature is a good guide through life, and the love of simple pleasures next, if not superior, to virtue; and we had on board an Irishman who based his claim to the widest and most affectionate popularity precisely upon these two qualities, that he was natural and happy. He boasted a fresh colour, a tight little figure, unquenchable gaiety, and indefatigable goodwill. His clothes puzzled the diagnostic mind, until you heard he had been once a private coachman, when they became eloquent and seemed a part of his biography. His face contained the rest, and, I fear, a prophecy of the future; the hawk's nose above accorded so ill with the pink baby's mouth below. His spirit and his pride belonged, you might say, to the nose; while it was the general shiftlessness expressed by the other that had thrown him from situation to situation, and at length on board the emigrant ship. Barney ate, so to speak, nothing from the galley; his own tea, butter and eggs supported him throughout the voyage; and about meal-time you might often find him up to the elbows in amateur cookery. His was the first voice heard singing among all the passengers; he was the first who fell to dancing. From Loch Foyle to Sandy Hook, there was not a piece of fun undertaken but there was Barney in the midst.

You ought to have seen him when he stood up to sing at our concerts – his tight little figure stepping to and fro, and his feet shuffling to the air, his eyes seeking and bestowing encouragement – and to have enjoyed the bow, so nicely calculated between jest and earnest, between grace and clumsiness, with which he brought each song to a conclusion. He was not only a great favourite among ourselves, but his songs attracted the lords of the saloon, who often leaned to hear him over the rails of the hurricane-deck. He was somewhat pleased, but not at all abashed by this attention; and one night in the midst of his famous performance of 'Billy Keogh,' I saw him spin half round in a pirouette and throw an audacious wink to an old gentleman above.

This was the more characteristic, as, for all his daffing,[60] he was a modest and very polite little fellow among ourselves.

He would not have hurt the feelings of a fly, nor throughout the passage did he give a shadow of offence; yet he was always, by his innocent freedoms and love of fun, brought upon that narrow margin where politeness must be natural to walk without a fall. He was once seriously angry, and that in a grave, quiet manner, because they supplied no fish on Friday;[61] for Barney was a conscientious Catholic. He had likewise strict notions of refinement; and when, late one evening, after the women had retired, a young Scotsman struck up an indecent song, Barney's drab clothes were immediately missing from the group. His taste was for the society of gentlemen, of whom, with the reader's permission, there was no lack in our five steerages and second cabin; and he avoided the rough and positive with a girlish shrinking. Mackay, partly from his superior powers of mind, which rendered him incomprehensible, partly from his extreme opinions, was especially distasteful to the Irishman. I have seen him slink off with backward looks of terror and offended delicacy, while the other, in his witty, ugly way, had been professing hostility to God, and an extreme theatrical readiness to be shipwrecked on the spot. These utterances hurt the little coachman's modesty like a bad word. ⟨His love for music was inborn and generous; none had so ready an applause as Barney; I have seen the delight with which he was introduced to Scotch dance music and his silent contempt for the melodies of the Music Hall. And it is àpropos of Barney that I must relate the great change which overtook the organization of our nightly concerts. Barney had no distaste for whiskey; and he and the young Jack-of-all-Trades received many a stiff glass from enthusiastic hearers. The fiddler, on the other hand, being silent and almost morose, fiddled away nightly and received no invitations to the bar. This partiality began to prey upon his mind; and one evening he made a clean breast of it to Jones and threatened to strike work. Here was a bomb shell in our camp. Barney and the Jack-of-all-Trades were certainly our two most esteemed vocalists; we might have continued to run the concerts on their attraction only; but it was not to be thought of that a valued collaborator should retire under a sense of neglect. The fiddler, too, should have his whiskey. It was decided to collect money, and offer a little collation upon deck to the performers in a body.

I am afraid we were all a little thoughtless, and I in the front rank; upon meeting Barney, I opened the matter to him without preparation and in terms that were perhaps too naked. He flushed to his neck. 'Well then,' he said, 'I do not sing at your concerts any more': adding he was glad enough to sing to amuse his friends, but would not sing at all for whiskey. I could only murmur that I thought he was right; and on that, he turned upon his heel and left me to my degradation. As everybody connected with the affair was now in a false position, and myself in the falsest, I retired to the cabin or, in so many words, hid myself.

What passed on deck, I never rightly knew. It appears, however, it was a scene of consternation for awhile; and Jones and young O'Reilly were cursing me for my defection. I must own I left them to bear the brunt that evening; but my time came too; for as I was sitting below and making some pretence to write my notes, I received a message that Barney wished to speak with me on deck. I went up with the resignation of the condemned criminal, feeling that if he wished my blood, it was no less than due to him, and, generally, that I had been blunt, inconsiderate and ungentlemanly. But there he was – bless his heart! – waiting to load me with apologies. He had spoken sharply; he had been impolite; he could not rest till he was pardoned. 'You have always been a good friend to me,' was his humble way of putting it, when the fact was that we had been good friends together. I protested that it was I alone who stood in need of pardon; but he would hear of no such thing; and I daresay we walked half an hour about the deck, before he consented to a compromise by which we were to pardon one another.

Meantime the system of concerts had been permanently destroyed, not at all, as Barney maintained, by his pride and ill-temper, but by a general want of tact among the rest of us; and instead, a select company moved by invitation into the second cabin. It was a kind of high life below stairs, which pleased me far less than our public and open air festivals of the past. But in this small way, they were not unsuccessful and offered some curious features. The fiddler combed his hair before appearing on this new and more select stage; and another performer, the young bride of whom the reader has been told, now lifted up a small and rather sweet pipe in little drawing-room ditties, sometimes alone, sometimes accompanied by her husband. But the point was the effect produced on Barney. In this small, quiet and, so to speak, genteel society, he opened like a rose. Pleasure looked out of his eyes. He seemed less merry than on deck, but his manners grew more affectionate and domestic; I have never seen a gallantry so kind as that with which he treated the ladies of this small circle; and he would have sung himself to death to give us pleasure. Nor can I find words to tell you with what enthusiasm he greeted the singing of the bride. These drawing room songs were exactly after his heart; he delighted in that music-mistress style; I believe the very smallness of the voice seemed to him a mark of refinement. Up to nearly midnight, he sat on deck declaring and exaggerating his delight.

His Irishisms and merry simplicities of speech were our current money and went round the steerage like the day's news. Once, he got two pills from the Doctor, took one, and brought the other back with scorn. He was of Captain Burnaby's mind,[62] it appeared; nothing would please him but Corkle's pills and not less than four of these. The Doctor protested he had but one box, which he reserved for his own use and that of the cabin passengers. 'Sure, Doctor,' said Barney, 'am n't I not the same Christian as yourself and the cabin passengers?' I need hardly say, the pills were given. Indeed he had only to spring the brogue on any one of us, and he could command what we had.

One story more I must relate, as I have some notes of what he said, and the incident besides completes the character of

Barney. I have spoken of a semi-official position, that of assistant to the Steerage steward, and how rapidly the semi-officials grew disgusted and resigned the place. The second of these had reigned, as I said, for a whole day. About noon on the morrow, a good many of us were hanging round the hatchway at the foot of companion No. 2 and 3, when round came the steerage steward, with his white sheet of loaves girt about him, like a man going forth to sow; and behind, carrying with both hands a huge tin dish of butter, who but Barney? He was greeted with acclamation; passed among us, rosy and smiling, half amused, half gratified with the distinction; and followed his superior down one of the galleries, with an overdone air of business, like a child helping to lay the table.

Perhaps ten minutes elapsed; and then Barney reappeared at full speed out of the steerage, set the dish down upon the hatchway with a bang, and threw himself rolling on the tarpaulin.

'The divel in your butter!' he cried, and buried his face in his hands.

The sheeted steward now followed and looked distressfully on his assistant amid shouts of laughter. It was some time before he found anything to say, and even then his voice came hollow from a profound consciousness that he should exhort in vain.

'Come along!' he cried feebly. 'Up with it, Johnny!'

'Sorry am I that iver you took Johnny in your mouth,' retorted Barney.

And the steward, seeing all was over, departed in search of other help; Barney had concluded his career as a semi official; how the rations were finally served out upon that occasion is more than I can tell.

Meantime Barney picked himself up, a rueful looking Barney.

'I must go on deck,' said he. 'I'm sick wid their butter. I can feel the smell of it!'

'It's rotten,' struck in an old woman.

'Rotten?' cried Barney, brightening up. 'Well, I'll tell ye. I gave a Dutchman down there the full of me hat of it. He wouldn't be plased[63] wid less!'

And so greatly comforted by having raised another laugh and callously unconcerned at his desertion, he departed upon deck and shall disappear from these pages.⟩

The Sick Man

One night Jones, the young O'Reilly, and myself were walking arm-in-arm and briskly up and down the deck. Six bells had rung; a head-wind blew chill and fitful, the fog was closing in with a sprinkle of rain, and the fog-whistle had been turned on, and now divided time with its unwelcome outcries, loud like a bull, thrilling and intense like a mosquito. ⟨The decks were deserted.⟩ Even the watch lay somewhere snugly out of sight. ⟨We passed the furnaces and through a blast of heat; and as we cleared the deck house, met the cold wind upon our cheek; and these alternations alone marked our promenade.⟩

For some time we observed something lying black and huddled in the scuppers, ⟨not far from where I was wakened by the fireman. At first we made light of it; but as we passed again and again, it began insensibly to occupy our minds; and as we reached the spot, the talk would languish, the pace would halt, and our three heads would all be inclined to that side. Almost unconsciously, we were beginning to grow interested in the black bundle; and before long by a natural process, we should have stopped of our own accord to satisfy our curiosity. But the matter was taken out of our hands; for the bundle⟩ at last heaved a little and moaned aloud. We ran to the rails. An elderly man, but whether passenger or seaman, ⟨whether beautiful or the reverse,⟩ it was impossible in the darkness to determine, lay grovelling on his belly in the wet scuppers, and kicking feebly with his outspread toes. ⟨He had been sick and his head was in his vomit.⟩ We asked him what was amiss, and he replied incoherently, with a strange accent and in a voice unmanned by terror, that he had cramp in the stomach, that he had been ailing all day, had seen the doctor twice, and had walked the deck against fatigue till he was overmastered and had fallen where we found him.

Jones remained by his side, while O'Reilly and I hurried off to seek the doctor. We knocked in vain at the doctor's cabin; there came no reply; nor could we find any one to guide us. It was no time for delicacy; so we ran once more forward; and I, whipping up a ladder and touching my hat to the officer of the watch, addressed him as politely as I could:

'I beg your pardon, sir; but there is a man lying bad with cramp in the lee scuppers; and I can't find the doctor.'

He looked at me peeringly in the darkness; and then somewhat harshly, 'Well, *I* can't leave the bridge, my man,' said he.

'No, sir, but you can tell me what to do,' I returned.

'Is it one of the crew?' he asked.

'I believe him to be a fireman,' I replied, ⟨going merely on my last experience.⟩

I daresay officers are much annoyed by complaints and alarmist information from their freight of human creatures, but certainly, whether it was the idea that the sick man was one of the crew, or from something conciliatory in my address, the officer in question was immediately relieved and mollified; and speaking in a voice much freer from constraint, advised me to find a steward and despatch him in quest of the doctor, who would now be in the smoking-room over his pipe.

One of the stewards was often enough to be found about this hour down our companion, Steerage No. 2 and 3; that was his smoking-room of a night. Let me call him Blackwood. ⟨I have asked myself repeatedly whether I should give his exact rank, and I find my heart fails me. If I call him Blackwood, I shall have a name answerable enough to his appearance, and leave him to the enjoyment of his privacy. I do not wish to bear tales out of school against an individual.⟩ O'Reilly and I rattled down the companion, breathing hurry; and in his shirt-sleeves and perched across the carpenter's bench upon one thigh, found Blackwood; a neat, bright, dapper, Glasgow-looking man, with a bead of an eye and a rank twang in his speech. I forget who was with him, but the pair were enjoying a deliberate talk over their pipes. I daresay he was tired with his day's work, and eminently comfortable at that moment; and the truth is, I did not stop to consider his feelings, but told my story in a breath.

'Steward,' said I, 'there's a man lying bad with cramp, and I can't find the doctor.'

He turned upon me as pert as a sparrow, but with a black look that is the prerogative of man; and taking his pipe out of his mouth—

'That's none of my business,' said he. 'I don't care.'

⟨So far as I have gone, I have not often heard an uglier speech; the French, in their academical manner, would call it cynical; brutal and devilish must serve the turn of a homely English speaker.⟩ I could have strangled the little ruffian where he sat. The thought of his cabin civility and cabin tips filled me with indignation. I glanced at O'Reilly; he was pale and quivering, and looked like assault and battery, every inch of him. But we had a better card than violence.

'You will have to make it your business,' said I, 'for I am sent to you by the officer on the bridge.'

Blackwood was fairly tripped. He made no answer, but put out his pipe, gave me one murderous look, and set off upon his errand strolling. From that day forward, I should say, he improved to me in courtesy, as though he had repented his evil speech and were anxious to leave a better impression. ⟨But I cannot help it: I hate every button upon that man's jacket.⟩

When we got on deck again, Jones was still beside the sick man; and two or three late stragglers had gathered round and were offering suggestions. One proposed to give the patient water, which was promptly negatived. Another bade us hold him up; he himself prayed to be let lie; but as it was at least as well to keep him off the streaming decks, O'Reilly and I supported him between us. It was only by main force that we did so, and neither an easy nor an agreeable duty; for he fought in his paroxysms like a frightened child, and moaned miserably when he resigned himself to our control.

⟨'Take care of your knee,' said I to O'Reilly. 'I have got mine in the vomit.'⟩

I thought the patient too much occupied to mind our observations; but he heard me, relaxed his struggles, and began to twist

in a new way with his arm across his body. I could not imagine
what he was at; till suddenly forth came a coloured handkerchief; and he held it out to me, saying 'Wipe your knee wi' that.'

We all know about Sir Philip Sidney: here is a Roland for his
Oliver.⁶⁴ It is easier to say a fine thing on the field of honour
than in such a scene of physical disgrace; and the number of
persons is considerable who would be shorn of all romantic
notions by having been dog-sick immediately before and on
the very spot where the occasion rose. It was the unaffected
courtliness of a good heart. You have wet your knee in my
service; well then, here is my handkerchief! It is true the man
thought he was come to his last hour: a thought to favour
dignity. That was indeed his argument against our friendly
violence.⟩

'O let me lie!' he pleaded. 'I'll no' get better anyway.' And
then, with a moan that went to my heart, 'O why did I come
upon this miserable journey?'

I was reminded of the song which I had heard a little while
before in the close, tossing steerage: 'O why left I my hame?'

Meantime Jones, relieved of his immediate charge, had gone
off to the galley, where we could see a light. There he found a
belated cook scouring pans by the radiance of two lanterns, and
one of these he sought to borrow. The scullion was backward.
'Was it one of the crew?' he asked. And when Jones, smitten
with my theory, had assured that it was a fireman, he reluctantly
left his scouring and came towards us at an easy pace, with one
of the lanterns swinging from his finger. The light, as it reached
the spot, showed us an elderly man, thick-set, and grizzled with
years; but the shifting and coarse shadows concealed from us
the expression and even the design of his face.

So soon as the cook set eyes on him he gave a sort of whistle.
'*It's only a passenger!*' said he; and turning about, made,
lantern and all, for the galley.

'He's a man anyway,' cried Jones in indignation.

'Nobody said he was a woman,' said a gruff voice, which I
recognised for that of the bo's'un. ⟨But I think he must have
made the remark to give himself a countenance, and because he

lacked the courage of his qualities; for, far from joining against us, he helped Jones to get the lantern from the cook.)

All this while there was no word of Blackwood or the doctor; and now the officer came to our side of the ship and asked, over the hurricane-deck rails, if the doctor were not yet come. We told him not.

'No?' he repeated with a breathing of anger; and we saw him hurry aft in person.

Ten minutes after the doctor made his appearance deliberately enough and examined our patient with the lantern. He made little of the case, had the man brought aft to the dispensary, dosed him, and sent him forward to his bunk. Two of his neighbours in the steerage had now come to our assistance, expressing loud sorrow that such 'a fine cheery body' should be sick; and these, claiming a sort of possession, took him entirely under their own care. The drug had probably relieved him, for he struggled no more, and was led along plaintive and patient, but protesting. His heart recoiled at the thought of the steerage. 'O let me lie down upon the bieldy side,' he cried; 'O dinna[65] take me down!' And again: 'O why did ever I come upon this miserable voyage?' And yet once more, with a gasp and a wailing prolongation of the fourth word: 'I had no *call* to come.' But there he was; and by the doctor's orders and the kind force of his two shipmates disappeared down the companion of Steerage No. 1 into the den allotted him.

At the foot of our own companion, just where I had found Blackwood, Jones and the bo's'un were now engaged in talk. This last was a gruff, cruel-looking seaman, who must have passed near half a century upon the seas; square-headed, goat-bearded, with heavy blond eyebrows, and an eye without radiance, but inflexibly steady and hard. I had not forgotten his rough speech; but I remembered also that he had helped us about the lantern; and now seeing him in conversation with Jones, and being choked with indignation, I proceeded to blow off my steam.

'Well,' said I, 'I make you my compliments upon your steward,' and furiously narrated what had happened.

'I've nothing to do with him,' replied the bo's'un. 'They're all alike. They wouldn't mind if they saw you all lying dead one upon the top of another.' ⟨And he made a quaint gesture with his pipe, expressive, so far as my imagination served me to interpret, of someone going up in an explosion.⟩

This was enough. A very little humanity went a long way with me after the experience of the evening. A sympathy grew up at once between the bo's'un and myself; and that night, and during the next few days, I learned to appreciate him better. He was a remarkable type, and not at all the kind of man you find in books. He had been at Sebastopol under English colours; and again in a States ship, 'after the *Alabama*, and praying God we shouldn't find her.' He was a high Tory[66] and a high Englishman. No manufacturer could have held opinions more hostile to the working man and his strikes. 'The workmen,' he said, 'think nothing of their country. They think of nothing but themselves. They're damned greedy, selfish fellows.' He would not hear of the decadence of England. 'They say they send us beef from America,' he argued; 'but who pays for it? All the money in the world's in England.' The Royal Navy was the best of possible services, according to him. 'Anyway the officers are gentlemen,' said he; 'and you can't get hazed[67] to death by a damned non-commissioned – as you can in the army.' Among nations, England was the first; then came France. He respected the French navy and liked the French people; and if he were forced to make a new choice in life, 'by God, he would try Frenchmen!' For all his looks and rough, cold manners, I observed that children were never frightened by him; they divined him at once to be a friend; and one night when he had chalked his hand and went about stealthily setting his mark on people's clothes, it was incongruous to hear this formidable old salt chuckling over his boyish monkey trick.

In the morning, my first thought was of the sick man. I was afraid I should not recognise him, so baffling had been the light of the lantern; and found myself unable to decide if he were Scots, English, or Irish. He had certainly employed north-country words and elisions; but the accent and the pronunciation seemed unfamiliar and incongruous in my ear.

To descend on an empty stomach into Steerage No. 1, was an adventure that required some nerve. The stench was atrocious; each respiration tasted in the throat like some horrible kind of cheese; and the squalid aspect of the place was aggravated by so many people worming themselves into their clothes in the twilight of the bunks. You may guess if I was pleased, not only for him, but for myself also, when I heard that the sick man was better and had gone on deck.

The morning was raw and foggy, though the sun suffused the fog with pink and amber; the fog-horn still blew, stertorous and intermittent; and to add to the discomfort, the seamen were just beginning to wash down the decks. But for a sick man this was heaven compared to the steerage. I found him standing on the hot-water pipe, just forward of the saloon deck-house. He was smaller than I had fancied, and plain-looking; but his face was distinguished by strange and fascinating eyes, limpid grey from a distance, but, when looked into, full of changing colours and grains of gold. His manners were mild and uncompromisingly plain; and I soon saw that, when once started, he delighted to talk. His accent and language had been formed in the most natural way, since he was born in Ireland, had lived a quarter of a century on the banks of Tyne, and was married to a Scots wife. A fisherman in the season, he had fished the east coast from Fisherrow to Whitby.[68] When the season was over, and the great boats, which required extra hands, were once drawn up on shore till the next spring, he worked as a labourer about chemical furnaces, or along the wharves unloading vessels. In this comparatively humble way of life he had gathered a competence, and could speak of his comfortable house, his hayfield, and his garden. On this ship, where so many accomplished artisans were fleeing from starvation, he was present on a pleasure trip to visit a brother in New York.

Ere he started, he informed me, he had been warned against the steerage and the steerage fare, and recommended to bring with him a ham and tea and a spice loaf. But he laughed to scorn such counsels. '*I'm* not afraid,' he had told his adviser; '*I'll* get on for ten days. I've not been a fisherman for nothing.' For it is no light matter, as he reminded me, to be in an open boat, perhaps waist-deep with herrings, day breaking with a scowl, and for miles on every hand lee-shores, unbroken, iron-bound, surf-beat, with only here and there an anchorage where you dare not lie, or a harbour impossible to enter with the wind that blows. The life of a North Sea fisher is one long chapter of exposure and hard work and insufficient fare; and even if he makes land at some bleak fisher port, perhaps the season is bad or his boat has been unlucky, and after fifty hours' unsleeping vigilance and toil, not a shop will give him credit for a loaf of bread. Yet the steerage of the emigrant ship had been too vile for the endurance of a man thus rudely trained. He had scarce eaten since he came on board, until the day before, when his appetite was tempted by some excellent pea-soup. We were all much of the same mind on board, and beginning with myself, had dined upon pea-soup not wisely but too well; only with him the excess had been punished, perhaps because he was weakened by former abstinence, and his first meal had resulted in a cramp. He had determined to live henceforth on biscuit; and when, two months later, he should return to England, to make the passage by saloon. The second cabin, after due inquiry, he scouted as another edition of the steerage.

He spoke apologetically of his emotion when ill. 'Ye see, I had no call to be here,' said he; 'and I thought it was by with me[69] last night. I've a good house at home, and plenty to nurse me, and I had no real call to leave them.' Speaking of the attentions he had received from his shipmates generally, 'they were all so kind,' he said, 'that there's none to mention.' And except in so far as I might share in this, he troubled me with no reference to my services. ⟨This was choice courtesy. I write with all measure, and except in the matter of bowing and scraping, I have never met a finer gentleman. He had the essentials of that business, in all senses of the expression, by heart.⟩

But what affected me in the most lively manner was the wealth of this day-labourer, paying a two months' pleasure visit to the States, and preparing to return in the saloon, and the new testimony rendered by his story, not so much to the horrors of the steerage as to the habitual comfort of the working classes. One foggy, frosty December evening, I encountered on Liberton

Hill,[70] near Edinburgh, an Irish labourer trudging homeward
from the fields. Our roads lay together, and it was natural
that we should fall into talk. He was covered with mud; an
inoffensive, ignorant creature, who thought the Atlantic Cable[71]
was a secret contrivance of the masters the better to oppress
labouring mankind; and I confess I was astonished to learn that
he had nearly three hundred pounds in the bank. But this man
had travelled over most of the world, and enjoyed wonderful
opportunities on some American railroad, with two dollars a
shift and double pay on Sunday and at night; whereas my
fellow-passenger had never quitted Tyneside, and had made all
that he possessed in that same accursed, down-falling England,
whence skilled mechanics, engineers, millwrights, and carpenters
were fleeing as from the native country of starvation.

Fitly enough, we slid off on the subject of strikes and wages
and hard times. Being from the Tyne, and a man who had gained
and lost in his own pocket by these fluctuations, he had much
to say, and held strong opinions on the subject. He spoke sharply
of the masters, and, when I led him on, of the men also. The
masters had been selfish and obstructive; the men selfish, silly,
and light-headed. He rehearsed to me the course of a meeting at
which he had been present, and the somewhat long discourse
which he had there pronounced, calling into question the wisdom and even the good faith of the Union delegates; and
although he had escaped himself through flush times and starvation times with a handsomely provided purse, he had so little
faith in either man or master, and so profound a terror for the
unerring Nemesis[72] of mercantile affairs, that he could think of
no hope for our country outside of a sudden and complete
political subversion. Down must go Lords and Church and
Army; and capital, by some happy direction, must change hands
from worse to better, or England stood condemned. Such
principles, he said, were growing 'like a seed.'

From this mild, soft, domestic man, these words sounded
unusually ominous and grave. I had heard enough revolutionary
talk among my workmen fellow-passengers; but most of it was
hot and turgid, and fell discredited from the lips of unsuccessful
men. This man was calm; he had attained prosperity and ease;

⟨he was a gentleman;⟩ he disapproved the policy which had been pursued by labour in the past; and yet this was his panacea, – to rend the old country from end to end, and from top to bottom, and in clamour and civil discord remodel it with the hand of violence. ⟨I thought of the Bo'swain, and wondered how such men and measures would recommend themselves to him and his like, if he had any. I thought too of the blessings of emigration: that men sufficiently instructed, who had for long times together received wages greater than many a man of letters and who yet, from drunkenness, shiftlessness and lack of balance, had failed flatly in life's battle, could still escape and make a new beginning somewhere else. For if the polity is to be subverted and the state's pedestals thrown down, let it be by clear-seeing people strung up by inborn generosity to the task, and not by waifs and beggars exasperated by external and perhaps well deserved reverses.⟩

The Stowaways

On the Sunday, among a party of men who were talking in our companion, Steerage No. 2 and 3, we remarked a new figure. He wore tweed clothes, well enough made if not very fresh, and a plain smoking-cap.[73] His face was pale, with pale eyes, and spiritedly enough designed; but though not yet thirty, a sort of blackguardly degeneration had already overtaken his features. The fine nose had grown fleshy towards the point, the pale eyes were sunk in fat. His hands were strong and elegant; his experience of life evidently varied; his speech full of pith and verve; his manners forward, but perfectly presentable. The lad who helped in the second cabin told me, in answer to a question, that he did not know who he was, but thought, 'by his way of speaking, and because he was so polite, that he was some one from the saloon.'

I was not so sure, for to me there was something equivocal in his air and bearing. He might have been, I thought, the son of some good family who had fallen early into dissipation and run from home(; though even then, he would have spoken with a clearer accent, and his pronunciation would either have respected orthography more thoroughly or slurred it in a different manner). But, making every allowance, how admirable was his talk! I wish you could have heard him tell his own stories. They were so swingingly set forth, in such dramatic language, and illustrated here and there by such luminous bits of acting, that they could only lose in any reproduction. There were tales of the P. and O. Company, where he had been an officer; of the East Indies, where in former years he had lived lavishly; of the Royal Engineers,[74] where he had served for a period; and of a dozen other sides of life, each introducing some vigorous thumb-nail portrait. He had the talk to himself that night, we were all so glad to listen. The best talkers usually addressed themselves to some particular society; there they are kings, elsewhere camp-followers, as a man may know Russian and yet be ignorant of Spanish; but this fellow had a frank, headlong power of style, and a broad, human choice of subject, that would have turned any circle in the world into a circle of hearers. He was a Homeric[75] talker, plain, strong, and cheerful; and the things and the people of which he spoke became readily and clearly present to the minds of those who heard him. This, with a certain added colouring of rhetoric and rodomontade, must have been the style of Burns,[76] who equally charmed the ears of duchesses and hostlers.

Yet freely and personally as he spoke, many points remained obscure in his narration. The Engineers, for instance, was a service which he praised highly; it is true there would be trouble with the sergeants; but then the officers were gentlemen, and his own, in particular, one among ten thousand. It sounded so far exactly like an episode in the rakish, topsy-turvy life of such an one as I had imagined. But then there came incidents more doubtful, which showed an almost impudent greed after gratuities, and a truly impudent disregard for truth. And then there was the tale of his departure. He had wearied, it seems, of Woolwich, and one fine day, with a companion, slipped up to London for a spree. I have a suspicion that spree was meant to be a long one; but God disposes all things; and one morning, near Westminster Bridge,[77] whom should he come across but the very sergeant who had recruited him at first! What followed? He himself indicated cavalierly that he had then resigned. Let us put it so. But these resignations are sometimes very trying.

At length, after having delighted us for hours, he took himself away from the companion; and I could ask Mackay who and what he was. 'That?' said Mackay. 'Why, that's one of the stowaways.'

'No man,' said the same authority, 'who has had anything to do with the sea, would ever think of paying for a passage.' I give the statement as Mackay's, without endorsement; yet I am tempted to believe that it contains a grain of truth; and if you add that the man should be impudent and thievish, or else dead-broke, it may even pass for a fair representation of the facts. We gentlemen of England who live at home at ease[78] have, I suspect, very insufficient ideas on the subject. All the world over, people are stowing away in coal-holes and dark corners, and when ships are once out to sea, appearing again, begrimed and bashful, upon deck. The career of these sea-tramps partakes largely of the adventurous. They may be poisoned by coal-gas, or die by starvation in their place of concealment; or when found they may be clapped at once and ignominiously into irons, thus to be carried to their promised land, the port of destination, and alas! brought back in the same way to that from which they started, and there delivered over to the magistrates and the seclusion of a county jail. Since I crossed the Atlantic, one miserable stowaway was found in a dying state among the fuel, uttered but a word or two, and departed for a farther country than America. ⟨On Jones's last passage before that on which I met him, no fewer than eleven had presented themselves from different quarters of the ship; and the captain had them all in irons until two of their number fainted and the passengers interposed to beg them off.

Just as the confraternity of beggars know and communicate among themselves the generous or saving character of different houses; just as, in the old days before the Prison Discipline Act, many indigent persons might have been observed on the approach of Christmas making for the neighbourhood of Wake-

field Jail,[79] where, for a petty theft or an aggravated misdemean-
our, the best sort of criminal entertainment might be had till the
return of Spring; so, among the stowaway class, one line of
steamers is distinguished from another by the nature of the
treatment which they may expect on board. Thus the line on
which I sailed was said to be particularly favoured by stowaways
with their faces towards the States; and thus such another,
greatly preferred by saloon passengers, is shunned like the
plague by a sea-tramp. On this last, he would invariably be
brought back and punished; on the former, he is half sure to make
out the voyage and be landed, a free citizen and independent
voter, at the harbour of New York.⟩

When the stowaway appears on deck, he had but one thing
to pray for: that he be set to work, which is the price and sign
of his forgiveness. After half an hour with a swab or a bucket,
he feels himself as secure as if he had paid for his passage. It is
not altogether a bad thing for the company, who get more or
less efficient hands for nothing but a few plates of junk and duff;
and every now and again find themselves better paid than by a
whole family of cabin passengers. Not long ago, for instance, a
packet was saved from nearly certain loss by the skill and
courage of a stowaway engineer. As was no more than just, a
handsome subscription rewarded him for his success; but even
without such exceptional good fortune, as things stand in England and America, the stowaway will often make a good profit
out of his adventure. Four engineers stowed away last summer
on the same ship, the *Circassia*;[80] and before two days after their
arrival each of the four had found a comfortable berth. This
was the most hopeful tale of emigration that I heard from first
to last; and as you see, the luck was for stowaways.

My curiosity was much inflamed by what I heard; and the
next morning, as I was making the round of the ship, I was
delighted to find the ex-Royal Engineer engaged in washing
down the white paint of a deck-house. There was another fellow
at work beside him, a lad not more than twenty, in the most
miraculous tatters, his handsome face sown with grains of
beauty and lighted up by expressive eyes. Four stowaways had
been found aboard our ship before she left the Clyde, but these

two had alone escaped the ignominy of being put ashore. Alick, my acquaintance of last night, was Scots by birth, and by trade a practical engineer; the other was from Devonshire, and had been to sea before the mast.[81] Two people more unlike by training, character, and habits, it would be hard to imagine; yet here they were together, scrubbing paint.

Alick had held all sorts of good situations, and wasted many opportunities in life. I have heard him end a story with these words: 'That was in my golden days, when I used finger-glasses.'[82] Situation after situation failed him; then followed the depression of trade, and for months he had hung round with other idlers, playing marbles all day in the West Park,[83] and going home at night to tell his landlady how he had been seeking for a job. I believe this kind of existence was not unpleasant to Alick himself, and he might have long continued to enjoy idleness and a life on tick;[84] but he had a comrade, let us call him Brown, who grew restive. This fellow was continually threatening to slip his cable for the States, and at last, one Wednesday, Glasgow was left widowed of her Brown. Some months afterwards, Alick met another old chum in Sauchiehall Street.[85]

'By the by, Alick,' said he, 'I met a gentleman in New York who was asking for you.'

'Who was that?' asked Alick.

'The second engineer on board the *So-and-so*,' was the reply.

'Well, and who is he?'

'Brown, to be sure.'

For Brown had been one of the fortunate quartette aboard the *Circassia*. If that was the way of it in the States, Alick thought it was high time to follow Brown's example. He spent his last day, as he put it, 'reviewing the yeomanry,'[86] and the next morning says he to his landlady, 'Mrs X., I'll not take porridge to-day, please; I'll take some eggs.'

'Why, have you found a job?' she asked, delighted.

'Well, yes,' returned the perfidious Alick; 'I think I'll start to-day.'

And so, well lined with eggs, start he did, but for America. I am afraid that landlady has seen the last of him.

It was easy enough to get on board in the confusion that

attends a vessel's departure; and in one of the dark corners of Steerage No. 1, flat in a bunk and with an empty stomach, Alick made the voyage from the Broomielaw to Greenock. That night, the ship's yeoman pulled him out by the heels and had him before the mate. Two other stowaways had already been found and sent ashore; but by this time darkness had fallen, they were out in the middle of the estuary, and the last steamer had left them till the morning.

'Take him to the forecastle and give him a meal,' said the mate, 'and see and pack him off the first thing to-morrow.'

In the forecastle he had supper, a good night's rest, and breakfast; and was sitting placidly with a pipe, fancying all was over and the game up for good with that ship, when one of the sailors grumbled out an oath at him, with a 'What are you doing there?' and 'Do you call that hiding, anyway?' There was need of no more; Alick was in another bunk before the day was older. Shortly before the passengers arrived, the ship was cursorily inspected. He heard the round come down the companion and look into one pen after another, until they came within two of the one in which he lay concealed. Into these last two they did not enter, but merely glanced from without; and Alick had no doubt that he was personally favoured in this escape. It was the character of the man to attribute nothing to luck and but little to kindness; whatever happened to him he had earned in his own right amply; favours came to him from his singular attraction and adroitness, and misfortunes he had always accepted with his eyes open. Half an hour after the searchers had departed, the steerage began to fill with legitimate passengers, and the worst of Alick's troubles was at an end. He was soon making himself popular, smoking other people's tobacco and politely sharing their private stock of delicacies, and when night came he retired to his bunk beside the others with composure.

Next day by afternoon, Lough Foyle being already far behind, and only the rough north-western hills of Ireland within view, Alick appeared on deck to court inquiry and decide his fate. As a matter of fact, he was known to several on board, and even intimate with one of the engineers; but it was plainly not the etiquette of such occasions for the authorities to avow their information. Every one professed surprise and anger on his appearance, and he was led prisoner before the captain.

'What have you got to say for yourself?' inquired the captain.

'Not much,' said Alick; 'but when a man has been a long time out of a job, he will do things he would not under other circumstances.'

'Are you willing to work?'

Alick swore he was burning to be useful.

'And what can you do?' asked the captain.

He replied composedly that he was a brass-fitter by trade.

'I think you will be better at engineering?' suggested the officer, with a shrewd look.

'No, sir,' says Alick simply. – 'There's few can beat me at a lie,' was his engaging commentary to me as he recounted the affair.

'Have you been to sea?' again asked the captain.

'I've had a trip on a Clyde steamboat, sir, but no more,' replied the unabashed Alick.

'Well, we must try and find some work for you,' concluded the officer.

And hence we behold Alick, clear of the hot engine-room, lazily scraping paint and now and then taking a pull upon a sheet.[87] 'You leave me alone,' was his deduction. 'When I get talking to a man, I can get round him.' ⟨For my own part, I should have drawn a different conclusion namely, that when a man is determined to be in a good business, nothing will put him out.⟩

The other stowaway, whom I will call the Devonian – it was noticeable that neither of them told his name – had both been brought up and seen the world in a much smaller way. His father, a confectioner, died and was closely followed by his mother. His sisters had taken, I think, to dress-making. He himself had returned from sea about a year ago and gone to live with his brother, who kept the 'George Hotel' – 'it was not quite a real hotel,' added the candid fellow – 'and had a hired man to mind the horses.' At first the Devonian was very welcome; but as time went on his brother not unnaturally grew cool towards him, and he began to find himself one too many at the 'George

Hotel.' 'I don't think brothers care much for you,' he said, as a general reflection upon life. Hurt at this change, nearly penniless, and too proud to ask for more, he set off on foot and walked eighty miles to Weymouth, living on the journey as he could. He would have enlisted, but he was too small for the army and too old for the navy; and thought himself fortunate at last to find a berth on board a trading dandy. Somewhere in the Bristol Channel, the dandy[88] sprung a leak and went down; and though the crew were picked up and brought ashore by fishermen, they found themselves with nothing but the clothes upon their back. His next engagement was scarcely better starred; for the ship proved so leaky, and frightened them all so heartily during a short passage through the Irish Sea, that the entire crew deserted and remained behind upon the quays of Belfast.

Evil days were now coming thick on the Devonian. He could find no berth in Belfast, and had to work a passage to Glasgow on a steamer. She reached the Broomielaw on a Wednesday: the Devonian had a bellyful that morning, laying in breakfast manfully to provide against the future, and set off along the quays to seek employment. But he was now not only penniless, his clothes had begun to fall in tatters; he had begun to have the look of a street Arab; and captains will have nothing to say to a ragamuffin; for in that trade, as in all others, it is the coat that depicts the man. You may hand, reef, and steer[89] like an angel, but if you have a hole in your trousers, it is like a millstone round your neck. The Devonian lost heart at so many refusals. He had not the impudence to beg; although, as he said, 'when I had money of my own, I always gave it.' It was only on Saturday morning, after three whole days of starvation, that he asked a scone from a milkwoman, who added of her own accord a glass of milk. He had now made up his mind to stow away, not from any desire to see America, but merely to obtain the comfort of a place in the forecastle and a supply of familiar sea-fare. He lived by begging, always from milkwomen, and always scones and milk, and was not once refused. It was vile wet weather, and he could never have been dry. By night he walked the streets, and by day slept upon Glasgow Green,[90] and heard, in the intervals of his dozing, the famous theologians of the spot clear up intricate points of doctrine and appraise the merits of the clergy. He had not much instruction; he could 'read bills on the street,' but was 'main bad at writing'; yet these theologians seem to have impressed him with a genuine sense of amusement. Why he did not go to the Sailor's Home[91] I know not; I presume there is in Glasgow one of these institutions, which are by far the happiest and the wisest effort of contemporaneous charity; but I must stand to my author, as they say in old books, and relate the story as I heard it. In the meantime, he had tried four times to stow away in different vessels, and four times had been discovered and handed back to starvation. The fifth time was lucky; and you may judge if he were pleased to be aboard ship again, at his old work, and with duff twice a week. He was, said Alick, 'a devil for the duff.' Or if devil was not the word, it was one if anything stronger.

The difference in the conduct of the two was remarkable. The Devonian was as willing as any paid hand, swarmed aloft among the first, pulled his natural weight and firmly upon a rope, and found work for himself when there was none to show him. Alick, on the other hand, was not only a skulker in the grain, but took a humorous and fine gentlemanly view of the transaction. He would speak to me by the hour in ostentatious idleness; and only if the bo's'un or a mate came by, fell-to languidly for just the necessary time till they were out of sight. 'I'm not breaking my heart with it,' he remarked. ⟨'So I observe,' said I, with cordial adhesion.⟩

Once there was a hatch to be opened near where he was stationed; he watched the preparations for a second or so suspiciously, and then, 'Hullo,' said he, 'here's some real work coming – I'm off,' and he was gone that moment. Again, calculating the six guinea passage-money, and the probable duration of the passage, he remarked pleasantly that he was getting six shillings a day for this job, 'and it's pretty dear to the company at that.' 'They are making nothing by me,' was another of his observations; 'they're making something by that fellow.' And he pointed to the Devonian, who was just then busy to the eyes.

The more you saw of Alick, the more, it must be owned, you learned to despise him. His natural talents were of no use either to himself or others; for his character had degenerated like his face, and become pulpy and pretentious. Even his power of persuasion, which was certainly very surprising, stood in some danger of being lost or neutralised by over-confidence. He lied in an aggressive, brazen manner, like a pert criminal in the dock; and he was so vain of his own cleverness that he could not refrain from boasting, ten minutes after, of the very trick by which he had deceived you. 'Why, now I have more money than when I came on board,' he said one night, exhibiting a sixpence, 'and yet I stood myself a bottle of beer before I went to bed yesterday. And as for tobacco, I have fifteen sticks of it.' That was fairly successful indeed; yet a man of his superiority, and with a less obtrusive policy, might, who knows? have got the length of half a crown. ⟨I warn Alick as a sort of well wisher: if he persist, the days of finger glasses are gone by for him forever, and he may have to clean paint in earnest or do yet dirtier work before the end. For instance, he spent a whole evening recounting to Jones and me a series of very cheap and black-guardly exploits, in which poor women were his easy and unpit-ied victims. A man of his talent and habit of the world, should have perceived the effect he was producing.⟩ A man who prides himself upon persuasion should learn the persuasive faculty of silence, above all as to his own misdeeds. It is only in the farce and for dramatic purposes that Scapin[92] enlarges on his peculiar talents to the world at large.

Scapin is perhaps a good name for this clever, unfortunate Alick; for at the bottom of all his misconduct there was a guiding sense of humour that moved you to forgive him. It was more than half as a jest that he conducted his existence. ⟨He was never entirely serious in a thought.⟩ 'Oh, man,' he said to me once with unusual emotion, like a man thinking of his mistress, 'I would give up anything for a lark.' ⟨And he stood for a while, smiling, with half shut eyes; and then proceeded to tell me how he would have passed the time on board, if he had been a passenger and free. It was fortunate for many that he had to mind his white paint, for his plan was unkind; yet I cannot deny that it was funny.⟩

It was in relation to his fellow-stowaway that Alick showed

the best, or perhaps I should say, the only, good points of his nature. 'Mind you,' he said suddenly, changing his tone, 'mind you that's a good boy. He wouldn't tell you a lie. A lot of them think he is a scamp because his clothes are ragged, but he isn't; he's as good as gold.' To hear him, you became aware that Alick himself had a taste for virtue. He thought his own idleness and the other's industry equally becoming. He was no more anxious to insure his own reputation as a liar than to uphold the truthfulness of his companion; and he seemed unaware of what was incongruous in his attitude, and was plainly sincere in both characters. ⟨But he was one who looked largely upon life, and would have been equally ready to adjudge the Montyon prize[93] for virtue or to sit as umpire in a competition of liars.⟩

It was not surprising that he should take an interest in the Devonian, for the lad worshipped and served him in love and wonder. Busy as he was, he would find time to warn Alick of an approaching officer, or even to tell him that the coast was clear, and he might slip off and smoke a pipe in safety. 'Tom,' he once said to him, for that was the name which Alick ordered him to use, 'if you don't like going to the galley, I'll go for you. You ain't used to this kind of thing, you ain't. But I'm a sailor; and I can understand the feelings of any fellow, I can.' Again, he was hard up, and casting about for some tobacco, for he was not so liberally used in this respect as others perhaps less worthy, when Alick offered him the half of one of his fifteen sticks. I think, for my part, he might have increased the offer to a whole one, or perhaps a pair of them, and not lived to regret his liberality. But the Devonian refused. 'No,' he said, 'you're a stowaway like me; I won't take it from you, I'll take it from some one who's not down on his luck.'

It was notable in this generous lad that he was strongly under the influence of sex. If a woman passed near where he was working, his eyes lit up, his hand paused, and his mind wandered instantly to other thoughts. ⟨'C'est Vénus tout entier.'[94]⟩ It was natural that he should exercise a fascination proportionally strong upon women. He begged, you will remember, from women only, and was never refused. Without wishing to explain away the charity of those who helped him, I cannot but fancy he may have owed a little to his handsome⟨, long nose, to his attractive eyes, to the grains of beauty on his⟩ face, and to that quick, responsive nature, formed for love, which speaks eloquently through all disguises, and can stamp an impression in ten minutes' talk or an exchange of glances. He was the more dangerous in that he was far from bold, but seemed to woo in spite of himself, and with a soft and pleading eye. Ragged as he was, and many a scarecrow is in that respect more comfortably furnished, even on board he was not without some curious admirers.

There was a girl among the passengers, a tall, blonde, handsome, strapping Irishwoman, with a wild, accommodating eye, whom Alick had dubbed Tommy, with that transcendental appropriateness that defies analysis. ⟨On her and her various admirers, and trusting implicitly in his own powers of talk, he based schemes of mystification that would have put a score of people by the ears in eight and forty hours and kept the rest of the ship's company in inextinguishable mirth. The Devonian, who always listened to him greedily as to a god, suggested some modification of the plan.

'You don't understand how to work these things,' observed Alick loftily.

'I suppose I don't, I suppose you do,' retorted the Devonian.

'God!' cried Alick with fervour, 'I've had a career of experience at least!'⟩

One day the Devonian was lying for warmth in the upper stoke-hole, which stands open on the deck, when Irish Tommy came past, very neatly attired, as was her custom.

'Poor fellow,' she said, stopping, 'you haven't a vest.'

'No,' he said; 'I wish I 'ad.'

Then she stood and gazed on him in silence, until, in his embarrassment, for he knew not how to look under this scrutiny, he pulled out his pipe and began to fill it with tobacco.

'Do you want a match?' she asked. And before he had time to reply, she ran off and presently returned with more than one.

That was the beginning and the end, as far as our passage is concerned, of what I will make bold to call this love-affair.

There are many relations which go on to marriage and last during a lifetime, in which less human feeling is engaged than in this scene of five minutes at the stoke-hole.

⟨It was perhaps because of this strong principle open in his character, that the Devonian's chief aspiration was after a clean shirt. That, and I hope many other things, have now been given him; for he worked so well and was so willing and pleasant on board, that he was offered a berth on the steamer into which he had crept unbidden.

I have already recommended the emigrant rather to go second cabin than steerage. Let me add, if he has the tact to carry it out and wisely to choose both his steamer and his hiding place on board, that he had better go as stowaway than either. The forecastle, I am told, is a far more desirable lodging than steerage No. 1; the fare is better and more cleanly served; and if his body be sound, the deck work will only benefit his health and keep his mind cheerful and disengaged. In point of economy, there is, of course, no comparison possible: the stowaway passage costing exactly nothing. At the same time, it is awkward to reach a foreign land with only sixpence, and that was all that the persuasive Alick had managed to scrape together on the passage. To be taken where you want to go and then brought back again for punishment in irons, is, to say the least of it, annoying. And to perish of hunger and bad air in a solitary coal hole, like a poisoned rat behind the skirting, is a tragical and ghastly death. There are the pro's and the con's, on which the reader may decide his own conduct for himself.⟩

Rigidly speaking, this would end the chapter of the stow-aways; but in a larger sense of the word I have yet more to add. Jones had discovered and pointed out to me a young woman who was remarkable among her fellows for a pleasing and inter-esting air. She was poorly clad, to the verge, if not over the line, of disrespectability, with a ragged old jacket and a bit of a sealskin cap no bigger than your fist; but her eyes, her whole expression, and her manner, even in ordinary moments, told of a true womanly nature, capable of love, anger, and devotion. She had a look, too, of refinement, like one who might have been a better lady than most, had she been allowed the opportunity. When alone she seemed pre-occupied and sad; but she was not often alone; there was usually by her side a heavy, dull, gross man in rough clothes, chary of speech and gesture – not from caution, but poverty of disposition; a man like a ditcher, unlovely and uninteresting; whom she petted and tended and waited on with her eyes as if he had been Amadis of Gaul. It was strange to see this hulking fellow dog-sick, and this delicate, sad woman caring for him. He seemed, from first to last, insensible of her caresses and attentions, and she seemed unconscious of his insensibility. The Irish husband, who sang his wife to sleep, and this Scottish girl serving her Orson,[95] were the two bits of human nature that most appealed to me throughout the voyage.

On the Thursday before we arrived, the tickets were collected; and soon a rumour began to go round the vessel; and this girl, with her bit of sealskin cap, became the centre of whispering and pointed fingers. She also, it was said, was a stowaway of a sort; for she was on board with neither ticket nor money; and the man with whom she travelled was the father of a family, who had left wife and children to be hers. The ship's officers discouraged the story, which may therefore have been a story and no more; but it was believed in the steerage, and the poor girl had to encounter many curious eyes from that day forth.

Personal Experience and Review

Travel is of two kinds; and this voyage of mine across the ocean combined both. 'Out of my country and myself I go,'[96] sings the old poet; and I was not only travelling out of my country in latitude and longitude, but out of myself in diet, associates, and consideration. Part of the interest and a great deal of the amusement flowed, at least to me, from this novel situation in the world.

I found that I had what they call fallen in life with absolute success and verisimilitude. I was taken for a steerage passenger; no one seemed surprised that I should be so; and there was nothing but the brass plate between decks to remind me that I had once been a gentleman. In a former book,[97] describing a former journey, I expressed some wonder that I could be readily and naturally taken for a pedlar, and explained the accident by the difference of language and manners between England and France. I must now take a humbler view; for here I was among my own countrymen, somewhat roughly clad, to be sure, but with every advantage of speech and manner; and I am bound to confess that I passed for nearly anything you please except an educated gentleman. The sailors called me 'mate,' the officers addressed me as 'my man,' my comrades accepted me without hesitation for a person of their own character and experience, but with some curious information. One, a mason himself, believed I was a mason; several, and among these at least one of the seamen, judged me to be a petty officer in the American navy; and I was so often set down for a practical engineer that at last I had not the heart to deny it. From all these guesses I drew one conclusion, which told against the insight of my companions. They might be close observers in their own way, and read the manners in the face; but it was plain that they did not extend their observation to the hands. ⟨There is nothing strange in the omission: the only marvel being that, where we are all as much interested about our neighbours, so few should have learned to look critically at a part of the body, uncovered like the face and nearly as eloquent and personal.⟩

To the saloon passengers also I sustained my part without a hitch. It is true I came little in their way; but when we did encounter, there was no recognition in their eye, although I confess I sometimes courted it in silence. All these, my inferiors and equals, took me, like the transformed monarch in the story,[98] for a mere common, human man. They gave me a hard, dead look, with the flesh about the eye kept unrelaxed.

With the women this surprised me less, as I had already experimented on the sex by going abroad through a suburban part of London simply attired in a sleeve-waistcoat. The result was curious. I then learned for the first time, and by the exhaustive process, how much attention ladies are accustomed to bestow on all male creatures of their own station; for, in my humble rig, each one who went by me caused me a certain shock of surprise and a sense of something wanting. In my normal circumstances, it appeared every young lady must have paid me some tribute of a glance; and though I had often not detected it when it was given, I was well aware of its absence when it was withheld. My height seemed to decrease with every woman who passed me, for she passed me like a dog. This is one of my grounds for supposing that what are called the upper classes may sometimes produce a disagreeable impression in what are called the lower; and I wish some one would continue my experiment, and find out exactly at what stage of toilette a man becomes invisible to the well-regulated female eye.

Here on shipboard the matter was put to a more complete test; for, even with the addition of speech and manner, I passed among the ladies for precisely the average man of the steerage. It was one afternoon that I saw this demonstrated. A very plainly dressed woman was taken ill on deck. I think I had the luck to be present at every sudden seizure during all the passage; and on this occasion found myself in the place of importance, supporting the sufferer. There was not only a large crowd immediately around us, but a considerable knot of saloon passengers leaning over our heads from the hurricane-deck. One of these, an elderly managing woman, hailed me with counsels. Of course I had to reply; and as the talk went on, I began to discover that the whole group took me for the husband. I looked upon my new wife, poor creature, with mingled feelings; and I must own she had not even the appearance of the poorest class of city servant-maids, but looked more like a country wench, who should have been employed at a roadside inn. ⟨I confess openly, I was chagrined at this.⟩ Now was the time for me to go and study the brass plate.

To such of the officers as knew about me – the doctor, the purser, and the stewards – I appeared in the light of a broad joke. The fact that I spent the better part of my day in writing had gone abroad over the ship and tickled them all prodigiously. Whenever they met me they referred to my absurd occupation with familiarity and breadth of humorous intention. Their manner was well calculated to remind me of my fallen fortunes. You may be sincerely amused by the amateur literary efforts of a gentleman, but you scarce publish the feeling to his face. 'Well!' they would say: 'still writing?' And the smile would widen into a laugh. The purser came one day into the cabin, and, touched to the heart by my misguided industry, offered me some other kind of writing, 'for which,' he added pointedly, 'you will be paid.' This was nothing else than to copy out the list of passengers. ⟨It was odd how my feeling of amusement was tempered by soreness. One of the sailors was the only man on board, besides my particular friends, who could be persuaded to take my literary character in earnest. I discussed the subject with him one night until his watch was over; he was much interested by all that I told him; and in return recommended me a work called *Tom Holt's Log*,[99] the principal incidents of which he obligingly described. I hand over the recommendation, fresh as I received it, to the reader; for I have not yet had an opportunity to see the book in question. But I will propose a wager, founding on a pretty large induction, that it is either excellent or downright penny trash. There seems to be no medium in the tastes of the unliterary class; mediocrity must tremble for its judgment; either strong, lively matter solidly handled, or mere ink and banditti, forms its literary diet.⟩

Another trick of mine which told against my reputation was my choice of roosting-place in an active draught upon the cabin floor. I was openly jeered and flouted for this eccentricity; and a considerable knot would sometimes gather at the door to see my last dispositions for the night. This was embarrassing, but I learned to support the trial with equanimity.

Indeed, I may say that, upon the whole, my new position sat lightly and naturally upon my spirits. I accepted the consequences with readiness, and found them far from difficult to bear. The steerage conquered me; I conformed more and more to the type of the place, not only in manner but at heart, growing hostile to the officers and cabin passengers who looked down upon me, and day by day greedier for small delicacies. Such was the result, as I fancy, of a diet of bread and butter, soup and porridge. We think we have no sweet tooth as long as we are full to the brim of molasses; but a man must have sojourned in the workhouse before he boasts himself indifferent to dainties.

Every evening, for instance, I was more and more pre-occupied about our doubtful fare at tea. If it was delicate my heart was much lightened; if it was but broken fish I was proportionally downcast. The offer of a little jelly from a fellow-passenger more provident than myself caused a marked elevation in my spirits. And I would have gone to the ship's end and back again for an oyster or a chipped fruit.

⟨Judge, then, of my delight, when a turn of events made me a sort of favoured inferior and welcome in the chief steward's office. It fell out thus. One day at dinner, the soup for the first time failed us. A despicable broth was followed by a piece of fresh meat no less despicable, and some salt horse racier than game. I left table, went off to the steward, told him I could eat nothing, and was at once supplied with bread and cheese for which he would not suffer me to pay. Meanwhile, during my absence, indignation had warmed up to the boiling point around the second cabin table. One of the company volunteered to write a letter of complaint, which he sealed, without showing it to any one, and handed over to the others to be laid before the captain in a deputation. The letter was brought and the plan explained to me on deck. As no one had seen the terms and the writer himself proposed to remain in the background, I discouraged the whole affair; the deputation fell through; and the missive was delivered single-handed by O'Reilly, who little imagined on what errand he had been dispatched. By three in the afternoon, the petard had burst; and the steward, the understewards and the whole second cabin were playing their parts in an absurd but most unpleasant tragi-comedy. The letter, on being opened, was found to be without a signature. With an odd alternation of dash and prudence, the man who hotly volunteered to lead the attack, had but given a run-away knock and disappeared, leaving O'Reilly in the breach. The prolonged consequences, the councils, the diplomacy, nay, the tears, which flowed from this ill-judged anonasume,[100] are too many to be set down here. But as I found myself unpleasantly situated, having made a complaint that very day, I sent a note disclaiming the authorship of the letter. That, like the famous pin which the young gentleman picked up before the merchant's window, was the beginning of my fortune. Thenceforth, I found myself a welcome visitor in the steward's box. I could see the cabin passengers at table; I was shown the bill of fare for the day; and when I left, the steward would fill my pocket with greengages. I have not been in such a situation since I was a child and prowled upon the frontiers of a dinner party. But I found myself unchanged by time. I looked with the same envy on the good things passing by for others. The bill of fare was mine; I pored over it, whetted my appetite, made a dozen dinners in ten minutes and grovelled soul and body in Barmecide[101] feasts; and when the talk was over, made my departure, happy like a tipped schoolboy, with my pocketful of fruit. I had regained the holy simplicity, the frank, piratical instincts of my youth; I was back in Eden and the glades of Arcady; and if I was still a gentleman on a brass plate,[102] in relation to these greengages I may call myself a savage. Perhaps I understand in a more human manner than before, the tithes exacted by domestic servants.⟩

In other ways I was content with my position. It seemed no disgrace to be confounded with my company; for I may as well declare at once I found their manners as gentle and becoming as those of any other class. I do not mean that my friends could have sat down without embarrassment and laughable disaster at the table of a duke. That does not imply an inferiority of breeding, but a difference of usage. Thus I flatter myself that I conducted myself well among my fellow-passengers; yet my most ambitious hope is not to have avoided faults, but to have committed as few as possible. I know too well that my tact is not the same as their tact, and that my habit of a different society constituted, not only no qualification, but a positive disability to move easily and becomingly in this. When Jones complimented me – because I 'managed to behave very pleasantly' to my fellow-passengers, was how he put it – I could follow the thought in his mind, and knew his compliment to be such as we pay foreigners on their proficiency in English. I dare say this praise was given me immediately on the back of some unpardonable solecism, which had led him to review my conduct as a whole. We are all ready to laugh at the ploughman among lords;

we should consider also the case of a lord among the ploughmen. I have seen a lawyer in the house of a Hebridean fisherman; and I know, but nothing will induce me to disclose, which of these two was the better gentleman. Some of our finest behaviour, though it looks well enough from the boxes, may seem even brutal to the gallery. We boast too often manners that are parochial rather than universal; that, like a country wine, will not bear transportation for a hundred miles, nor from the parlour to the kitchen. To be a gentleman is to be one all the world over, and in every relation and grade of society. It is a high calling, to which a man must first be born, and then devote himself for life. And, unhappily, the manners of a certain so-called upper grade have a kind of currency, and meet with a certain external acceptation throughout all the others, and this tends to keep us well satisfied with slight acquirements and the amateurish accomplishments of a clique. But manners, like art, should be human and central.

Some of my fellow-passengers, as I now moved among them in a relation of equality, seemed to me excellent gentlemen. They were not rough, nor hasty, nor disputatious; debated pleasantly, differed kindly; were helpful, gentle, patient, and placid. The type of manners was plain, and even heavy; there was little to please the eye, but nothing to shock; and I thought gentleness lay more nearly at the spring of behaviour than in many more ornate and delicate societies. I say delicate, where I cannot say refined; a thing may be fine like ironwork, without being delicate like lace. There was here less delicacy; the skin supported more callously the natural surface of events, the mind received more bravely the crude facts of human existence; but I do not think that there was less effective refinement, less consideration for others, less polite suppression of self. (Of Barney and the old fisher, for instance, I may hope the reader has now some notion of his own; let him ask himself if he meets gentlemen so accomplished at his club. Not every day by many, I am sure. And I know for my part, that I have had a great opportunity, and should have learned some better manners for the future.

It will be understood that⟩ I speak of the best among my

fellow-passengers; for in the steerage, as well as in the saloon, there is a mixture. ⟨The women, in particular, too often displeased me by something hard and forward, by something alternately sullen and jeering both in speech and conduct. But, to begin with, this may have been my own fault, for the game of manners is more easily played with a good partner; and in the second place, it may have depended entirely on the difference of sex. I am led to fancy this, because it was in the younger women alone that I was thus displeased. The elder and the married women behaved to me in my capacity of steerage passenger and their co-equal, exactly as they would if I had come on horseback with a groom behind me. What, then, ailed the girls? May I not construe these taunts and tiffs and sulks, as so many challenges into the field of courtship? Many animals and the youth of even the most delicate classes, conduct their love dalliance under the similitude of a quarrel; and something of this modest subterfuge survives perhaps in every marriage or advanced flirtation. Now the girls of our company and perhaps the people of that class (among themselves) may prefer at least to open the campaign on these aggressive tactics. They are forward and backward to provoke the men, that the first kiss may be taken in a tussle and furiously resented. At least I was not amenable to these advances, if such they were; and I thought the women greatly and even surprisingly inferior to the men. It is true that the class of women who emigrate is not likely, for many reasons, to be the best. And I should add, what seems hardly necessary, for it is involved in every word that I have written on the subject, that these were all Scotch and Irish girls; not one from England.⟩

Those, then, with whom I found myself in sympathy, and of whom I may therefore hope to write with a greater measure of truth, were not only as good in their manners, but endowed with very much the same natural capacities, and about as wise in deduction, as the bankers and barristers of what is called society. One and all were too much interested in disconnected facts, and loved information for its own sake with too rash a devotion; but people in all classes display the same appetite as they gorge themselves daily with the miscellaneous gossip of the newspaper. Newspaper reading, as far as I can make out, is often rather a sort of brown study than an act of culture. I have myself palmed off yesterday's issue on a friend, and seen him re-peruse it for a continuance of minutes with an air at once refreshed and solemn. Workmen, perhaps, pay more attention; but though they may be eager listeners, they have rarely seemed to me either willing or careful thinkers. Culture is not measured by the greatness of the field which is covered by our knowledge, but by the nicety with which we can perceive relations in that field, whether great or small. Workmen, certainly those who were on board with me, I found wanting in this quality or habit of the mind. They did not perceive relations, ⟨mutually reactive and conditioned by a million others;⟩ but leaped to a so-called cause, and thought the problem settled. Thus the cause of everything in England was the form of government, and the cure for all evils was, by consequence, a revolution. It is surprising how many of them said this, and that none should have had a definite thought in his head as he said it. Some hated the Church because they disagreed with it; some hated Lord Beaconsfield[103] because of war and taxes; all hated the masters, possibly with reason. But these feelings were not at the root of the matter; the true reasoning of their souls ran thus – I have not got on; I ought to have got on; if there was a revolution I should get on. How? They had no idea. Why? Because – because – well, look at America!

To be politically blind is no distinction; we are all so, if you come to that. At bottom, as it seems to me, there is but one question in modern home politics, though it appears in many shapes, and that is the question of money; and but one political remedy, that the people should grow wiser and better. My workmen fellow-passengers were as impatient and dull of hearing on the second of these points as any member of Parliament; but they had some glimmerings of the first. They would not hear of improvement on their part, but wished the world made over again in a crack, so that they might remain improvident and idle and debauched, and yet enjoy the comfort and respect that should accompany the opposite virtues; and it was in this expectation, as far as I could see, that many of them were now on their way to America. But on the point of money they saw clearly enough that inland politics, so far as they were concerned, were reducible to the question of annual income; a question which should long ago have been settled by a revolution, they did not know how, and which they were now about to settle for themselves, once more they knew not how, by crossing the Atlantic in a steamship of considerable tonnage.

And yet it has been amply shown them that the second or income question is in itself nothing, and may as well be left undecided, if there be no wisdom and virtue to profit by the change. It is not by a man's purse, but by his character, that he is rich or poor. ⟨What have the colliers done with their great earnings? My Irish labourer had his three hundred pounds in bank, and was still young. My old North Sea fisher took a pleasure trip to see the States, and had his house and hayfield by the Tyne. There come periods in every country when the struggle for existence grows too fierce to be endured, and a man will do well, if he is able, to escape where the forces are balanced more evenly and daily bread is an affair of course. But to travel after high wages, I have been told by workmen, is never the way to come to easy circumstances, even for the best. And as for those who have already had their opportunity, and lost it, and come out of the flush times in England as poor as they began, we may well wonder with what hope they take to emigration. Wages must fluctuate; work must come and go; the power of manual labour is a gift so common that none but the exceptionally skilled can count upon employment; and when the evil days are here again, the rest shall emigrate once more and once more with empty pockets. I do not at all despise the relief of a time, however brief and passing, of comparative ease in money matters; for while any man can be poor for a month or two with equanimity and even merriment, it is the long continuous drag and the daily recurrence of the same small cares that weary patience and lead on despair. Let them follow high wages, by all means; but let them not suppose that either a change of country or a change of government will make those rich or contented who are without the virtues of the state.⟩ Barney will be poor, Alick will be poor, Mackay will be poor; let them go where they will, and wreck all the governments under heaven, they will be poor until they die.

Nothing is perhaps more notable in the average workman than his surprising idleness, and the candour with which he confesses to the failing. It has to me been always something of a relief to find the poor, as a general rule, so little oppressed with work. I can in consequence enjoy my own more fortunate beginning with a better grace. The other day I was living with a farmer in America, an old frontiersman, who had worked and fought, hunted and farmed, from his childhood up. He excused himself for his defective education on the ground that he had been overworked from first to last. Even now, he said, anxious as he was, he had never the time to take up a book. In consequence of this, I observed him closely; he was occupied for four or, at the extreme outside, for five hours out of the twenty-four, and then principally in walking; and the remainder of the day he passed in born idleness, either eating fruit or standing with his back against a door. I have known men do hard literary work all morning, and then undergo quite as much physical fatigue by way of relief as satisfied this powerful frontiersman for the day. He, at least, like all the educated class, did so much homage to industry as to persuade himself he was industrious. But the average mechanic recognises his idleness with effrontery; he has even, as I am told, organised it.

I give the story as it was told me, and it was told me for a fact. A man fell from a housetop in the city of Aberdeen,[104] and was brought into hospital with broken bones. He was asked what was his trade, and replied that he was a *tapper*. No one had ever heard of such a thing before; the officials were filled with curiosity; they besought an explanation. It appeared that when a party of slaters were engaged upon a roof, they would now and then be taken with a fancy for the public-house. Now a seamstress, for example, might slip away from her work and no one be the wiser; but if these fellows adjourned, the tapping of the mallets would cease, and thus the neighbourhood be advertised of their defection. Hence the career of the tapper. He has to do the tapping and keep up an industrious bustle on the

housetop during the absence of the slaters. When he taps for
only one or two the thing is child's-play, but when he has to
represent a whole troop, it is then that he earns his money in
the sweat of his brow. Then must he bound from spot to spot,
reduplicate, triplicate, sexduplicate his single personality, and
swell and hasten his blows, until he produce a perfect illusion
for the ear, and you would swear that a crowd of emulous
masons were continuing merrily to roof the house. It must be a
strange sight from an upper window.

I heard nothing on board of the tapper; but I was astonished
at the stories told by my companions. Skulking, shirking, mal-
ingering, were all established tactics, it appeared. They could
see no dishonesty where a man who is paid for an hour's work
gives half an hour's consistent idling in its place. Thus the tapper
would refuse to watch for the police during a burglary, and call
himself an honest man. It is not sufficiently recognised that our
race detests to work. If I thought that I should have to work
every day of my life as hard as I am working now, I should be
tempted to give up the struggle. And the workman early begins
on his career of toil. He has never had his fill of holidays in the
past, and his prospect of holidays in the future is both distant
and uncertain. In the circumstances, it would require a high
degree of virtue not to snatch alleviations for the moment.

There were many good talkers on the ship; and I believe good
talking of a certain sort is a common accomplishment among
working men. Where books are comparatively scarce, a greater
amount of information will be given and received by word of
mouth; and this tends to produce good talkers, and, what is no
less needful for conversation, good listeners. They could all tell
a story with effect. I am sometimes tempted to think that the
less literary class show always better in narration; they have so
much more patience with detail, are so much less hurried to
reach the points, and preserve so much juster a proportion
among the facts. At the same time their talk is dry; they pursue
a topic ploddingly, have not an agile fancy, do not throw sudden
lights from unexpected quarters, and when the talk is over they
often leave the matter where it was. They mark time instead of
marching. They think only to argue, not to reach new con-

clusions, and use their reason rather as a weapon of offence than as a tool for self-improvement. Hence the talk of some of the cleverest was unprofitable in result, because there was no give and take; they would grant you as little as possible for premise, and begin to dispute under an oath to conquer or to die.

But the talk of a workman is apt to be more interesting than that of a wealthy merchant, because the thoughts, hopes, and fears of which the workman's life is built lie nearer to necessity and nature. They are more immediate to human life. An income calculated by the week is a far more human thing than one calculated by the year, and a small income, simply from its smallness, than a large one. I never wearied listening to the details of a workman's economy, because every item stood for some real pleasure. If he could afford pudding twice a week, you know that twice a week the man ate with genuine gusto and was physically happy; while if you learn that a rich man has seven courses a day, ten to one the half of them remain untasted, and the whole is but misspent money and a weariness to the flesh.

The difference between England and America to a working man was thus most humanly put to me by a fellow-passenger: 'In America,' said he, 'you get pies and puddings.' I do not hear enough, in economy books, of pies and pudding. A man lives in and for the delicacies, adornments, and accidental attributes of life, such as pudding to eat and pleasant books and theatres to occupy his leisure. The bare terms of existence would be rejected with contempt by all. If a man feeds on bread and butter, soup and porridge, his appetite grows wolfish after dainties. And the workman dwells in a borderland, and is always within sight of those cheerless regions where life is more difficult to sustain than worth sustaining. Every detail of our existence, where it is worth while to cross the ocean after pie and pudding, is made alive and enthralling by the presence of genuine desire; but it is all one to me whether Crœsus has a hundred or a thousand thousands in the bank. There is more adventure in the life of the working man who descends as a common soldier into the battle of life, than in that of the millionaire who sits apart in an office, like Von Moltke,[105] and only directs the manœuvres by telegraph. Give me to hear about the career of him who is in the thick of the business; to whom one change of market means an empty belly, and another a copious and savoury meal. This is not the philosophical, but the human side of economics; it interests like a story; and the life of all who are thus situated partakes in a small way of the charm of *Robinson Crusoe*;[106] for every step is critical, and human life is presented to you naked and verging to its lowest terms.

New York

As we drew near to New York I was at first amused, and then somewhat staggered, by the cautious and the grisly tales that went the round. You would have thought we were to land upon a cannibal island. You must speak to no one in the streets, as they would not leave you till you were rooked and beaten. You must enter a hotel with military precautions; for the least you had to apprehend was to awake next morning without money or baggage, or necessary raiment, a lone forked radish in a bed; and if the worst befell, you would instantly and mysteriously disappear from the ranks of mankind.

I have usually found such stories correspond to the least modicum of fact. Thus I was warned, I remember, against the roadside inns of the Cévennes, and that by a learned professor; and when I reached Pradelles[107] the warning was explained; it was but the far-away rumour and reduplication of a single terrifying story already half a century old, and half forgotten in the theatre of the events. So I was tempted to make light of these reports against America. But we had on board with us a man whose evidence it would not do to put aside. He had come near these perils in the body; he had visited a robber inn. The public has an old and well-grounded favour for this class of incident, and shall be gratified to the best of my power.

My fellow-passenger, whom we shall call M'Naughten,[108] had come from New York to Boston with a comrade, seeking work. They were a pair of rattling blades; and, leaving their baggage at the station, passed the day in beer-saloons, and with congenial spirits, until midnight struck. Then they applied themselves to find a lodging, and walked the streets till two, knocking at houses of entertainment and being refused admittance, or themselves declining the terms. By two the inspiration of their liquor had begun to wear off; they were weary and humble, and after a great circuit found themselves in the same street where they had begun their search, and in front of a French hotel where they had already sought accommodation. Seeing the house still open, they returned to the charge. A man in a white cap sat in an office by the door. He seemed to welcome them more warmly than when they had first presented themselves, and the charge for the night had somewhat unaccountably fallen from a dollar to a quarter. They thought him ill-looking, but paid their quarter apiece, and were shown upstairs to the top of the house. There, in a small room, the man in the white cap wished them pleasant slumbers.

It was furnished with a bed, a chair, and some conveniences. The door did not lock on the inside; and the only sign of adornment was a couple of framed pictures, one close above the head of the bed, and the other opposite the foot, and both curtained, as we may sometimes see valuable water-colours, or the portraits of the dead, or works of art more than usually skittish in the subject. It was perhaps in the hope of finding something of this last description that M'Naughten's comrade pulled aside the curtain of the first. He was startlingly disappointed. There was no picture. The frame surrounded, and the curtain was designed to hide, an oblong aperture in the partition, through which they looked forth into the dark corridor. A person standing without could easily take a purse from under the pillow, or even strangle a sleeper as he lay abed. M'Naughten and his comrade stared at each other like Balboa and his men, 'with a wild surmise',[109] and then the latter, catching up the lamp, ran to the other frame and roughly raised the curtain. There he stood, petrified; and M'Naughten, who had followed, grasped him by the wrist in terror. They could see into another room, larger in size than that which they occupied, where three men sat crouching and silent in the dark. For a second or so these five persons looked each other in the eyes, then the curtain was dropped, and M'Naughten and his friend made but one bolt of it out of the room and downstairs. The man in the white cap said nothing as they passed him; and they were so pleased to be once more in the open night that they gave up all notion of a bed, and walked the streets of Boston till the morning.

No one seemed much cast down by these stories, but all inquired after the address of a respectable hotel; and I, for my part, put myself under the conduct of Mr Jones. Before noon of the second Sunday we sighted the low shores outside of New York harbour; the steerage passengers must remain on board to pass through Castle Garden[110] on the following morning; but we of the second cabin made our escape along with the lords of the saloon; and by six o'clock Jones and I issued into West Street, sitting on some straw in the bottom of an open baggage-wagon. It rained miraculously; and from that moment till on the following night I left New York, there was scarce a lull, and no cessation of the downpour. The roadways were flooded; a loud strident noise of falling water filled the air; the restaurants smelt heavily of wet people and wet clothing.

It took us but a few minutes, though it cost us a good deal of money, to be rattled along West Street to our destination: 'Reunion House, No. 10 West Street, one minute's walk from Castle Garden; convenient to Castle Garden, the Steamboat Landings, California Steamers and Liverpool Ships; Board and Lodging per day 1 dollar, single meals 25 cents, lodging per night 25 cents; private rooms for families; no charge for storage or baggage; satisfaction guaranteed to all persons; Michael Mitchell, Proprietor.' Reunion House was, I may go the length of saying, a humble hostelry. You entered through a long bar-room, thence passed into a little dining-room, and thence into a still smaller kitchen. The furniture was of the plainest; but the bar was hung in the American taste, with encouraging and hospitable mottoes. ⟨There is something youthful in this fashion which pleases me; it runs into the advertisements; they do not merely offer you your money's worth of perfunctory attendance, but hold out golden prospects and welcome you with both hands; such a proprietor defies black care to follow you into his saloon; such another, touching the keynote with precision, invites you to his bar 'to have a good time with the boys.' So they not only insure their own attention but the wit and friendly spirit of their guests.⟩

Jones was well known; we were received warmly; and two minutes afterwards I had refused a drink from the proprietor, and was going on, in my plain European fashion, to refuse a cigar, when Mr Mitchell sternly interposed, and explained the situation. He was offering to treat me, it appeared; whenever an American bar-keeper proposes anything, it must be borne in mind that he is offering to treat; and if I did not want a drink, I must at least take the cigar. I took it bashfully, feeling I had begun my American career on the wrong foot. I did not enjoy that cigar; but this may have been from a variety of reasons, even the best cigar often failing to please if you smoke three-quarters of it in a drenching rain.

For many years America was to me a sort of promised land. 'Westward the march of empire holds its way';[111] the race is for the moment to the young; what has been and what is we imperfectly and obscurely know; what is to be yet lies beyond the flight of our imaginations. Greece, Rome and Judæa are gone by for ever, leaving to generations the legacy of their accomplished work; China still endures, an old-inhabited house in the brand-new city of nations; England has already declined, since she has lost the States; and to these States, therefore, yet undeveloped, full of dark possibilities, and grown, like another Eve, from one rib out of the side of their own old land, the minds of young men in England turn naturally at a certain hopeful period of their age. It will be hard for an American to understand the spirit. But let him imagine a young man, who shall have grown up in an old and rigid circle, following bygone fashions and taught to distrust his own fresh instincts, and who now suddenly hears of a family of cousins, all about his own age, who keep house together by themselves and live far from restraint and tradition; let him imagine this, and he will have some imperfect notion of the sentiment with which spirited

English youths turn to the thought of the American Republic. It seems to them as if, out west, the war of life was still conducted in the open air, and on free barbaric terms; as if it had not yet been narrowed into parlours, nor begun to be conducted, like some unjust and dreary arbitration, by compromise, costume,[112] forms of procedure, and sad, senseless self-denial. Which of these two he prefers, a man with any youth still left in him will decide rightly for himself. He would rather be homeless than denied a pass-key; rather go without food than partake of a stalled ox in stiff, respectable society; rather be shot out of hand than direct his life according to the dictates of the world.

He knows or thinks nothing of the Maine Laws,[113] the Puritan sourness, the fierce, sordid appetite for dollars, or the dreary existence of country towns. A few wild story-books which delighted his childhood form the imaginative basis of his picture of America. In course of time, there is added to this a great crowd of stimulating details – vast cities that grow up as by enchantment; the birds, that have gone south in autumn, returning with the spring to find thousands camped upon their marshes, and the lamps burning far and near along populous streets; forests that disappear like snow; countries larger than Britain that are cleared and settled, one man running forth with his household gods before another, while the bear and the Indian are yet scarce aware of their approach; oil that gushes from the earth; gold that is washed or quarried in the brooks or glens of the Sierras; and all that bustle, courage, action, and constant kaleidoscopic change that Walt Whitman[114] has seized and set forth in his vigorous, cheerful, and loquacious verses. ⟨Even the shot-gun, the navy revolver and the bowie knife, seem more connected with courage than with cruelty. I remember a while ago when Chicago was burned,[115] hearing how a man, ere he began to rebuild his house, put up a board with some such inscription as the following: 'All lost. Have a wife and three children. Have the world to begin again;' and then in large capitals the word: '*Energy*.' The pluck and the expansion are alike youthful, and go straight to a young heart. Yes, it seemed to me, here was the country after all; here the undaunted stock of mankind, worthy to earn a new world.

I think Americans are scarce aware of this romantic attraction exercised by their land upon their cousins over sea. Perhaps they are unable to detect it under a certain jealousy and repentant soreness with which we regard a prosperity that might have been ours but for our own misconduct. Perhaps, too, we purposely conceal it; for we do not yet despair of the old ship. And perhaps the feeling flourishes more freely in the absence of any embodied and gently disappointing Uncle Sam.[116] Europe is visited yearly by a crowd of preposterous fellows who, stung by some inattention or merely sick with patriotism, decline their titles of superiority in our ears and insult us with statistics by the page. From some such excursion, they return full of bitterness because the English show so small an interest and so modified a pleasure in the progress of the States. Truly; but perhaps we should please them better, if they would measure the growth of America on some different standard from the decline of England. That capital essayist, Mr Lowell,[117] suffered much from 'a certain condescension in foreigners,' by which they made him feel that America was still young and incomplete; there is, I fear, a certain assumption in the American, by which he manages to taunt us with our age and debility. And since I am on this subject, let me courteously invite each American citizen who purposes travelling in Europe, either to hold his peace upon the subject of the Alabama claims; or if he must discuss the matter, to first refund from his own pocket the money which was paid by the one party and accepted by the other to conclude and definitively bury the dispute. The first American I ever encountered after I had begun to adore America, quarrelled with me, or else I quarrelled with him, about the Alabama claims. He has not been the last. Yet I never started the subject; indeed I know nothing about it, except that the money was paid; and fight for my flag in ignorance like a man before the mast.

It is possible that some people are always best at home, though the reverse is scandalously true of others. I have just been reading Mr Charles Reade's *Woman Hater* (for which I wish to thank him), and I am reminded of Zoe Vizard's remark: 'What does that matter? We are abroad.'[118] Sedentary, respectable people seem to leave some vital qualities behind them when they travel:

non omnia sua secum; they are not themselves, and with all that
mass of baggage, have forgotten to put up their human virtues.
A Bohemian[119] may not have much to recommend him, but
what he has, is at least his own and indefeasible. You may rely
as surely upon his virtues as upon his vices, for they are both
bred in the bone. Neither have been assumed to suit the temper
of society, or depend in any degree on the vicinity of Portman
Square.[120] But respectable people, transplanted from their own
particular zone of respectability, too often lose their manners,
their good sense, and a considerable part of their religion. For
instance I have not yet seen the Sabbatarian[121] who did not
visibly relax upon the continent. Hence perhaps the difference
between the American abroad and the American at home. If one
thing were deeply written on my mind, it was this: that the
American dislikes England and the English; and yet I had no
sooner crossed the Atlantic, than I began to think it an
unfounded notion. The old country – so they called it with an
accent of true kindliness – was plainly not detested; they spoke
of it with a certain emotion, as of a father from whom they had
parted in anger and who was since dead; and wherever I went,
I found my nationality an introduction. I am old-fashioned
enough to be patriotic, particularly when away from home; and
thus the change delighted and touched me. Up to the moment
of my arrival, I had connected Americans with hostility, not to
me indeed, but to my land; from that moment forward, I found
that was a link which I had thought to be a barrier, and knew
that I was among blood relations.

So much had I written some time ago, with great good sense,
as I thought, and complete catholicity of view. But it began at
first to dawn upon me slowly, and was then forced upon me in
a thunderclap, that I had myself become one of those uncivil
travellers whom I so heartily condemned: that while here I was,
kindly received, I could not find a good word nor so much as a
good thought for the land that harboured me; that I was eager
to spy its faults and shrank from the sight of virtues as if they
were injustices to England. Such was the case; explain it how
you may. It was too like my home, and yet not like enough. It
stood to me like a near relation who is scarce a friend, and who

may disgrace us by his mis-conduct and yet cannot greatly please by his prosperity. I can bear to read the worst word of a Frenchman about England, and can do so smiling; but let an American take up the tale, and I am all quivering susceptibility from head to foot. There is still a sense of domestic treachery when we fall out, and a sense of unwarrantable coolness even when we agree.

Did you ever read the parable of the Prodigal Son?[122] Or do you fancy, if things had been reversed and the prodigal come home in broadcloth and a chaise and four, that his brother who had stayed at home and stood by the old concern, would be better satisfied with the result? He might have been; not I. I have not enough justice in me for a case so trying. And then in one version of the parable, the prodigal was driven from home with barbarous usage; and O! what a bitterness is added to the cup! Your own Benjamin Franklin[123] has foreseen my case. 'Were it possible for *us* to forget and forgive,' he wrote, 'it is not possible for *you* (I mean the British nation) to forgive the people you have so heavily injured.' Incisive Franklin! Yours is the prophecy, mine the ill-feeling. I have all the faults of my forefathers on my stomach; I have historical remorse; I cannot see America but through the jaundiced spectacles of criminality.

And surely if jealousy be, as I believe it is, only the most radical, primeval and naked form of admiration – admiration in war paint, so to speak – then every word of my confession proves a delicate flattery like incense. Sail on, O mighty Union! God knows I wish you a noble career. Only somehow, when I was younger, I used to feel as if I had some portion in your future; but first I began to meet Americans in my own home, and they did not run to greet me as I hoped; and then I came myself into these states, and found my own heart not pure of ancient hatred. With that I knew I was a stranger, and you did but justice to refuse me copyright.[124] Yet it is with disappointed tenderness that I behold you steaming off to glory in your new and elegant turret ship, while I remain behind to go down with the old three decker.[125] We have feelings that will not be uttered in prose; and where poetry is absent, jingle must serve the turn.

With half a heart I wander here
    As from an age gone by,
A brother – yet, though young in years,
    An elder brother I!

You speak another tongue from mine,
    Though both were English born.
I towards the night of time decline:
    You mount into the morn.

Youth shall grow great and strong and free
    But age must still decay.
Tomorrow for the States – for me
    England and yesterday!⟩

Here I was at last in America, and was soon out upon New York streets, spying for things foreign. The place had to me an air of Liverpool;[126] but such was the rain that not Paradise itself would have looked inviting. We were a party of four, under two umbrellas; Jones and I and two Scots lads, recent immigrants, and not indisposed to welcome a compatriot. They had been six weeks in New York, and neither of them had yet found a single job or earned a single halfpenny. Up to the present they were exactly out of pocket by the amount of the fare.

The lads soon left us. Now I had sworn by all my gods to have such a dinner as would rouse the dead; there was scarce any expense at which I should have hesitated; the devil was in it but Jones and I should dine like heathen emperors. I set to work, asking after a restaurant; and I chose the wealthiest and most gastronomical-looking passers-by to ask from. Yet, although I had told them I was willing to pay anything in reason, one and all sent me off to cheap, fixed-price houses, where I would not have eaten that night for the cost of twenty dinners. I do not know if this were characteristic of New York, or whether it was only Jones and I who looked un-dinerly and discouraged enterprising suggestions. But at length, by our own sagacity, we found a French restaurant, where there was a French waiter, some fair French cooking, some so-called French wine, and French coffee to conclude the whole. I never entered into the feelings of Jack on land so completely as when I tasted that coffee.

I suppose we had one of the 'private rooms for families' at Reunion House. It was very small, furnished with a bed, a chair, and some clothes-pegs; and it derived all that was necessary for the life of the human animal through two borrowed lights:[127] one looking into the passage, and the second opening, without sash, into another apartment, where three men fitly snored, or in intervals of wakefulness, drearily mumbled to each other all night long. It will be observed that this was almost exactly the disposition of the room in M'Naughten's story. Jones had the bed; I pitched my camp upon the floor; he did not sleep until near morning, and I, for my part, never closed an eye. ⟨Some of this wakefulness was due to the change from shipboard; but the better part, in my case, to a certain distressing malady which had been growing on me during the last few days and of which more anon.⟩

At sunrise I heard a cannon fired; and shortly afterwards the men in the next room gave over snoring for good, and began to rustle over their toilettes. The sound of their voices as they talked was low and moaning, like that of people watching by the sick. Jones, who had at last begun to doze, tumbled and murmured, and every now and then opened unconscious eyes upon me where I lay. I found myself growing eerier and eerier, for I daresay I was a little fevered by my restless night, and hurried to dress and get downstairs.

You had to pass through the rain, which still fell thick and resonant, to reach a lavatory on the other side of the court. There were three basin-stands, and a few crumpled towels and pieces of wet soap, white and slippery like fish; nor should I forget a looking-glass and a pair of questionable combs. Another Scots lad was here, scrubbing his face with a good will. He had been three months in New York and had not yet found a single job nor earned a single halfpenny. Up to the present, he also was exactly out of pocket by the amount of the fare.[128] I began to grow sick at heart for my fellow-emigrants.

Of my nightmare wanderings in New York I spare to tell. I had a thousand and one things to do; only the day to do them

in, and a journey across the continent before me in the evening.
It rained with patient fury; every now and then I had to get under
cover for a while in order, so to speak, to give my mackintosh a
rest; for under this continued drenching it began to grow damp
on the inside. I went to banks, post-offices, railway-offices,
restaurants, publishers, booksellers, money-changers, and wherever I went a pool would gather about my feet, and those who
were careful of their floors would look on with an unfriendly eye.
Wherever I went, too, the same traits struck me: the people were
all surprisingly rude and surprisingly kind. The money-changer
cross-questioned me like a French commissary, asking my age,
my business, my average income, and my destination, beating
down my attempts at evasion, and receiving my answers in
silence; and yet when all was over, he shook hands with me up
to the elbows, and sent his lad nearly a quarter of a mile in the
rain to get me books at a reduction. Again, in a very large
publishing and bookselling establishment a man, who seemed
to be the manager, received me as I had certainly never before
been received in any human shop, indicated squarely that he
put no faith in my honesty, and refused to look up the names of
books or give me the slightest help of information, on the
ground, like the steward, that it was none of his business. I lost
my temper at last, said I was a stranger in America and not
learned in their etiquette; but I would assure him, if he went to
any bookseller in England, of more handsome usage. The boast
was perhaps exaggerated; but like many a long shot, it struck
the gold. The manager passed at once from one extreme to the
other; I may say that from that moment he loaded me with
kindness; he gave me all sorts of good advice, wrote me down
addresses, and came bareheaded into the rain to point me out a
restaurant, where I might lunch, nor even then did he seem to
think that he had done enough. These are (it is as well to be
bold in statement) the manners of America. It is this same
opposition that has most struck me in people of almost all
classes and from east to west. By the time a man had about
strung me up to be the death of him by his insulting behaviour,
he himself would be just upon the point of melting into confidence and serviceable attention. Yet I suspect, although I have

met with the like in so many parts, that this must be the character of some particular State or group of States; for in America, and this again in all classes, you will find some of the softest-mannered gentlemen in the world.

⟨I returned to Mitchell's to write some letters, and then made the acquaintance of his stripling daughter. She was a slip of a girl at that attractive period of life when the girl just begins to put on the forms of the woman, and yet retains an accent and character of her own. Her looks were dark, strange and comely. Her eyes had a caressing fixity, which made you inclined to turn aside your own. She was what is called a reading girl, and it was because she saw books in my open knapsack as I sat writing at a table near the bar, that she plucked up courage to address me. Had I any songs? she asked me, touching a volume with her finger. I told her I had not; but she still hovered by, and again inquired, if any of the books were nice? I gave her a volume of my own, not because I thought it so nice, but because it had a likeness of myself in the frontispiece, which I thought it would amuse the child to recognise. She was delighted beyond measure, and read a good many pages aloud to her sister as I sat writing; the sister, I must confess, soon wearied and ran away; but the other child, with admirable courage, persevered till it was time for me to go. I wish her a kind husband who will have, without my wishing it, a most desirable wife, particularly for an author.

I went to a chemist's in Broadway, a great temple near the Post Office, where I was examined and prescribed for by a fine gentleman in fine linen and with the most insinuative manners. My wrists were a mass of sores; so were many other parts of my body. The itching was at times overwhelming; at times, too, it was succeeded by furious stinging pains, like so many cuts with a carriage whip. There were moments when even a stoic or an Indian Gymnosophist[129] might have been excused for some demonstration of interest; and for my part, I was ready to roll upon the floor in my paroxysms. The gentleman in fine linen told me, with admirable gravity, that my liver was out of order, and presented me with a blue pill, a seidlitz powder and a little bottle of some salt and colourless fluid to take night and morning on the journey. He might as well have given me a cricket bat and a copy of Johnson's dictionary,[130] I might have lived exclusively on blue pills and been none the better. But the diagnosis of the gentleman in fine linen was hopelessly at fault. Perhaps he had moved too exclusively in elegant circles; perhaps he was too noble-minded to suspect me of anything disgraceful. The true name of my complaint,[131] I will never divulge, for I know what is due to the reader and to myself; but there is every reason to believe that I am not the only emigrant who has arrived in the Western world with similar symptoms. It is indeed a piece of emigrant experience, though one which I had not desired to share. Should any person be so intoxicated by my descriptions of an emigrant's career, as to desire to follow in my footsteps, here is a consideration which may modify if not eradicate the wish. But I have since been told that with a ring of red sublimate about the wrist, a man may plunge into the vilest company unfearing. I had no red sublimate: that is my story; hence these tears.[132])

I was so wet when I got back to Mitchell's towards the evening, that I had simply to divest myself of my shoes, socks and trousers, and leave them behind for the benefit of New York City. No fire could have dried them ere I had to start; and to pack them in their present condition was to spread ruin among my other possessions. With a heavy heart I said farewell to them as they lay a pulp in the middle of a pool upon the floor of Mitchell's kitchen. I wonder if they are dry by now. Mitchell hired a man to carry my baggage to the station, which was hard by, accompanied me thither himself, and recommended me to the particular attention of the officials. No one could have been kinder. Those who are out of pocket may go safely to Reunion House, where they will get decent meals and find an honest and obliging landlord. I owed him this word of thanks, before I enter fairly on the second and far less agreeable chapter of my emigrant experience.

II

ACROSS THE PLAINS

Leaves from the Notebook of an Emigrant between New York and San Francisco

Notes by the Way to Council Bluffs[1]

Monday. – It was, if I remember rightly, five o'clock when we were all signalled to be present at the Ferry Depot of the railroad. An emigrant ship had arrived at New York on the Saturday night, another on the Sunday morning, our own on Sunday afternoon, a fourth early on Monday; and as there is no emigrant train on Sunday, a great part of the passengers from these four ships was concentrated on the train by which I was to travel. There was a Babel of bewildered men, women, and children. The wretched little booking-office, and the baggage-room, which was not much larger, were crowded thick with emigrants, and were heavy and rank with the atmosphere of dripping clothes. Open carts full of bedding stood by the half-hour in the rain. The officials loaded each other with recriminations. A bearded, mildewed little man, whom I take to have been an emigrant agent, was all over the place, his mouth full of brimstone, blustering and interfering. It was plain that the whole system, if system there was, had utterly broken down under the strain of so many passengers.

My own ticket was given me at once, and an oldish man, who preserved his head in the midst of this turmoil, got my baggage registered, and counselled me to stay quietly where I was till he should give me the word to move. I had taken along with me a small valise, a knapsack, which I carried on my shoulders, and in the bag of my railway rug the whole of Bancroft's *History of the United States*,[2] in six fat volumes. It was as much as I could carry with convenience even for short distances, but it ensured me plenty of clothing, and the valise was at that moment, and often after, useful for a stool. I am sure I sat for an hour in the baggage-room, and wretched enough it was; yet, when at last the word was passed to me and I picked up my bundles and got under way, it was only to exchange discomfort for downright misery and danger.

I followed the porters into a long shed reaching downhill from West Street to the river. It was dark, the wind blew clean through it from end to end; and here I found a great block of passengers and baggage, hundreds of one and tons of the other. I feel I shall have a difficulty to make myself believed; and certainly the scene must have been exceptional, for it was too dangerous for daily repetition. It was a tight jam; there was no fair way through the mingled mass of brute and living obstruction. Into the upper skirts of the crowd, porters, infuriated by hurry and overwork, clove their way with shouts. I may say that we stood like sheep, and that the porters charged among us like so many maddened sheep-dogs; and I believe these men were no longer answerable for their acts. It mattered not what they were carrying, they drove straight into the press, and when they could get no farther, blindly discharged their barrowful. With my own hand, for instance, I saved the life of a child as it sat upon its mother's knee, she sitting on a box; and since I heard of no accident, I must suppose that there were many similar interpositions in the course of the evening. It will give some idea of the state of mind to which we were reduced if I tell you that neither the porter nor the mother of the child paid the least attention to my act. It was not till some time after that I understood what I had done myself, for to ward off heavy boxes seemed at the moment a natural incident of human life. Cold, wet, clamour, dead opposition to progress, such as one encounters in an evil dream, had utterly daunted the spirits. We had accepted this purgatory as a child accepts the conditions of the world. For my part, I shivered a little, and my back ached wearily; but I believe I had neither a hope nor a fear, and all the activities of my nature had become tributary to one massive sensation of discomfort.

At length, and after how long an interval I hesitate to guess, the crowd began to move, heavily straining through itself. About the same time some lamps were lighted, and threw a sudden flare over the shed. We were being filtered out into the river boat for Jersey City.[3] You may imagine how slowly this filtering proceeded, through the dense, choking crush, every one over-laden with packages or children, and yet under the necessity of fishing out his ticket by the way; but it ended at length for me, and I found myself on deck under a flimsy awning and with a trifle of elbow-room to stretch and breathe in. This was on the starboard; for the bulk of the emigrants stuck hopelessly on the port side, by which we had entered. In vain the seamen shouted to them to move on, and threatened them with shipwreck. These poor people were under a spell of stupor, and did not stir a foot. It rained as heavily as ever, but the wind now came in sudden claps and capfuls, not without danger to a boat so badly bal-lasted as ours; and we crept over the river in the darkness, trailing one paddle in the water like a wounded duck, and passed ever and again by huge, illuminated steamers running many knots, and heralding their approach by strains of music. The contrast between these pleasure embarkations and our own grim vessel, with her list to port and her freight of wet and silent emigrants, was of that glaring description which we count too obvious for the purposes of art.

The landing at Jersey was done in a stampede. I had a fixed sense of calamity, and to judge by conduct, the same persuasion was common to us all. A panic selfishness, like that produced by fear, presided over the disorder of our landing. People pushed, and elbowed, and ran, their families following how they could. Children fell, and were picked up to be rewarded by a blow. One child, who had lost her parents, screamed steadily and with increasing shrillness, as though verging towards a fit; an official kept her by him, but no one else seemed so much as to remark her distress; and I am ashamed to say that I ran among the rest. I was so weary that I had twice to make a halt and set down my bundles in the hundred yards or so between the pier and the railway station, so that I was quite wet by the time that I got under cover. There was no waiting-room, no refreshment-room; the cars were locked; and for at least another hour, or so it seemed, we had to camp upon the draughty, gas-lit platform.

I sat on my valise, too crushed to observe my neighbours; but as they were all cold, and wet, and weary, and driven stupidly crazy by the mismanagement to which we had been subjected, I believe they can have been no happier than myself. I bought half a dozen oranges from a boy, for oranges and nuts were the only refection to be had. As only two of them had even a pretence of juice, I threw the other four under the cars, and beheld, as in a dream, grown people and children groping on the track after my leavings. 〈God knows they would get little comfort from these balls of yellow fibre. But the touch completes the misery of the picture.

You will tell me, perhaps, that people are jostled, driven, and condemned to wait in the cold and rain, to get upon an excursion train or to see a new piece in a theatre; and that these discomforts are constantly, if not always cheerfully supported. I cannot deny it; but whether it was because the trial lasted so long, or because we were here whole families together, carrying all their worldly goods and bent upon a serious end, I know only that I have never seen fellow creatures so stricken down, nor suffered, in my own person, such complete paralysis of mind. The whole business was a nightmare while it lasted, and is still a nightmare to remember. If the railway company cared – but then it does not, and I should address the winds.[4] The officials, who are to blame for this unnecessary suffering, are without doubt humane men and subscribe to public charities; but when all hands are piped,[5] they may find their duty lay some other way. Kindness is the first of virtues; and capacity in a man's own business the greatest kindness in his reach.〉

At last we were admitted into the cars,[6] utterly dejected, and far from dry. For my own part, I got out a clothes-brush, and brushed my trousers as hard as I could till I had dried them and warmed my blood into the bargain; but no one else, except my next neighbour to whom I lent the brush, appeared to take the least precaution. As they were, they composed themselves to sleep. I had seen the lights of Philadelphia, and been twice ordered to change carriages and twice countermanded, before I allowed myself to follow their example.

Tuesday. – When I awoke, it was already day; the train was standing idle; I was in the last carriage, and, seeing some others strolling to and fro about the lines, I opened the door and stepped forth, as from a caravan by the wayside. We were near no station, nor even, as far as I could see, within reach of any signal. A green, open, undulating country stretched away upon all sides. Locust trees and a single field of Indian corn[7] gave it a foreign grace and interest; but the contours of the land were soft and English. It was not quite England, neither was it quite France; yet like enough either to seem natural in my eyes. And it was in the sky, and not upon the earth, that I was surprised to find a change. Explain it how you may, and for my part I cannot explain it at all, the sun rises with a different splendour in America and Europe. There is more clear gold and scarlet in our old country mornings; more purple, brown, and smoky orange in those of the new. It may be from habit, but to me the coming of day is less fresh and inspiriting in the latter; it has a duskier glory, and more nearly resembles sunset; it seems to fit some subsequential, evening epoch of the world, as though America were in fact, and not merely in fancy, farther from the orient of Aurora[8] and the springs of day. I thought so then, by the railroad side in Pennsylvania, and I have thought so a dozen times since in far distant parts of the continent. If it be an illusion it is one very deeply rooted, and in which my eyesight is accomplice.

Soon after a train whisked by, announcing and accompanying its passage by the swift beating of a sort of chapel-bell upon the engine; and as it was for this we had been waiting, we were summoned by the cry of 'All aboard!' and went on again upon our way. The whole line, it appeared, was topsy-turvy; an accident at midnight having thrown all the traffic hours into arrear. We paid for this in the flesh, for we had no meals all that day. Fruit we could buy upon the cars; and now and then we had a few minutes at some station with a meagre show of rolls and sandwiches for sale; but we were so many and so ravenous that, though I tried at every opportunity, the coffee was always exhausted before I could elbow my way to the counter.

Our American sunrise had ushered in a noble summer's day. There was not a cloud; the sunshine was baking; yet in the woody river-valleys among which we wound our way, the atmosphere preserved a sparkling freshness till late in the afternoon. It had an inland sweetness and variety to one newly from the sea; it smelt of woods, rivers, and the delved earth. These, though in so far a country, were airs from home. I stood on the platform[9] by the hour; and as I saw one after another, pleasant villages, carts upon the highway and fishers by the stream, and heard cockcrows and cheery voices in the distance, and beheld the sun, no longer shining blankly on the plains of ocean, but striking among shapely hills and his light dispersed and coloured by a thousand accidents of form and surface, I began to exult with myself upon this rise in life like a man who had come into a rich estate. ⟨For we are creatures of the shore; and it is only on shore that our senses are supplied with a variety of matter, or that the heart can find her proper business. There is water enough for one by the coasts of any running stream; or if I must indeed look upon the ocean, let it be from along the seaboard, surf-bent, strewn with wreck[10] and dotted at sundown with the clear lights that pilot home bound vessels. The revolution in my surroundings was certainly joyful and complete.⟩ And when I had asked the name of a river from the brakesman, ⟨the least surly of his class whom I encountered,⟩ and heard that it was called the Susquehanna, the beauty of the name seemed to be part and parcel of the beauty of the land. As when Adam[11] with divine fitness named the creatures, so this word Susquehanna was at once accepted by the fancy. That was the name, as no other could be, for that shining river and desirable valley.

None can care for literature in itself who do not take a special pleasure in the sound of names; and there is no part of the world where nomenclature is so rich, poetical, humorous, and picturesque as the United States of America. All times, races, and languages have brought their contribution. Pekin is in the same State[12] with Euclid, with Bellefontaine, and with Sandusky. Chelsea, with its London associations of red brick, Sloane Square, and the King's Road, is own suburb to stately and primeval Memphis; there they have their seat, translated names of cities, where the Mississippi runs by Tennessee and Arkansas;[13] and both, while I was crossing the continent, lay, watched by armed men, in the horror and isolation of a plague.[14]

Old, red Manhattan lies, like an Indian arrow-head under a steam factory, below Anglified New York. The names of the States and Territories themselves form a chorus of sweet and most romantic vocables: Delaware, Ohio, Indiana, Florida, Dakota, Iowa, Wyoming, Minnesota, and the Carolinas; there are few poems with a nobler music for the ear: a songful, tuneful land; and if the new Homer shall arise from the Western continent, his verse will be enriched, his pages sing spontaneously, with the names of states and cities that would strike the fancy in a business circular.

Late in the evening we were landed in a waiting-room at Pittsburg.[15] I had now under my charge a young and sprightly Dutch widow with her children; these I was to watch over providentially for a certain distance farther on the way; but as I found she was furnished with a basket of eatables, I left her in the waiting-room to seek a dinner for myself.

I mention this meal, not only because it was the first of which I had partaken for about thirty hours, but because it was the means of my first introduction to a coloured gentleman. He did me the honour to wait upon me after a fashion, while I was eating; and with every word, look, and gesture marched me farther into the country of surprise. He was indeed strikingly unlike the negroes of Mrs Beecher Stowe, or the Christy Minstrels[16] of my youth. Imagine a gentleman, certainly somewhat dark, but of a pleasant warm hue, speaking English with a slight and rather odd foreign accent, every inch a man of the world, and armed with manners so patronisingly superior that I am at a loss to name their parallel in England. A butler perhaps rides as high over the unbutlered, but then he sets you right with a reserve and a sort of sighing patience which one is often moved to admire. And again, the abstract butler never stoops to familiarity. But the coloured gentleman will pass you a wink at a time; he is familiar like an upper-form boy to a fag; he unbends to you like Prince Hal with Poins and Falstaff.[17] He makes himself at home and welcome. Indeed, I may say, this waiter behaved himself to me throughout that supper much as, with us, a young, free, and not very self-respecting master might behave to a good-looking chambermaid. I had come prepared to pity the poor negro, to put him at his ease, to prove in a thousand condescensions that I was no sharer in the prejudice of race; but I assure you I put my patronage away for another occasion, and had the grace to be pleased with that result.

Seeing he was a very honest fellow, I consulted him upon a point of etiquette: if one should offer to tip the American waiter? Certainly not, he told me. Never. It would not do. They considered themselves too highly to accept. They would even resent the offer. As for him and me, we had enjoyed a very pleasant conversation; he, in particular, had found much pleasure in my society; I was a stranger; this was exactly one of those rare conjunctures ... Without being very clear-seeing, I can still perceive the sun at noonday; and the coloured gentleman deftly pocketed a quarter.

Wednesday. – A little after midnight I convoyed my widow and orphans on board the train; and morning found us far into Ohio. This had early been a favourite home of my imagination; I have played at being in Ohio by the week, and enjoyed some capital sport there with a dummy gun, my person being still unbreeched. My preference was founded on a work which appeared in *Cassell's Family Paper*, and was read aloud to me by my nurse. It narrated the doings of one Custaloga, an Indian brave,[18] who, in the last chapter, very obligingly washed the paint off his face and became Sir Reginald Somebody-or-other; a trick I never forgave him. The idea of a man being an Indian brave, and then giving up that to be a baronet, was one which my mind rejected. It offended verisimilitude, like the pretended anxiety of Robinson Crusoe and others to escape from uninhabited islands. ⟨Just you put me on an uninhabited island, I thought, and then we'll see!⟩

But Ohio was not at all as I had pictured it. We were now on those great plains which stretch unbroken to the Rocky Mountains. The country was flat like Holland, but far from being dull. All through Ohio, Indiana, Illinois, and Iowa, or for as much as I saw of them from the train and in my waking moments, it was rich and various, and breathed an elegance peculiar to itself. The tall corn pleased the eye; the trees were graceful in themselves, and framed the plain into long, aerial vistas; and the clean, bright, gardened townships spoke of country fare and pleasant summer evenings on the stoop. It was a sort of flat paradise; but, I am afraid, not unfrequented by the devil. That morning dawned with such a freezing chill as I have rarely felt; a chill that was not perhaps so measurable by instrument, as it struck home upon the heart and seemed to travel with the blood. Day came in with a shudder. White mists lay thinly over the surface of the plain, as we see them more often on a lake; and though the sun had soon dispersed and drunk them up, leaving an atmosphere of fever-heat and crystal pureness from horizon to horizon, the mists had still been there, and we knew that this paradise was haunted by killing damps and foul malaria. The fences along the line bore but two descriptions of advertisement; one to recommend tobaccos, and the other to vaunt remedies against the ague. At the point of day, and while we were all in the grasp of that first chill, a native of the State, who had got in at some way-station, pronounced it, with a doctoral air, 'a fever and ague morning.'

The Dutch widow was a person of some character. She had conceived at first sight a great aversion for the present writer, which she was at no pains to conceal. But, being a woman of a practical spirit, she made no difficulty about accepting my attentions, and encouraged me to buy her children fruits and candies, to carry all her parcels, and even to sleep upon the floor that she might profit by my empty seat. Nay, she was such a rattle[19] by nature, and so powerfully moved to autobiographical talk, that she was forced, for want of a better, to take me into confidence and tell me the story of her life. I heard about her late husband, who seemed to have made his chief impression by taking her out pleasuring on Sundays. I could tell you her prospects, her hopes, the amount of her fortune, the cost of her house-keeping by the week, and a variety of particular matters that are not usually disclosed except to friends. At one station she shook up her children to look at a man on the platform and say if he were not like Mr Z.; while to me she explained how she had been keeping company with this Mr Z., how far matters had proceeded, and how it was because of his desistance that she was now travelling to the West. Then, when I was thus put in possession of the facts, she asked my judgment on that type of manly beauty. I admired it to her heart's content. She was not, I think, remarkably veracious in talk but broidered as fancy prompted, and built castles in the air out of her past; yet she had that sort of candour, to keep me, in spite of all these confidences, steadily aware of her aversion. Her parting words were ingeniously honest. 'I am sure,' said she, 'we all *ought* to be very much obliged to you.' I cannot pretend that she put me at my ease; but I had a certain respect for such a genuine dislike. A poor nature would have slipped, in the course of these familiarities, into a sort of worthless toleration for me.

We reached Chicago in the evening. I was turned out of the cars, bundled into an omnibus, and driven off through the streets to the station of a different railroad. Chicago seemed a great and gloomy city. I remember having subscribed, let us say sixpence, towards its restoration at the period of the fire; and now when I beheld street after street of ponderous houses and crowds of comfortable burghers, I thought it would be a graceful act for the corporation to refund that sixpence, or, at the least, to entertain me to a cheerful dinner. But there was no word of restitution. I was that city's benefactor, yet I was received in a third-class waiting-room, and the best dinner I could get was a dish of ham and eggs at my own expense.

I can safely say, I have never been so dog-tired as that night in Chicago. ⟨I sat, or rather lay, on some steps in the station, and was gratefully conscious of every point of contact between my body and the boards. My one ideal of pleasure was to stretch myself flat on my back with arms extended, like a dying hermit in a picture, and to move no more. I bought a newspaper, but could not summon up the energy to read it; I debated with myself if it were worth while to make a cigarette, and unanimously decided that it was not.⟩ When it was time to start, I descended the platform like a man in a dream. It was a long train, lighted from end to end; and car after car, as I came up with it, was not only filled but overflowing. My valise, my knapsack, my rug, with those six ponderous tomes of Bancroft, weighed me double; I was hot, feverish, painfully athirst; and there was a great darkness over me, an internal darkness, not to be dispelled by gas. When at last I found an empty bench, I sank into it like a bundle of rags, the world seemed to swim away into the distance, and my consciousness dwindled within me to a mere pin's head, like a taper on a foggy night.

When I came a little more to myself, I found that there had sat down beside me a very cheerful rosy little German gentleman, somewhat gone in drink, who was talking away to me, nineteen to the dozen, as they say. I did my best to keep up the conversation; for it seemed to me dimly as if something depended upon that. I heard him relate, among many other things, that there were pickpockets on the train, who had already robbed a man of forty dollars and a return ticket; but though I caught the words, I do not think I properly understood the sense until next morning; and I believe I replied at the time that I was very glad to hear it. What else he talked about I have no guess; I remember a gabbling sound of words, his profuse gesticulation, and his smile, which was highly explanatory; but no more. And I suppose I must have shown my confusion very plainly; for, first, I saw him knit his brows at me like one who has conceived a doubt; next, he tried me in German, supposing perhaps that I was unfamiliar with the English tongue; and finally, in despair, he rose and left me. I felt chagrined; but my fatigue was too crushing for delay, and, stretching myself as far as that was possible upon the bench, I was received at once into a dreamless stupor.

The little German gentleman was only going a little way into the suburbs after a *dîner fin*,[20] and was bent on entertainment while the journey lasted. Having failed with me, he pitched next upon another emigrant, who had come through from Canada, and was not one jot less weary than myself. Nay, even in a natural state, as I found next morning when we scraped acquaintance, he was a heavy, uncommunicative man. After trying him on different topics, it appears that the little German gentleman flounced into a temper, swore an oath or two, and departed from that car in quest of livelier society. Poor little gentleman! I suppose he thought an emigrant should be a rollicking, free-hearted blade, with a flask of foreign brandy and a long, comical story to beguile the moments of digestion. (He should have met Alick; Alick and he would have been like brothers.)

Thursday. – I suppose there must be a cycle in the fatigue of travelling, for when I awoke next morning, I was entirely renewed in spirits and ate a hearty breakfast of porridge, with sweet milk, and coffee and hot cakes at Burlington, upon the Mississippi. Another long day's ride followed, with but one feature worthy of remark. At a place called Creston,[21] a drunken man got in. He was aggressively friendly, but, according to English notions, not at all unpresentable upon a train. For one stage he eluded the notice of the officials; but just as we were beginning to move out of the next station, Cromwell by name, by came the conductor. There was a word or two of talk; and then the official had the man by the shoulders, twitched him from his seat, marched him through the car, and sent him flying on to the track. It was done in three motions, as exact as a piece of drill. The train was still moving slowly, although beginning to mend her pace, and the drunkard got his feet without a fall. He carried a red bundle, though not so red as his cheeks; and he shook this menacingly in the air with one hand, while the other stole behind him to the region of the kidneys. It was the first indication that I had come among revolvers, and I observed it with some emotion. The conductor stood on the steps with one hand on his hip, looking back at him; and perhaps this attitude imposed upon the creature, for he turned without further ado, and went off staggering along the track towards Cromwell, followed by a peal of laughter from the cars. They were speaking English all about me, but I knew I was in a foreign land.

Twenty minutes before nine that night we were deposited at the Pacific Transfer Station near Council Bluffs, on the eastern banks of the Missouri river. Here we were to stay the night at a kind of caravanserai, set apart for emigrants. But I gave way to a thirst for luxury, separated myself from my companions, and marched with my effects into the Union Pacific Hotel. A white clerk and a coloured gentleman whom, in my plain European way, I should call the boots,[22] were installed behind a counter like bank tellers. They took my name, assigned me a number, and proceeded to deal with my packages. And here came the tug of war. I wished to give up my packages into safe keeping; but I did not wish to go to bed. And this, it appeared, was impossible in an American hotel.

It was, of course, some inane misunderstanding, and sprang from my unfamiliarity with the language. For although two nations use the same words and read the same books, intercourse is not conducted by the dictionary. The business of life is not carried on by words, but in set phrases, each with a special and almost a slang signification. ⟨Thus every difference of habit modifies the spoken tongue, and even to send off a telegram or order a dish of oysters without some foreign indirectness, an Englishman must have partly learned to be an American. I speak of oysters, because that was the last example that I came across: in San Francisco, if you ask to have your oysters opened, it means they are to be taken from the shell.⟩ Some international obscurity prevailed between me and the coloured gentleman at Council Bluffs; so that what I was asking, which seemed very natural to me, appeared to him a monstrous exigency. He refused, and that with the plainness of the West. This American manner of conducting matters of business is, at first, highly unpalatable to the European. When we approach a man in the way of his calling, and for those services by which he earns his bread, we consider him for the time being our hired servant. But in the American opinion, two gentlemen meet and have a friendly talk with a view to exchanging favours if they shall agree to please. I know not which is the more convenient, nor even which is the more truly courteous. The English stiffness unfortunately tends to be continued after the particular trans-action is at an end, and thus favours class separations. But on the other hand these equalitarian plainnesses leave an open field for the insolence of Jack-in-office.

I was nettled by the coloured gentleman's refusal, and unbuttoned my wrath under the similitude of ironical sub-mission. I knew nothing, I said, of the ways of American hotels; but I had no desire to give trouble. If there was nothing for it but to get to bed immediately, let him say the word, and though it was not my habit, I should cheerfully obey.

He burst into a shout of laughter. 'Ah!' said he, 'you do not know about America. They are fine people in America. Oh! you will like them very well. But you mustn't get mad. I know what you want. You come along with me.'

And issuing from behind the counter, and taking me by the arm like an old acquaintance, he led me to the bar of the hotel.

'There,' said he, pushing me from him by the shoulder, 'go and have a drink!'

The Emigrant Train

All this while I had been travelling by mixed trains, where I might meet with Dutch widows and little German gentry fresh from table. I had been but a latent emigrant; now I was to be branded once more, and put apart with my fellows. It was about two in the afternoon of Friday that I found myself in front of the Emigrant House, with more than a hundred others, to be sorted and boxed for the journey. A white-haired official, with a stick under one arm, and a list in the other hand, stood apart in front of us, and called name after name in the tone of a command. At each name you would see a family gather up its brats and bundles and run for the hindmost of the three cars that stood awaiting us, and I soon concluded that this was to be set apart for the women and children. The second or central car, it turned out, was devoted to men travelling alone, and the third to the Chinese.[23] The official was easily moved to anger at the least delay; but the emigrants were both quick at answering their names, and speedy in getting themselves and their effects on board.

The families once housed, we men carried the second car without ceremony by simultaneous assault. I suppose the reader has some notion of an American railroad-car, that long, narrow wooden box, like a flat-roofed Noah's ark,[24] with a stove and a convenience, one at either end, a passage down the middle, and transverse benches upon either hand. Those destined for emigrants on the Union Pacific are only remarkable for their extreme plainness, nothing but wood entering in any part into their constitution, and for the usual inefficacy of the lamps, which often went out and shed but a dying glimmer even while they burned. The benches are too short for anything but a young child. Where there is scarce elbow-room for two to sit, there will not be space enough for one to lie. Hence the company, or rather, as it appears from certain bills about the Transfer Station, the company's servants, have conceived a plan for the better accommodation of travellers. They prevail on every two to chum together. To each of the chums they sell a board and three square cushions stuffed with straw, and covered with thin cotton. The benches can be made to face each other in pairs, for the backs are reversible. On the approach of night the boards are laid from bench to bench, making a couch wide enough for two, and long enough for a man of the middle height; and the chums lie down side by side upon the cushions with the head to the conductor's van and the feet to the engine. When the train is full, of course this plan is impossible, for there must not be more than one to every bench, neither can it be carried out unless the chums agree. It was to bring about this last condition that our white-haired official now bestirred himself. He made a most active master of ceremonies, introducing likely couples, and even guaranteeing the amiability and honesty of each. The greater the number of happy couples the better for his pocket, for it was he who sold the raw material of the beds. His price for one board and three straw cushions began with two dollars and a half; but before the train left, and I am sorry to say long after I had purchased mine, it had fallen to one dollar and a half. ⟨I cannot suppose that emigrants are thus befooled and robbed with the connivance of the Company; yet this was the Company's servant. It is never pleasant to bear tales; but this is a system; the emigrants are many of them foreigners and therefore easy to cheat, and they are all so poor that it is unmanly to cheat them; and if the white-haired leach is not contumeliously discharged in this world, I leave him with all confidence to the devil in the next. As for the emigrant, I have better news for him. Let him quietly agree with a chum, but bid the official harpy from his sight; and if he will read a few pages farther, he shall see the profit of his reticence.⟩

The match-maker had a difficulty with me; perhaps, like some ladies, I showed myself too eager for union at any price; but certainly the first who was picked out to be my bedfellow, declined the honour without thanks. He was an old, heavy, slow-spoken man, I think from Yankeeland,[25] looked me all over with great timidity, and then began to excuse himself in broken phrases. He didn't know the young man, he said. The young man might be very honest, but how was he to know that? There was another young man whom he had met already in the train; he guessed *he* was honest, and would prefer to chum with *him* upon the whole. All this without any sort of excuse, as though I had been inanimate or absent. I began to tremble lest every one should refuse my company, and I be left rejected. But the next in turn was a tall, strapping, long-limbed, small-headed, curly-haired Pennsylvania Dutchman,[26] with a soldierly smartness in his manner. To be exact, he had acquired it in the navy. But that was all one; he had at least been trained to desperate resolves, so he accepted the match, and the white-haired swindler pronounced the connubial benediction, and pocketed his fees.

The rest of the afternoon was spent in making up the train. I am afraid to say how many baggage-waggons followed the engine – certainly a score; then came the Chinese, then we, then the families, and the rear was brought up by the conductor in what, if I have it rightly, is called his caboose. The class to which I belonged was of course far the largest, and we ran over, so to speak, to both sides; so that there were some Caucasians among the Chinamen, and some bachelors among the families. But our own car was pure from admixture, save for one little boy of eight or nine, who had the whooping-cough. At last, about six, the long train crawled out of the Transfer Station and across the wide Missouri river to Omaha, westward bound.

It was a troubled uncomfortable evening in the cars. There was thunder in the air, which helped to keep us restless. A man played many airs upon the cornet, and none of them were much attended to, until he came to 'Home, sweet Home.'[27] It was truly strange to note how the talk ceased at that, and the faces began to lengthen. I have no idea whether musically this air is to be considered good or bad; but it belongs to that class of art which may be best described as a brutal assault upon the feelings. Pathos must be relieved by dignity of treatment. If you wallow naked in the pathetic, like the author of 'Home, sweet Home,' you make your hearers weep in an unmanly fashion; and even while yet they are moved, they despise themselves and hate the occasion of their weakness. It did not come to tears that night, for the experiment was interrupted. An elderly, hard-looking man, with a goatee beard and about as much appearance of sentiment as you would expect from a retired slaver, turned with a start and bade the performer stop that 'damned thing.' 'I've heard about enough of that,' he added; 'give us something about the good country we're going to.' A murmur of adhesion ran round the car; the performer took the instrument from his lips, laughed and nodded, and then struck into a dancing measure; and, like a new Timotheus,[28] stilled immediately the emotion he had raised.

The day faded; the lamps were lit; a party of wild young men, who got off next evening at North Platte, stood together on the stern platform, singing 'The Sweet By-and-bye'[29] with very tuneful voices; the chums began to put up their beds; and it seemed as if the business of the day were at an end. But it was not so; for, the train stopping at some station, the cars were instantly thronged with the natives, wives and fathers, young men and maidens, some of them in little more than nightgear, some with stable lanterns, and all offering beds for sale. Their charge began with twenty-five cents a cushion, but fell, before the train went on again, to fifteen, with the bed-board gratis, or less than one-fifth of what I had paid for mine at the Transfer. This is my contribution to the economy of future emigrants.

A great personage on an American train is the newsboy. He sells books (such books!), papers, fruit, lollipops, and cigars; and on emigrant journeys, soap, towels, tin washing-dishes, tin coffee pitchers, coffee, tea, sugar, and tinned eatables, mostly hash or beans and bacon. Early next morning the newsboy went around the cars, and chumming on a more extended principle became the order of the hour. It requires but a co-partnery of two to manage beds; but washing and eating can be carried on

most economically by a syndicate of three. I myself entered a
little after sunrise into articles of agreement, and became one of
the firm of Pennsylvania, Shakespeare, and Dubuque. Shakespeare was my own nickname on the cars; Pennsylvania that of
my bedfellow; and Dubuque, the name of a place in the State of
Iowa, that of an amiable young fellow going west to cure an
asthma, and retarding his recovery by incessantly chewing or
smoking, and sometimes chewing and smoking together. I have
never seen tobacco so sillily abused. Shakespeare bought a tin
washing-dish, Dubuque a towel, and Pennsylvania a brick of
soap. The partners used these instruments, one after another,
according to the order of their first awaking; and when the firm
had finished there was no want of borrowers. Each filled the tin
dish at the water filter opposite the stove, and retired with the
whole stock in trade to the platform of the car. There he knelt
down, supporting himself by a shoulder against the woodwork,
or one elbow crooked about the railing, and made a shift to
wash his face and neck and hands, – a cold, an insufficient, and,
if the train is moving rapidly, a somewhat dangerous toilet.

On a similar division of expense, the firm of Pennsylvania,
Shakespeare, and Dubuque supplied themselves with coffee,
sugar, and necessary vessels; and their operations are a type of
what went on through all the cars. Before the sun was up the
stove would be brightly burning; at the first station the natives
would come on board with milk and eggs and coffee cakes; and
soon from end to end the car would be filled with little parties
breakfasting upon the bed-boards. It was the pleasantest hour
of the day.

There were meals to be had, however, by the wayside: a
breakfast in the morning, a dinner somewhere between eleven
and two, and supper from five to eight or nine at night. We had
rarely less than twenty minutes for each; and if we had not spent
many another twenty minutes waiting for some express upon a
side track among miles of desert, we might have taken an hour
to each repast and arrived at San Francisco up to time. For
haste is not the foible of an emigrant train. It gets through on
sufferance, running the gauntlet among its more considerable
brethren; should there be a block, it is unhesitatingly sacrificed;

and they cannot, in consequence, predict the length of the passage within a day or so. ⟨The meals, taken overland, were palateable; and they were not dear, at least for us. I had the pleasure, at one station, of dining in the same room, with express passengers eastward bound, getting dish for dish the identical same dinner, and paying exactly half the charge. It was an experience in which I delighted, and I began to see the advantages of a state of Emigrancy.⟩ Civility is the main comfort that you miss. Equality, though conceived very largely in America, does not extend so low down as to an emigrant. Thus in all other trains, a warning cry of 'All aboard!' recalls the passengers to take their seats; but as soon as I was alone with emigrants, and from the Transfer all the way to San Francisco, I found this ceremony was pretermitted; the train stole from the station without note of warning, and you had to keep an eye upon it even while you ate. The annoyance is considerable, and the disrespect both wanton and petty.

Many conductors, again, will hold no communication with an emigrant. I asked a conductor one day at what time the train would stop for dinner; as he made no answer I repeated the question, with a like result; a third time I returned to the charge, and then Jack-in-office looked me coolly in the face for several seconds and turned ostentatiously away. I believe he was half-ashamed of his brutality; for when another person made the same inquiry, although he still refused the information, he condescended to answer, and even to justify his reticence in a voice loud enough for me to hear. It was, he said, his principle not to tell people where they were to dine; for one answer led to many other questions, as what o'clock it was? or, how soon should we be there? and he could not afford to be eternally worried.

As you are thus cut off from the superior authorities, a great deal of your comfort depends on the character of the newsboy. He has it in his power indefinitely to better and brighten the emigrant's lot. The newsboy with whom we started from the Transfer was a dark, bullying, contemptuous, insolent scoundrel, who treated us like dogs. Indeed, in his case, matters came nearly to a fight. It happened thus: he was going his rounds through the cars with some commodities for sale, and coming

to a party who were at Seven-up or Cascino[30] (our two games),
upon a bed-board, slung down a cigar-box in the middle of the
cards, knocking one man's hand to the floor. It was the last
straw. In a moment the whole party were upon their feet, the
cigars were upset, and he was ordered to 'get out of that directly,
or he would get more than he reckoned for.' The fellow grumbled and muttered, but ended by making off, and was less openly
insulting in the future. On the other hand, the lad who rode
with us in this capacity from Ogden to Sacramento[31] made
himself the friend of all, and helped us with information, attention, assistance, and a kind countenance. He told us where and
when we should have our meals, and how long the train would
stop; kept seats at table for those who were delayed, and watched
that we should neither be left behind nor yet unnecessarily
hurried. You, who live at home at ease, can hardly realise the
greatness of this service, even had it stood alone. When I think
of that lad coming and going, train after train, with his bright
face and civil words, I see how easily a good man may become
the benefactor of his kind. Perhaps he is discontented with
himself, perhaps troubled with ambitions; why, if he but knew
it, he is a hero of the old Greek stamp; and while he thinks he is
only earning a profit of a few cents, and that perhaps exorbitant,
he is doing a man's work, and bettering the world.

I must tell here an experience of mine with another newsboy.
I tell it because it gives so good an example of that uncivil
kindness of the American, which is perhaps their most bewilder-
ing character to one newly landed. It was immediately after I
had left the emigrant train; and I am told I looked like a man at
death's door, so much had this long journey shaken me. I sat at
the end of a car, and the catch being broken, and myself feverish
and sick, I had to hold the door open with my foot for the sake
of air. In this attitude my leg debarred the newsboy from his
box of merchandise. I made haste to let him pass when I observed
that he was coming; but I was busy with a book, and so once or
twice he came upon me unawares. On these occasions he most
rudely struck my foot aside; and though I myself apologised, as
if to show him the way, he answered me never a word. ⟨I conceive
I had a right to do as I was doing; it was no fault of mine if the

car was out of repair; he must have seen, besides, my willingness to spare him trouble; and had I been Obstruction in person, it would not have justified either his violence or his silence.⟩ I chafed furiously, and I fear the next time it would have come to words. But suddenly I felt a touch upon my shoulder, and a large juicy pear was put into my hand. It was the newsboy, who had observed that I was looking ill and so made me this present out of a tender heart. For the rest of the journey I was petted like a sick child; he lent me newspapers, thus depriving himself of his legitimate profit on their sale, and came repeatedly to sit by me and cheer me up. ⟨I hate myself now, to think how little I encouraged him; but as was said by one of the best of men, taciturnity is another word for selfishness.⟩

The Plains of Nebraska

It had thundered on the Friday night, but the sun rose on Saturday without a cloud. We were at sea – there is no other adequate expression – on the plains of Nebraska. I made my observatory on the top of a fruit-waggon, and sat by the hour upon that perch to spy about me, and to spy in vain for something new. It was a world almost without a feature; an empty sky, an empty earth; front and back, the line of railway stretched from horizon to horizon, like a cue across a billiard-board; on either hand, the green plain ran till it touched the skirts of heaven. Along the track innumerable wild sunflowers, no bigger than a crown-piece,[32] bloomed in a continuous flower-bed; grazing beasts were seen upon the prairie at all degrees of distance and diminution; and now and again we might perceive a few dots beside the railroad which grew more and more distinct as we drew nearer till they turned into wooden cabins, and then dwindled and dwindled in our wake until they melted into their surroundings, and we were once more alone upon the billiard-board. The train toiled over this infinity like a snail; and being the one thing moving, it was wonderful what huge proportions it began to assume in our regard. It seemed miles in

length, and either end of it within but a step of the horizon.
Even my own body or my own head seemed a great thing in
that emptiness. I note the feeling the more readily as it is the
contrary of what I have read of in the experience of others. Day
and night, above the roar of the train, our ears were kept busy
with the incessant chirp of grasshoppers – a noise like the
winding up of countless clocks and watches, which began after
a while to seem proper to that land.

To one hurrying through by steam there was a certain exhilaration in this spacious vacancy, this greatness of the air, this
discovery of the whole arch of heaven, this straight, unbroken
prison-line of the horizon. Yet one could not but reflect upon
the weariness of those who passed by there in old days, at the
foot's pace of oxen, painfully urging their teams, and with no
landmark but that unattainable evening sun for which they
steered, and which daily fled them by an equal stride. They had
nothing, it would seem, to overtake; nothing by which to reckon
their advance; no sight for repose or for encouragement; but
stage after stage, only the dead green waste under foot, and the
mocking, fugitive horizon. But the eye, as I have been told,
found differences even here; and at the worst the emigrant came,
by perseverance, to the end of his toil. It is the settlers, after all,
at whom we have a right to marvel. Our consciousness, by
which we live, is itself but the creature of variety. Upon what
food does it subsist in such a land? What livelihood can repay a
human creature for a life spent in this huge sameness? He is cut
off from books, from news, from company, from all that can
relieve existence but the prosecution of his affairs. A sky full of
stars is the most varied spectacle that he can hope. He may walk
five miles and see nothing; ten, and it is as though he had not
moved; twenty, and still he is in the midst of the same great
level, and has approached no nearer to the one object within
view, the flat horizon which keeps pace with his advance. We
are full at home of the question of agreeable wall-papers, and
wise people are of opinion that the temper may be quieted by
sedative surroundings. But what is to be said of the Nebraskan
settler? His is a wall-paper with a vengeance – one quarter of
the universe laid bare in all its gauntness. His eye must embrace

at every glance the whole seeming concave of the visible world; it quails before so vast an outlook, it is tortured by distance; yet there is no rest or shelter, till the man runs into his cabin, and can repose his sight upon things near at hand. Hence, I am told, a sickness of the vision peculiar to these empty plains.

Yet perhaps with sunflowers and cicadæ,[33] summer and winter, cattle, wife and family, the settler mày create a full and various existence. ⟨We exaggerate the difficulties of a situation when we conceive and criticise it in fancy; for we forget that people live in this world by the day or week. Theory shows us an unbroken tenor to the last sickness; but the actual man lives it in pieces, and begins afresh with every morning. The blind can comfortably exist while seeing nothing; but there is this difference that they are not blind by choice. A man who is married is no longer master of his destiny, and carries a compensation along with him wherever he may go. But what can bring to Nebraska a lone, unfettered bachelor, who has all the world before him and might starve, if he preferred, in London or New York?⟩

One person at least I saw upon the plains who seemed in every way superior to her lot. This was a woman who boarded us at a way-station, selling milk. She was largely formed; her features were more than comely; she had that great rarity – a fine complexion which became her; and her eyes were kind, dark, and steady. She sold milk with patriarchal grace. There was not a line in her countenance, not a note in her soft and sleepy voice, but spoke of an entire contentment with her life. It would have been fatuous arrogance to pity such a woman. Yet the place where she lived was to me almost ghastly. Less than a dozen wooden houses, all of a shape and all nearly of a size, stood planted along the railway lines. Each stood apart in its own lot. Each opened direct off the billiard-board, as if it were a billiard-board indeed, and these only models that had been set down upon it ready-made. Her own, into which I looked, was clean but very empty, and showed nothing home-like but the burning fire. This extreme newness, above all in so naked and flat a country, gives a strong impression of artificiality. With none of the litter and discoloration of human life; with the paths unworn, and the houses still sweating from the axe, such a settlement as this seems purely scenic. The mind is loth to accept it for a piece of reality; and it seems incredible that life can go on with so few properties, or the great child, man, find entertainment in so bare a play-room.

And truly it is as yet an incomplete society in some points; or at least it contained, as I passed through, one person incompletely civilised. At North Platte, where we supped that evening, one man asked another to pass the milk-jug. This other was well-dressed and of what we should call a respectable appearance; a darkish man, high spoken, eating as though he had some usage of society; but he turned upon the first speaker with extraordinary vehemence of tone——

'There's a waiter here!' he cried.

'I only asked you to pass the milk,' explained the first.

Here is the retort verbatim——

'Pass! Hell! I'm not paid for that business; the waiter's paid for it. You should use civility at table, and, by God, I'll show you how!'

⟨He would show him how! I wonder what would be his charge for the twelve lessons. And this explosion, you will not forget, was to save himself the trouble of moving a milk jug a distance of perhaps thirty inches.⟩

The other man very wisely made no answer, and the bully went on with his supper as though nothing had occurred. It pleases me to think that some day soon he will meet with one of his own kidney; and that perhaps both may fall.

The Desert of Wyoming

To cross such a plain is to grow home-sick for the mountains. I longed for the Black Hills of Wyoming, which I knew we were soon to enter, like an ice-bound whaler for the spring. Alas! and it was a worse country than the other. All Sunday and Monday we travelled through these sad mountains, or over the main ridge of the Rockies, which is a fair match to them for misery of aspect. Hour after hour it was the same unhomely and unkindly

world about our onward path; tumbled boulders, cliffs that
drearily imitate the shape of monuments and fortifications –
how drearily, how tamely, none can tell who has not seen them;
not a tree, not a patch of sward, not one shapely or commanding
mountain form; sage-brush, eternal sage-brush;[34] over all, the
same weariful and gloomy colouring, greys warming into
brown, greys darkening towards black; and for sole sign of life,
here and there a few fleeing antelopes; here and there, but at
incredible intervals, a creek running in a cañon.[35] The plains
have a grandeur of their own; but here there is nothing but a
contorted smallness. Except for the air, which was light and
stimulating, there was not one good circumstance in that
God-forsaken land.

⟨I had, as I must tell you, been suffering a good deal all the
way, from what the gentleman at New York was pleased to call
my liver. The hot weather and the fever put into my blood by
so much continuous travel, had aggravated these symptoms till
they were strangely difficult to bear. When the fit was on me, I
grew almost light headed. I had to make a second cigarette
before the first was smoked, for tobacco alone gave me self
command under these paroxysms of irritation. Fancy will give
you no clew to what I endured; the basis was, as you might say,
a mere annoyance; but when an annoyance is continued day
and night and assumes by starts an absolute control upon your
mind, not much remains to distinguish it from pain. I am obliged
to touch upon this, but with a delicacy which the reader will
appreciate, not only because it is a part of emigrant experience,
but because it must stand as my excuse for many sins of omission
in this chronicle.⟩

I had been suffering in my health a good deal all the way; and
at last, whether I was exhausted by my complaint or poisoned
in some wayside eating-house, the evening we left Laramie,[36] I
fell sick outright. That was a night which I shall not readily
forget. The lamps did not go out; each made a faint shining in
its own neighbourhood, and the shadows were confounded
together in the long, hollow box of the car. The sleepers lay in
uneasy attitudes; here two chums alongside, flat upon their
backs like dead folk; there a man sprawling on the floor, with

his face upon his arm; there another half-seated with his head and shoulders on the bench. The most passive were continually and roughly shaken by the movement of the train; others stirred, turned, or stretched out their arms like children; it was surprising how many groaned and murmured in their sleep; and as I passed to and fro, stepping across the prostrate, and caught now a snore, now a gasp, now a half-formed word, it gave me a measure of the worthlessness of rest in that unresting vehicle. Although it was chill, I was obliged to open my window, for the degradation of the air soon became intolerable to one who was awake and using the full supply of life. Outside, in a glimmering night, I saw the black, amorphous hills shoot by unweariedly into our wake. They that long for morning have never longed for it more earnestly than I.

And yet when day came, it was to shine upon the same broken and unsightly quarter of the world. Mile upon mile, and not a tree, a bird, or a river. Only down the long, sterile cañons, the train shot hooting and awoke the resting echo. That train was the one piece of life in all the deadly land; it was the one actor, the one spectacle fit to be observed in this paralysis of man and nature. And when I think how the railroad has been pushed through this unwatered wilderness and haunt of savage tribes, and now will bear an emigrant for some twelve pounds from the Atlantic to the Golden Gates;[37] how at each stage of the construction, roaring, impromptu cities, full of gold and lust and death, sprang up and then died away again, and are now but wayside stations in the desert; how in these uncouth places pig-tailed Chinese pirates worked side by side with border ruffians and broken men from Europe, talking together in a mixed dialect, mostly oaths, gambling, drinking, quarrelling and murdering like wolves; how the plumed hereditary lord of all America heard, in this last fastness, the scream of the 'bad medicine-waggon' charioting his foes; and then when I go on to remember that all this epical turmoil was conducted by gentlemen in frock coats, and with a view to nothing more extraordinary than a fortune and a subsequent visit to Paris, it seems to me, I own, as if this railway were the one typical achievement of the age in which we live, as if it brought together into one plot all the ends of the world and all the degrees of social rank, and offered to some great writer the busiest, the most extended, and the most varied subject for an enduring literary work. If it be romance, if it be contrast, if it be heroism that we require, what was Troy[38] town to this? But, alas! it is not these things that are necessary – it is only Homer.

Here also we are grateful to the train, as to some god who conducts us swiftly through these shades and by so many hidden perils. Thirst, hunger, the sleight and ferocity of Indians are all no more feared, so lightly do we skim these horrible lands; as the gull, who wings safely through the hurricane and past the shark. Yet we should not be forgetful of these hardships of the past; and to keep the balance true, since I have complained of the trifling discomforts of my journey, perhaps more than was enough, let me add an original document. It was not written by Homer, but by a boy of eleven[39] long since dead, and is dated only twenty years ago. I shall punctuate, to make things clearer, but not change the spelling.

> 'My dear sister Mary, – I am afraid you will go nearly crazy when you read my letter. If Jerry' (the writer's eldest brother) 'has not written to you before now, you will be surprised to heare that we are in California, and that poor Thomas' (another brother, of fifteen) 'is dead. We started from —— in July, with plenty of provisions and too yoke oxen. We went along very well till we got within six or seven hundred miles of California, when the Indians attacked us. We found places where they had killed the emigrants. We had one passenger with us, too guns, and one revolver; so we ran all the lead We had into bullets (and) hung the guns up in the wagon so that we could get at them in a minit. It was about two o'clock in the afternoon; droave the cattel a little way; when a prairie chicken[40] alited a little way from the wagon.

> 'Jerry took out one of the guns to shoot it, and told Tom to drive the oxen. Tom and I drove the oxen, and Jerry and the passenger went on. Then, after a little, I left Tom and caught up with Jerry and the other man. Jerry stopped for Tom to come up; me and the man went on and sit down by a little stream. In a few

minutes, we heard some noise; then three shots (they all struck poor Tom, I suppose); then they gave the war hoop,[41] and as many as twenty of the red skins came down upon us. The three that shot Tom was hid by the side of the road in the bushes.

'I thought the Tom and Jerry were shot; so I told the other man that Tom and Jerry were dead, and that we had better try to escape, if possible. I had no shoes on; having a sore foot, I thought I would not put them on. The man and me run down the road, but We was soon stopt by an Indian on a pony. We then turend the other way, and run up the side of the Mountain, and hid behind some cedar trees, and stayed there till dark. The Indians hunted all over after us, and verry close to us, so close that we could here there tomyhawks Jingle. At dark the man and me started on, I stubing my toes against sticks and stones. We traveld on all night; and next morning, Just as it was getting gray, we saw something in the shape of a man. It layed Down in the grass. We went up to it, and it was Jerry. He thought we ware Indians. You can imagine how glad he was to see me. He thought we was all dead but him, and we thought him and Tom was dead. He had the gun that he took out of the wagon to shoot the prairie Chicken; all he had was the load that was in it.

'We traveld on till about eight o'clock, We caught up with one wagon with too men in it. We had traveld with them before one day; we stopt and they Drove on; we knew that they was ahead of us, unless they had been killed to. My feet was so sore when we caught up with them that I had to ride; I could not step. We traveld on for too days, when the men that owned the cattle said they would (could) not drive them another inch. We unyoked the oxen; we had about seventy pounds of flour; we took it out and divided it into four packs. Each of the men took about 18 pounds apiece and a blanket. I carried a little bacon, dried meat, and little quilt; I had in all about twelve pounds. We had one pint of flour a day for our alloyance. Sometimes we made soup of it; sometimes we (made) pancakes; and sometimes mixed it up with cold water and eat it that way. We traveld twelve or fourteen days. The time came at last when we should have to reach some place or starve. We saw fresh horse and cattle tracks. The morning come, we scraped all the flour out of the sack, mixed it up, and baked it

*into bread, and made some soup, and eat everything we had. We
traveld on all day without anything to eat, and that evening we
Caught up with a sheep train of eight wagons. We traveld with
them till we arrived at the settlements; and know I am safe in
California, and got to good home, and going to school.*

*'Jerry is working in——. It is a good country. You can get from
50 to 60.75 Dollars for cooking. Tell me all about the affairs in
the States, and how all the folks get along.'*

And so ends this artless narrative. The little man was at school
again, God bless him! while his brother lay scalped upon the
deserts

Fellow-Passengers

At Ogden we changed cars from the Union Pacific to the Central
Pacific line of railroad. The change was doubly welcome; for,
first, we had better cars on the new line; and, second, those in
which we had been cooped for more than ninety hours had
begun to stink abominably. Several yards away, as we returned,
let us say from dinner, our nostrils were assailed by rancid air.
I have stood on a platform while the whole train was shunting;
and as the dwelling-cars drew near, there would come a whiff
of pure menagerie, only a little sourer, as from men instead of
monkeys. I think we are human only in virtue of open windows.
Without fresh air, you only require a bad heart, and a remarkable command of the Queen's English, to become such another
as Dean Swift;[42] a kind of leering, human goat, leaping and
wagging your scut on mountains of offence. I do my best to
keep my head the other way, and look for the human rather
than the bestial in this Yahoo-like business of the emigrant train.
But one thing I must say, the car of the Chinese was notably the
least offensive⟨, and that of the women and children by a good
way the worst. A stroke of nature's satire⟩.

The cars on the Central Pacific were nearly twice as high, and
so proportionally airier; they were freshly varnished, which gave

us all a sense of cleanliness as though we had bathed; the seats drew out and joined in the centre, so that there was no more need for bed boards; and there was an upper tier of berths which could be closed by day and opened at night. ⟨Thus in every way the accommodation was more cheerful and comfortable, and every one might have a bed to lie on if he pleased. The company deserve our thanks. It was the first sign I could observe of any kindly purpose towards the emigrant. For myself it was, in some ways, a fatal change; for it fell to me to sleep in one of the lofts; and that I found to be impossible. The air was always bad enough at the level of the floor. But my bed was four feet higher, immediately under the roof, and shut into a kind of Saratoga trunk with one side partly open. And there, unless you were the Prince of Camby,[43] it were madness to attempt to sleep. Though the fumes were narcotic and weighed upon the eyelids, yet they so smartly irritated the lungs that I could only lie and cough. I spent the better part of one night walking to and fro and envying my neighbours.⟩

I had by this time some opportunity of seeing the people whom I was among. They were in rather marked contrast to the emigrants I had met on board ship while crossing the Atlantic. ⟨There was both less talent and less good manners; I believe I should add less good feeling, though that is implied. Kindness will out; and a man who is gentle will contrive to be a gentleman.⟩ They were mostly lumpish fellows, silent and noisy, a common combination; somewhat sad, I should say, with an extraordinary poor taste in humour, and little interest in their fellow-creatures beyond that of a cheap and merely external curiosity. If they heard a man's name and business, they seemed to think they had the heart of that mystery; but they were as eager to know that much as they were indifferent to the rest. Some of them were on nettles till they learned your name was Dickson and you a journeyman baker; but beyond that, whether you were Catholic or Mormon, dull or clever, fierce or friendly, was all one to them. Others who were not so stupid, gossiped a little, and, I am bound to say, unkindly. A favourite witticism was for some lout to raise the alarm of 'All aboard!' while the rest of us were dining, thus contributing his mite to the general discomfort. Such a one was always much applauded for his high spirits. When I was ill coming through Wyoming, I was astonished – fresh from the eager humanity on board ship – to meet with little but laughter. One of the young men even amused himself by incommoding me, as was then very easy; and that not from ill-nature, but mere clod-like incapacity to think, for he expected me to join the laughter. I did so, but it was phantom merriment. Later on, a man from Kansas had three violent epileptic fits, and though, of course, there were not wanting some to help him, it was rather superstitious terror than sympathy that his case evoked among his fellow-passengers. 'Oh, I hope he's not going to die!' cried a woman; 'it would be terrible to have a dead body!' And there was a very general movement to leave the man behind at the next station. This, by good fortune, the conductor negatived.

There was a good deal of story-telling in some quarters; in others, little but silence. In this society, more than any other that ever I was in, it was the narrator alone who seemed to enjoy the narrative. It was rarely that any one listened for the listening. If he lent an ear to another man's story, it was because he was in immediate want of a hearer for one of his own. Food and the progress of the train were the subjects most generally treated; many joined to discuss these who otherwise would hold their tongues. One small knot had no better occupation than to worm out of me my name; and the more they tried, the more obstinately fixed I grew to baffle them. They assailed me with artful questions and insidious offers of correspondence in the future; but I was perpetually on my guard, and parried their assaults with inward laughter. I am sure Dubuque would have given me ten dollars for the secret. He owed me far more, had he understood life, for thus preserving him a lively interest throughout the journey. I met one of my fellow-passengers months after, driving a street tramway car in San Francisco; and, as the joke was now out of season, told him my name without subterfuge. You never saw a man more chop-fallen. But had my name been Demogorgon,[44] after so prolonged a mystery he had still been disappointed.

There were no emigrants direct from Europe – save one

German family and a knot of Cornish miners who kept grimly
by themselves, one reading the New Testament all day long
through steel spectacles, the rest discussing privately the secrets
of their old-world, mysterious race. Lady Hester Stanhope[45]
believed she could make something great of the Cornish; for my
part, I can make nothing of them at all. A division of races,
older and more original than that of Babel, keeps this close,
esoteric family apart from neighbouring Englishmen. Not even
a Red Indian seems more foreign in my eyes. This is one of the
lessons of travel – that some of the strangest races dwell next
door to you at home.

The rest were all American born, but they came from almost
every quarter of that continent. All the States of the North had
sent out a fugitive to cross the plains with me. From Virginia,
from Pennsylvania, from New York, from far western Iowa and
Kansas, from Maine that borders on the Canadas, and from the
Canadas themselves – some one or two were fleeing in quest of
a better land and better wages. The talk in the train, like the talk
I heard on the steamer, ran upon hard times, short commons,[46]
and hope that moves ever westward. I thought of my shipful
from Great Britain with a feeling of despair. They had come
3,000 miles, and yet not far enough. Hard times bowed them
out of the Clyde, and stood to welcome them at Sandy Hook.
Where were they to go? Pennsylvania, Maine, Iowa, Kansas?
These were not places for immigration, but for emigration, it
appeared; not one of them, but I knew a man who had lifted up
his heel and left it for an ungrateful country. And it was still
westward that they ran. Hunger, you would have thought, came
out of the east like the sun, and the evening was made of edible
gold. And, meantime, in the car in front of me, were there not
half a hundred emigrants from the opposite quarter? Hungry
Europe and hungry China, each pouring from their gates in
search of provender, had here come face to face. The two waves
had met; east and west had alike failed; the whole round world
had been prospected and condemned; there was no El Dorado[47]
anywhere; and till one could emigrate to the moon, it seemed as
well to stay patiently at home. Nor was there wanting another
sign, at once more picturesque and more disheartening; for, as

we continued to steam westward toward the land of gold, we were continually passing other emigrant trains upon the journey east; and these were as crowded as our own. Had all these return voyagers made a fortune in the mines? Were they all bound for Paris, and to be in Rome by Easter? It would seem not, for, whenever we met them, the passengers ran on the platform and cried to us through the windows, in a kind of wailing chorus, to 'Come back.' On the plains of Nebraska, in the mountains of Wyoming, it was still the same cry, and dismal to my heart, 'Come back!' That was what we heard by the way 'about the good country we were going to.' And at that very hour the Sand-lot[48] of San Francisco was crowded with the unemployed, and the echo from the other side of Market Street was repeating the rant of demagogues.

If, in truth, it were only for the sake of wages that men emigrate, how many thousands would regret the bargain! But wages, indeed, are only one consideration out of many; for we are a race of gipsies, and love change and travel for themselves.

Despised Races

Of all stupid ill-feelings, the sentiment of my fellow-Caucasians towards our companions in the Chinese car was the most stupid and the worst. They seemed never to have looked at them, listened to them, or thought of them, but hated them *a priori*.[49] The Mongols were their enemies in that cruel and treacherous battle-field of money. They could work better and cheaper in half a hundred industries, and hence there was no calumny too idle for the Caucasians to repeat, and even to believe. They declared them hideous vermin, and affected a kind of choking in the throat when they beheld them. Now, as a matter of fact, the young Chinese man is so like a large class of European women, that on raising my head and suddenly catching sight of one at a considerable distance, I have for an instant been deceived by the resemblance. I do not say it is the most attractive class of our women, but for all that many a man's wife is less

pleasantly favoured. Again, my emigrants declared that the
Chinese were dirty. I cannot say they were clean, for that was
impossible upon the journey; but in their efforts after cleanliness
they put the rest of us to shame. We all pigged and stewed in
one infamy, wet our hands and faces for half a minute daily on
the platform, and were unashamed. But the Chinese never lost
an opportunity, and you would see them washing their feet – an
act not dreamed of among ourselves – and going as far as
decency permitted to wash their whole bodies. I may remark by
the way that the dirtier people are in their persons the more
delicate is their sense of modesty. A clean man strips in a
crowded boathouse; but he who is unwashed slinks in and out
of bed without uncovering an inch of skin. Lastly, these very foul
and malodorous Caucasians entertained the surprising illusion
that it was the Chinese waggon, and that alone, which stank. I
have said already that it was the exception, and notably the
freshest of the three.

These judgments are typical of the feeling in all Western
America. The Chinese are considered stupid, because they are
imperfectly acquainted with English. They are held to be base
because their dexterity and frugality enable them to underbid
the lazy, luxurious Caucasian. They are said to be thieves; I am
sure they have no monopoly of that. They are called cruel; the
Anglo-Saxon and the cheerful Irishman may each reflect before
he bears the accusation. ⟨It comes amiss from John Bull, who the
other day forced that unhappy Zazel, all bruised and tottering
from a dangerous escape, to come forth again upon the theatre,
and continue to risk her life for his amusement; or from Pat,[50]
who makes it his pastime to shoot down the compliant farmer
from behind a wall in Europe, or to stone the solitary Chinaman
in California.⟩ I am told, again, that they are of the race of river
pirates, and belong to the most despised and dangerous class in
the Celestial Empire. But if this be so, what remarkable pirates
have we here! and what must be the virtues, the industry, the
education, and the intelligence of their superiors at home!

A while ago it was the Irish, now it is the Chinese that must
go. Such is the cry. It seems, after all, that no country is bound
to submit to immigration any more than to invasion: each is

war to the knife, and resistance to either but legitimate defence. Yet we may regret the free tradition of the republic, which loved to depict herself with open arms, welcoming all unfortunates. And certainly, as a man who believes that he loves freedom, I may be excused some bitterness when I find her sacred name misused in the contention. It was but the other day that I heard a vulgar fellow[51] in the Sand-lot, the popular tribune of San Francisco, roaring for arms and butchery. 'At the call of Abreham Lincoln,' said the orator, 'ye rose in the name of freedom to set free the negroes; can ye not rise and liberate yourselves from a few dhirty Mongolians?'[52] ⟨It exceeds the license of an Irishman to rebaptise our selfish interests by the name of virtue. Defend your bellies, if you must; I, who do not suffer, am no judge in your affairs; but let me defend language, which is the dialect and one of the ramparts of virtue.⟩

For my own part, I could not look but with wonder and respect on the Chinese. Their forefathers watched the stars before mine had begun to keep pigs. Gunpowder and printing, which the other day we imitated, and a school of manners which we never had the delicacy so much as to desire to imitate, were theirs in a long-past antiquity. They walk the earth with us, but it seems they must be of different clay. They hear the clock strike the same hour, yet surely of a different epoch. They travel by steam conveyance, yet with such a baggage of old Asiatic thoughts and superstitions as might check the locomotive in its course. Whatever is thought within the circuit of the Great Wall;[53] what the wry-eyed, spectacled schoolmaster teaches in the hamlets round Pekin; religions so old that our language looks a halfling boy alongside; philosophy so wise that our best philosophers find things therein to wonder at; all this travelled alongside of me for thousands of miles over plain and mountain. Heaven knows if we had one common thought or fancy all that way, or whether our eyes, which yet were formed upon the same design, beheld the same world out of the railway windows. And when either of us turned his thoughts to home and childhood, what a strange dissimilarity must there not have been in these pictures of the mind – when I beheld that old, grey, castled city,[54] high throned above the firth, with the flag of Britain flying, and the red-coat sentry pacing over all; and the man in the next car to me would conjure up some junks and a pagoda and a fort of porcelain, and call it, with the same affection, home.

Another race shared among my fellow-passengers in the disfavour of the Chinese; and that, it is hardly necessary to say, was the noble red man of old story – he over whose own hereditary continent we had been steaming all these days. I saw no wild or independent Indian; indeed, I hear that such avoid the neighbourhood of the train; but now and again at waystations, a husband and wife and a few children, disgracefully dressed out with the sweepings of civilisation, came forth and stared upon the emigrants. The silent stoicism of their conduct, and the pathetic degradation of their appearance, would have touched any thinking creature, but my fellow-passengers danced and jested round them with a truly Cockney[55] baseness. I was ashamed for the thing we call civilisation. We should carry upon our consciences so much at least, of our forefathers' misconduct as we continue to profit by ourselves.

If oppression drives a wise man mad, what should be raging in the hearts of these poor tribes, who have been driven back and back, step after step, their promised reservations torn from them one after another as the States extended westward, until at length they are shut up into these hideous mountain deserts of the centre – and even there find themselves invaded, insulted, and hunted out by ruffianly diggers? The eviction of the Cherokees[56] (to name but an instance), the extortion of Indian agents, the outrages of the wicked, the ill-faith of all, nay, down to the ridicule of such poor beings as were here with me upon the train, make up a chapter of injustice and indignity such as a man must be in some ways base if his heart will suffer him to pardon or forget. These old, well-founded, historical hatreds have a savour of nobility for the independent. That the Jew should not love the Christian, nor the Irishman love the English, nor the Indian brave tolerate the thought of the American, is not disgraceful to the nature of man; rather, indeed, honourable, since it depends on wrongs ancient like the race, and not personal to him who cherishes the indignation.

⟨As for the Indians, there are of course many unteachable and wedded to war and their wild habits; but many also who, with fairer usage, might learn the virtues of the peaceful state. You will find a valley in the county of Monterey, drained by the river of Carmel: a true Californian valley, bare, dotted with chaparral,[57] overlooked by quaint, unfinished hills. The Carmel runs by many pleasant farms, a clear and shallow river, loved by wading kine; and at last, as it is falling towards a quicksand and the great Pacific, passes a ruined mission on a hill. From the church the eye embraces a great field of ocean, and the ear is filled with a continuous sound of distant breakers on the shore. The roof has fallen; the ground squirrel[58] scampers on the graves; the holy bell of St Charles is long dismounted; yet one day in every year the church awakes from silence, and the Indians return to worship in the church of their converted fathers. I have seen them trooping thither, young and old, in their clean print dresses, with those strange, handsome, melancholy features, which seem predestined to a national calamity and it was notable to hear the old Latin words and old Gregorian music sung, with nasal fervour, and in a swift, staccato style, by a trained chorus of Red Indian men and women. In the huts of the Rancherie[59] they have ancient European Mass-books, in which they study together to be perfect. An old blind man was their leader. With his eyes bandaged, and leaning on a staff, he was led into his place in church by a little grandchild. He had seen changes in the world since first he sang that music sixty years ago, when there was no gold and no Yankees, and he and his people lived in plenty under the wing of the kind priests. The mission church is in ruins; the Rancherie, they tell me, encroached upon by Yankee newcomers; the little age of gold is over for the Indian; but he has had a breathing-space in Carmel valley before he goes down to the dust with his red fathers.)

To the Golden Gates

A little corner of Utah is soon traversed, and leaves no particular impressions on the mind. By an early hour on Wednesday morning we stopped to breakfast at Toano,[60] a little station on a bleak, high-lying plateau in Nevada. The man who kept the station eating-house was a Scot, and learning that I was the same, he grew very friendly, and gave me some advice on the country I was now entering. 'You see,' said he, 'I tell you this, because I come from your country.' Hail, brither[61] Scots!

His most important hint was on the moneys of this part of the world. There is something in the simplicity of a decimal coinage[62] which is revolting to the human mind; thus the French, in small affairs, reckon strictly by halfpence; and you have to solve, by a spasm of mental arithmetic, such posers as thirty-two, forty-five, or even a hundred halfpence. In the Pacific states they have made a bolder push for complexity, and settle their affairs by a coin that no longer exists – the *bit*, or old Mexican real. The supposed value of the bit is twelve and a half cents, eight to the dollar. When it comes to two bits, the quarter-dollar stands for the required amount. But how about an odd bit? The nearest coin to it is a dime,[63] which is short by a fifth. That, then, is called a *short bit*. If you have one, you lay it triumphantly down, and save two and a half cents. But if you have not, and lay down a quarter, the bar-keeper or shopman calmly tenders you a dime by way of change; and thus you have paid what is called a *long bit*, and lost two and a half cents, or even, by comparison with a short bit, five cents. In country places all over the Pacific coast, nothing lower than a bit is ever asked or taken, which vastly increases the cost of life; as even for a glass of beer you must pay fivepence or sevenpence-halfpenny, as the case may be. You would say that this system of mutual robbery was as broad as it was long; but I have discovered a plan to make it broader, with which I here endow the public. It is brief and simple – radiantly simple. There is one place where five cents are recognised, and that is the post-office. A quarter is only worth two bits, a short and a long. Whenever you have a quarter, go to the post-office and buy five cents' worth of postage-stamps; you will receive in change two dimes, that is, two short bits. The purchasing power of your money is undiminished. You can go and have your two glasses of beer all the same; and you have made yourself a present of five cents' worth of postage-stamps into the bargain. Benjamin Franklin would have patted me on the head for this discovery.

From Toano we travelled all day through deserts of alkali and sand, horrible to man, and bare sage-brush country that seemed little kindlier, and came by supper-time to Elko.[64] As we were standing, after our manner, outside the station, I saw two men whip suddenly from underneath the cars, and take to their heels across country. They were tramps, it appeared, who had been riding on the beams since eleven of the night before; and several of my fellow-passengers had already seen and conversed with them while we broke our fast at Toano. These land stowaways play a great part over here in America, and I should have liked dearly to become acquainted with them.

At Elko an odd circumstance befell me. I was coming out from supper, when I was stopped by a small, stout, ruddy man, followed by two others taller and ruddier than himself.

'Ex-cuse me, sir,' he said, 'but do you happen to be going on?'

I said I was, whereupon he said he hoped to dissuade me to desist from that intention. He had a situation to offer me, and if we could come to terms, why, good and well. 'You see,' he continued, 'I'm running a theatre here, and we're a little short in the orchestra. You're a musician, I guess?'

I assured him that, beyond a rudimentary acquaintance with 'Auld Lang Syne' and 'The Wearing of the Green,'[65] I had no pretension whatever to that style. He seemed much put out of countenance; and one of his taller companions asked him, on the nail, for five dollars.

'You see, sir,' added the latter to me, 'he bet you were a musician; I bet you weren't. No offence, I hope?'

'None whatever,' I said, and the two withdrew to the bar, where I presume the debt was liquidated.

This little adventure woke bright hopes in my fellow-travellers, who thought they had now come to a country where situations went a-begging. But I am not so sure that the offer was in good faith. Indeed, I am more than half persuaded it was but a feeler to decide the bet.

Of all the next day I will tell you nothing, for the best of all reasons, that I remember no more than that we continued through desolate and desert scenes, fiery hot and deadly weary. But some time after I had fallen asleep that night, I was awakened by one of my companions. It was in vain that I resisted. A fire of enthusiasm and whisky burned in his eyes; and he declared we were in a new country, and I must come forth upon the platform and see with my own eyes. The train was then, in its patient way, standing halted in a by-track. It was a clear, moonlit night; but the valley was too narrow to admit the moonshine direct, and only a diffused glimmer whitened the tall rocks and relieved the blackness of the pines. A hoarse clamour filled the air; it was the continuous plunge of a cascade somewhere near at hand among the mountains. The air struck chill, but tasted good and vigorous in the nostrils – a fine, dry, old mountain atmosphere. I was dead sleepy, but I returned to roost with a grateful mountain feeling at my heart.

When I awoke next morning, I was puzzled for a while to know if it were day or night, for the illumination was unusual. I sat up at last, and found we were grading slowly downward through a long snowshed; and suddenly we shot into an open; and before we were swallowed into the next length of wooden tunnel, I had one glimpse of a huge pine-forested ravine upon my left, a foaming river, and a sky already coloured with the fires of dawn. I am usually very calm over the displays of nature; but you will scarce believe how my heart leaped at this. It was like meeting one's wife. I had come home again – home from unsightly deserts to the green and habitable corners of the earth. Every spire of pine along the hill-top, every trouty pool along that mountain river, was more dear to me than a blood relation. Few people have praised God more happily than I did. And thenceforward, down by Blue Cañon, Alta, Dutch Flat,[66] and all the old mining camps, through a sea of mountain forests, dropping thousands of feet toward the far sea-level as we went, not I only, but all the passengers on board, threw off their sense of dirt and heat and weariness, and bawled like school boys, and thronged with shining eyes upon the platform and became new creatures within and without. The sun no longer oppressed us with heat, it only shone laughingly along the mountain-side, until we were fain to laugh ourselves for glee. At every turn we could see farther into the land and our own happy futures. At every town the cocks were tossing their clear notes into the golden air, and crowing for the new day and the new country. For this was indeed our destination; this was 'the good country' we had been going to so long.

By afternoon we were at Sacramento, the city of gardens in a plain of corn; and the next day before the dawn we were lying-to upon the Oakland side of San Francisco Bay. The day was breaking as we crossed the ferry; the fog was rising over the citied hills of San Francisco; the bay was perfect – not a ripple, scarce a stain, upon its blue expanse; everything was waiting, breathless, for the sun. A spot of cloudy gold lit first upon the head of Tamalpais,[67] and then widened downward on its shapely shoulder; the air seemed to awaken, and began to sparkle; and suddenly

'The tall hills Titan discovered,'[68]

and the city of San Francisco, and the bay of gold and corn, were lit from end to end with summer daylight.

Notes

TRAVELS WITH A DONKEY IN THE CÉVENNES

CJ = Cévennes Journal

DEDICATION

1. *Sidney Colvin*: Sir Sidney Colvin (1845–1927), Slade Professor of Fine Art at Cambridge and Keeper of Prints at the British Museum. He was Stevenson's literary executor and published editions of his works and letters.
2. *John Bunyan*: Puritan writer (1628–88), whose most famous work is *The Pilgrim's Progress* (1678), an allegory of life as a journey past the temptations of this world to salvation in the next.

VELAY

1. *Velay*: A region in the Massif Central, covering most of the Haute-Loire department.
2. *Sophocles*: From his play *Antigone*, second chorus, 332f. Sophocles, the Greek tragedian, lived in Athens in the fifth century BC.
3. *Job*: 39:5.
4. *Legitimists, Orleanists, Imperialists, and Republicans*: Nineteenth-century French political factions: the Legitimists wished to see the restoration of the Bourbon kings of France; the Orleanists were also monarchists, but supported a rival branch of the royal family; the Imperialists desired a return to the glory of the reign of the Emperor Napoleon; and the Republicans stood for the principles of the French Revolution at the end of the eighteenth century.

5.   *Poland ... Babylon*: Polish political factionalism, which was thought to have encouraged the dismemberment of Poland by Austria, Prussia and Russia in the eighteenth century, was almost proverbial. Babylon, the ancient city in Mesopotamia (modern Iraq), was the centre of the Assyrian Empire; but here Stevenson may mean Babel, synonymous with verbal discord, for according to Genesis 11:9 it was here that God made people speak different languages.

6.   *Father Adam*: A pedlar whose name was in fact Surrel. He sold calendars, almanacs and other goods in the local villages.

7.   *pilot-coat ... spencer*: The first, also known as a reefer or pea-coat, was a short, heavy topcoat made of thick blue cloth worn by sailors; the second was a waist-length jacket.

8.   *Bologna sausage*: Cooked, smoked sausage, originally from Bologna in Italy.

9.   *Christian*: The hero of Bunyan's *Pilgrim's Progress*; his burden represents his sins.

10. *as an ox goeth to the slaughter*: Proverbs 7:22.

11. *through the common*: Instead of this sentence *CJ* (p. 29) has: 'The bells of Monastier were just knocking nine as I got quit of all my troubles and descended through the common.' Such stylistic adjustments are typical of the more minor changes Stevenson made to his journal in preparing it for publication.

12. *Englishman*: Stevenson often refers to himself as English, perhaps in this instance ironically. When later he arrives at the monastery of Our Lady of the Snows, he introduces himself as a Scotsman.

13. *Alais*: This French spelling was replaced after Stevenson's time by the local dialect version Alès.

14. *Et vous marchez comme ça*: And you walk like that!

15. *deus ex machinâ*: Literally, the god out of the machine (Latin), a reference to the convention of divine intervention to settle the characters' difficulties at the climax of a classical drama.

16. *Proot*: Surely an Anglicized spelling of 'Proute!', the singular imperative of the French verb *prouter*, 'to fart'. The peasant was making fun of Stevenson, but he probably realized (see the reference to orthography later in the paragraph) and used the joke himself.

17. *It is only a traveller ... the warmth of sunlight*: These three sentences replace the following passage in *CJ* (pp. 30–31):

     A whole country laid at rest, with its going ploughs and mills arrested, and no one without doors but yourself, is surely striking

to behold, and seems a noble way to worship God and recognise the
littleness of our pursuits. The far-spread unusual silence, which
makes the birds sing so much louder, impresses you with the sense
as of a great sea, and the two ideas of the Sabbath and the Ocean
are, I find, inextricably connected in my mind. The great ascetic
feast; one day of Buddhism after every six of striving Xtianity. The
sounds of Psalms from a church, the thought of a similar sound in
every parish throughout the length and breadth of the land, streaming to heaven and away over Europe to where 'Kedar's wilderness
afar, lifts up its lonely voice'.

The quotation in the line above is from *Scottish Paraphrase 23*
(Isaiah 42:1–13), 53f. The *Scottish Paraphrases* are a collection
of biblical passages versified for singing, often to psalm tunes,
and used in the Church of Scotland since the eighteenth century.

18. *Homer's Cyclops*: The one-eyed giant Polyphemus who captures
Odysseus and his crew in Book 9 of Homer's epic poem the *Odyssey*.

19. *Régis Senac*: French fencing instructor who arrived in New York
in 1872; he set up a fencing school and took part in fencing
competitions and displays, including some at Tammany Hall,
notorious now as the centre of a political pressure group that
became synonymous with local government corruption.

20. *like a sucking-dove*: In Shakespeare's *A Midsummer Night's
Dream* Bottom, offering to play the part of a lion without frighten-
ing the audience, declares he will 'roar you as gently as any
sucking dove' (I.ii).

21. *bastinado*: Beating with a stick, a form of punishment or torture,
especially when applied to the soles of the feet.

22. *the whole hypothec*: A Scots expression meaning 'everything',
'the whole lot'.

23. *It was the most despicable fix*: This sentence replaces in *CJ* (p. 32):
'Just then, one of the children came in my road, as I was stepping
backwards, and my fury, rejoicing to find a vent, poured forth
upon the urchin in a few well-selected terms. That was a relief,
which I do not mean to despise; it was timely and did me good
service; but it did not alter the circumstances.'

24. *through the village*: Stevenson here omits the interjection 'Venom-
ous animal!' (*CJ*, p. 33).

25. *general average*: A legal principle according to which all parties
in a sea venture proportionately share any losses resulting from a
voluntary and successful sacrifice of part of the ship or cargo to
save the whole in an emergency; here Stevenson means that,

having thrown away his own bread supply, he did not apply general average and discard Modestine's as well.

26. *although this last was dear to my heart*: This continues in *CJ* (p. 33): 'and had been presented to me not long before by the lady of a castle in the neighbourhood of Shepherd's Bush'. The lady was the wife of Stevenson's friend, the poet and critic W. E. Henley (1849–1903); Shepherd's Bush is a district of London.

27. *cruelly I chastised her*: The following passage from *CJ* (pp. 33–4) is here omitted:

> As I passed through Costaros, an ugly village on the highroad, the people pretended to be hurt and shocked by my brutality. 'Ah,' they cried, 'look how tired she is, the poor beast!' And one man, into whose front apartment the little, cross-grained, long-eared limmer [bitch] made a bolt, had the indecency to tell me she was overladen. 'Have you a donkey of your own?' cried I, the devil once more rising into my mouth. He admitted he had. 'How much does she carry?' said I. I think it was five quintals [hundredweights: approximately 560 pounds] that he said. 'Very well then, feel the weight of that and mind your own affairs – unless you would like to help me carry my basket?' It was my first popular success of the day; all the Sunday loiterers joined in a laugh against my interlocutor. 'Cependant,' added another Costarosian, 'elle est petite – il ne faut pas trop la presser.' The miserable creature did not know I was fighting against time . . .

The French remark may be translated: 'But she's small – you should not hurry her too much.'

28. *my unwearying bastinado*: This sentence in *CJ* (p. 34) is omitted here: 'I used to think General Scarlet must have been a very strong man to do moulinade for eight minutes, and yet here am I, no very athletic figure, a thread-paper, drawing room being, who beat a donkey, unremittingly, up all the long hill from Goudet.' General James Scarlet commanded the Heavy Brigade at the Battle of Balaclava (1854) where, by continuous whirling of their sabres over their heads in what are termed 'moulinets' (not 'moulinades' – Stevenson's word is incorrect) they beat off an attack by a vastly superior force of Russian cavalry.

29. *still cursing*: *CJ* (p. 35) hints at the oaths used: 'F—, B—re', obviously standing for '*Foutre!*' ('Screw it!') and '*Bougre!*' ('Bugger!').

30. *Mount Mézenc*: Mont Mézenc, at 5,750ft (1,753m), is the highest
     mountain in the area.
31. *wandered in a gorge*: In *CJ* (p. 36) the paragraph ends: 'I was too
     cold and weary to admire, or I believe I might have paused a little
     longer.'
32. *auberge*: Inn.
33. *grouting*: [Grout:] 'Of a pig: to "muzzle" or turn up the ground
     with the snout' (*Oxford English Dictionary*).
34. *amateur*: In the French sense of 'lover' or 'enthusiast'.
35. *whang*: Thick slice (a Scots word).
36. *dur comme un âne*: Tough as an ass.
37. *what he was offering*: Stevenson here omits the following incident
     recorded in *CJ* (p. 38):

> The youngest daughter, it would seem, was but a careless
> herdswoman, and her father, to teach her better manners in the
> future, told her he had sold her to me, to be my little servant, and
> appealed to me for confirmation. 'Yes,' said I, 'I paid ten halfpence;
> it was a little dear, but . . .' 'But,' the father cut in, 'Monsieur was
> willing to make a sacrifice.' A little after, she strode out of the
> kitchen and soon the noise of sobs came to our ears, along with the
> munching and stamping of the cattle and horses. The poor thing
> was crying her eyes out in the stable. Made all right.

38. *beautiful arms*: *CJ* (p. 38) adds 'full white and shapely', and
     continues: 'whether she slept naked or in her slip, I declare I know
     not; only her arms were bare'. The journal contains correspond-
     ingly less than the published version about Stevenson's embarrass-
     ment at sharing a room with a married couple.
39. *the fatal calling of a maker of matches*: Workers ran the risk of
     poisoning from the phosphorus used to make the matches.
40. *aftermath*: New grass growing after mowing or harvest (the literal
     meaning of this word).
41. *Gévaudan*: In the southern part of the Massif Central, and charac-
     terized by granite plateaux.
42. *the ever-memorable* BEAST *. . . Vivarais*: The Beast of Gévaudan
     was a mysterious animal, usually thought to be a large wolf, that
     terrorized parts of the Auvergne during 1764–7, killing over a
     hundred people, mainly women and children. Some suspect there
     was more than one wolf and legend has portrayed the Beast as a
     werewolf and other monsters. Its victims were often horribly

mutilated or completely consumed. The Beast became notorious throughout France and King Louis XV offered a reward for slaying it. As a result, a large wolf was shot and displayed at Versailles; Stevenson's description of it as 'a common wolf, and even small for that' goes against tradition. But the killings in the Auvergne continued and only ended when Jean Chastel, a local farmer, shot another wolf, said to have been of great size. The mystery of the Beast of Gévaudan is the subject of a feature film released in 2001, *Le Pacte des Loups* (Brotherhood of the Wolf), directed by Christophe Gans. The Vivarais corresponds to the Ardèche department.

43. *Versailles*: The magnificent palace of the Kings of France outside Paris.

44. *Alexander Pope . . . the Little Corporal . . . M. Elie Berthet*: The first is the English poet (1688–1744), though the quotation is not from him, but resembles line 29 of 'False Greatness', a hymn by the religious poet Isaac Watts (1674–1748). The second is a reference to Napoleon: after he displayed his courage at the Battle of Lodi (1796) in his first Italian campaign, his troops nicknamed him *'le Petit Caporal'* (the Little Corporal). Élie Berthet was a French novelist (1818–91).

45. *hoe*: Here *CJ* (p. 41) has the word 'grape', which Stevenson presumably meant for the Scots word 'graip', meaning an implement like a rake.

46. *D'où'st-ce-que vous venez*: Where do you come from?

UPPER GÉVAUDAN

1. *Pilgrim's Progress*: Part 2 (1684), p. 201.

2. *marish*: An old form of the word 'marsh'.

3. *Herbert Spencer*: English philosopher (1820–1903), who based his ideas on the theory of evolution and scientific principles. Stevenson means that his knowledge of Spencer did not prevent a feeling of superstitious awe at this point.

4. *patois*: Local dialect.

5. *a little farther lend thy guiding hand*: The opening line of Milton's *Samson Agonistes* (1671), slightly misquoted.

6. *sensible*: Able to be felt, tangible.

7. *C'est que, voyez-vous . . . farceuse*: *C'est que, voyez-vous, il fait noir*: It's just that it's dark, you see. *mais – c'est – de la peine*: But – there's a difficulty. *Ce n'est pas ça*: it's not that . . . *C'est vrai*,

ça: That's true. *oui, c'est vrai. Et d'où venez-vous?*: Yes, it's true. And where do you come from? *farceuse*: Joker.

8. *Filia barbara pater barbarior*: A barbarous daughter, a more barbarous father (Latin).

9. *bambino*: Child (Italian).

10. *Pastors of the Desert*: Napoléon Peyrat (1809–81), *Histoire des pasteurs du désert depuis la révocation de l'édit de Nantes jusqu'à la Révolution française, 1685–1789* (1842), a standard nineteenth-century history of the Camisards; Stevenson relied on this book for much of the information about the Camisards later in *Travels with a Donkey*. In a letter to his mother just before his journey, he wrote: 'I am reading up the Camisards and shall go a walk in the scene of their wars, the Hautes Cévennes' (*The Letters of Robert Louis Stevenson*, ed. Bradford A. Booth and Ernest Mehew (New Haven: Yale University Press, 1994–5), vol. 2, p. 263).

11. *Ulysses, left on Ithaca*: Stevenson may have in mind here the Ulysses of Tennyson's poem (1842) in which the restless hero longs to travel again, despite the tribulations of his voyage home to Ithaca from Troy (the subject of Homer's *Odyssey*, in which Ulysses is inspired and guided by the goddess Athene).

12. *What went ye out for to see*: Matthew 11: 8–9 and Luke 7: 24–6; Jesus asks people why they went into the wilderness to see John the Baptist (the rest of this paragraph is not in *CJ*).

13. *Balquhidder and Dunrossness*: The first is a town in the Scottish Highlands; the second, an area at the south end of the mainland of Shetland. Like most of Scotland, these are Protestant communities.

14. *ill-judged light-heartedness*: *CJ* (p. 53) adds 'I could have seen her led to the gelatine manufactory without a pang.'

15. *Æsop . . . short day's march*: Aesop was the legendary author of a set of animal fables handed down from classical times; in the fable of the miller, his son and their ass, the men end up carrying the animal. Instead of the last sentence of the published paragraph, *CJ* (p. 53) has:

> But the crowd had the facts on their side for the moment; for there was the raw beef and there was the trickle of blood. I assure you, I set out with heavy thoughts upon my little day's march. For I had given up my favourite cut through the Forest of Mercoire; and in honour of real or feigned fatigue upon the part of my loathly donkey,

had determined to strike humbly back into the valley of the Allier
and stay the night at Luc.

16. *I travel for travel's sake*: *CJ* (p. 54) adds: 'And to write about it
     afterwards, if only the public will be so condescending as to read.'
17. *where fifty might have dined*: *CJ* (p. 55) gives here the details of
     the meal Stevenson ate that evening: 'with capital trout, stewed
     hare, a famous cheese, and a palatable little wine of the Vivarais
     to wash all down, I would not have envied a diner at Bignon's [a
     Paris restaurant]'.

OUR LADY OF THE SNOWS

1.   *Our Lady of the Snows*: A monastery, founded in 1850. It burned
     down in 1912 and the present buildings were erected on a different
     site.
2.   *Matthew Arnold*: English poet (1822–88); in addition to quoting
     lines 64–6 of Arnold's poem 'Stanzas from the Grande Char-
     treuse' (1855), *CJ* (p. 57) also here includes a poem by Stevenson
     himself, written during his stay at the monastery and expressing
     his feelings about monastic life:

> O better in the great wild world tempest tossed,
> To serve and sin,
> Than here, grave-clad, an empty peace to win;
> With love and joy and laughing service lost.
> Than here, unkindly quiet in a cell,
> To breathe your breath
> Where, neighbouring with the royalty of death,
> Mankind's deserters, mankind's wounded dwell.
>
> Here the tongue ceases; here the heart is dead;
> Here in a cell
> Mankind's deserters, mankind's wounded dwell,
> And life continues with life's purpose fled.
> O better in the wild world tempest tossed,
> To serve and sin,
> Than, O ironically perfect, lost
> To man and mankind, deadly dwell herein!

The poem is signed 'W. P. Bannatyne', one of Stevenson's
pseudonyms; Bannatyne is a Scots name, best known in George

Bannatyne (1545–1609), whose manuscript collection of poetry is one of the most important sources of Renaissance Scottish verse.

3.   *Next morning . . . along the line of march*: This short paragraph replaces two longer ones in *CJ* (pp. 58–9) in which Stevenson explains the new arrangement of his baggage which 'would plainly relieve the brute of all further annoyance' (p. 58). In *CJ* (p. 59) he begins the next paragraph with: 'The morning dawned dark, with low, flying mists upon the hillsides. With my Scotch weather wisdom, I predicted that the mists would rise and give me a fine day; the people at the inn prophesied a day's rain. I am proud to say that I was in the right.'

4.   *Mende*: The main town of the Lozère department, 120 miles south of Clermont-Ferrand.

5.   *Wordsworth . . . whistle*: William Wordsworth (1770–1850), English poet. In *heard YE that whistle* Stevenson combines two half-lines from one of Wordsworth's sonnets of 1845 protesting against the building of a railway line through the Lake District in north-west England. *CJ* (p. 59) adds: 'All the time I saw this pleasing line, I saw nothing but baggage trains; transporting, as I imagined, the goods of those who were enabled to flee from such an unfriendly neighbourhood: for themselves, as soon as they were set free, I presume they could not so much as wait for a train, but giving some inarticulate directions, flung themselves across a horse and galloped for their lives.'

6.   *Trappist*: Belonging to a branch of the Cistercian order of monks started at the French monastery of La Trappe in the seventeenth century. The Trappists' restrained use of spoken words is often taken for a vow of silence.

7.   *penny plain and twopence coloured*: The title of Stevenson's essay, published in *Memories and Portraits* (1887), on the cardboard sheets of characters and scenery for toy theatres which he used to buy as a boy.

8.   *passed a bourne*: Reminiscent of the image of death as the 'undiscover'd country, from whose bourn / No traveller returns' in *Hamlet* III.1.79–80.

9.   *Marco Sadeler*: Marcus Christoph Sadeler (1614–60) was born in Munich of a family of Flemish artists and etchers. Stevenson possessed a book of engravings by J. and R. Sadeler showing scenes of hermit life.

10. *Scotsman*: This appears as 'Scotchman' in *CJ* (p. 61), where Stevenson consistently uses 'Scotch' instead of 'Scots', the spelling

preferred in the published version, and by modern Scots, who usually apply the word 'Scotch' only to whisky.

11. *drew landscapes*: Stevenson did some sketches as well as writing his journal.

12. *Dr Pusey . . . virtue in prayer*: Edward Bouverie Pusey (1800–82) was a leading figure in the Oxford Movement, an attempt to revive the Church of England's spirituality by appealing to its medieval traditions. The movement seemed to lead back to the Roman Catholicism England had broken with in the sixteenth-century Reformation, and after a time some of Pusey's companions became Roman Catholics, though he did not. The quoted sentence is not in *CJ*.

13. *Father Apollinaris*: Apollinaire Rey was born in 1825, entered the monastery in 1851 and was ordained in 1892. 'According to monastery records, he was a simple man, a bit naive, without a trace of malice' (*CJ*, p. 143, n. 8).

14. *I summoned the place in form . . . Father Michael*: Like a knight-errant or besieging general, Stevenson formally requests admittance. Father Michael (Michel Eymard, 1847–90) entered the monastery in 1866 and was ordained in 1872. 'Hospitaller of the monastery in 1878, he was later sent to Mexico, where he died suddenly on March 16, 1890' (*CJ*, p. 144, n. 9).

15. *Brother Ambrose*: Ambroise Auruolle (1830–1910) lived for sixty years in the monastery, 'a friar who had received only a rudimentary education and whose somewhat unstable temperament sometimes caused him to hesitate in his choices' (*CJ*, p. 144, n. 11).

16. *MM. les retraitants*: The retreating gentlemen (*MM.* is the abbreviation for *messieurs*), visitors to the monastery making a retreat or religious withdrawal from the world.

17. *the late Pope . . . Imitation*: The pope was presumably Pius IX, who died in February 1878. *De Imitatione Christi* is usually attributed to Thomas à Kempis (1380–1471), German religious writer and Augustinian monk.

18. *Life of Elizabeth Seton*: Elizabeth Ann Seton (1774–1821) founded several Roman Catholic schools and the Order of the Sisters of Charity (1813) in Emmitsburg, Maryland; she was canonized in 1975, becoming the first American-born saint.

19. *Cotton Mather*: A Boston Puritan (1663–1728) of strict Protestant views. He was involved in the Salem witchcraft trials of 1692 but also interested in science, and the first native-born American to be elected to the Royal Society.

20. *Le temps libre ... de bonnes résolutions*: Free time is used for examining the conscience, for confession, for making good resolutions.

21. *little Irishman of fifty*: Michael O'Callaghan was confined to the monastery by a mild mental illness. He died there in 1889. 'His illness only manifested itself from time to time and was character-ised by an over-scrupulosity, and sometimes mystical exaltation. The other monks were probably polite enough not to mention anything to Stevenson' (*CJ*, p. 144, n. 16).

22. *Waverley Novels*: The novels of Sir Walter Scott (1771–1832), named after the first, *Waverley* (1814).

23. *Veuillot ... Chateaubriand ... Molière*: Louis Veuillot (1813–83) was a French journalist and supporter of the Catholic Church in France. François-René, Vicomte de Chateaubriand (1768–1848), was a French writer whose most famous work is *Le Génie du Christianisme* (1802). *Odes et Ballades* is a collection of poems published in 1826 by the French poet, novelist and dramatist Victor Hugo (1802–85). Molière, born Jean-Baptiste Poquelin (1622–73), is the French comic dramatist.

24. *For in a Trappist monastery ... they let her in*: Stevenson revised this passage to make it more decorous; for example, he originally described thus a monk's personal activities: 'for all the world has his labour in a Trappist monastery, what he likes, whither his inclination leads him; literature, potatoes, photography; as you please; you don the habit and you take your choice' (*CJ*, p. 65).

25. *phalansteries*: A phalanstery is a community of the followers of Charles Fourier (1772–1837), a Utopian socialist. Stevenson applies the term to the artists' colonies such as that at Grez where he met Fanny Osbourne.

26. *this worldly criticism of a religious rule*: Stevenson's inclusion of this apology in a passage that is a considerable revision of the corresponding text of *CJ* indicates his acute nervousness about his comments on the life of the Trappist monks, as he struggles to treat them fairly while evidently disturbed by their silent and isolated existence.

27. *Algiers*: Part of France's colonial empire in North Africa.

28. *compline ... Regina*: Compline is the last service of the day in the Roman Catholic ritual. *Salve Regina*: The opening words and title of the most celebrated Roman Catholic hymn to the Virgin Mary, used in monasteries since the twelfth century at least.

29. *and when I remember ... Que t'as de belles filles ... and free to love*: From *and when I remember* (end of preceding paragraph)

to the end of 'The Monks', *CJ* (pp. 68–9) differs considerably from the published version:

> these things have a flavour and a significance that cannot be rendered in words. Only to the faithful can this be made clear; or to one like myself who is faithful all the world over and finds no form of worship silly or distasteful.
>
> Apart from all other considerations, the thought of this perpetual succession of prayers made the time seem pleasant to me in the monastery of Our Lady of the Snows. I have, like other people, my own thoughts about prayer; I find some prayers among the noblest reading in the world. Often when I am alone, I find a pleasure in making them for myself, as one would make a sonnet. I share, but cannot approve, the superstition that a man may change, by his supplications, the course of the seasons or the linked events of life. I have prayed in my day, like others, for wicked, foolish, or senseless alterations in the scheme of things. But these gasping complaints are not prayer; it is in prayer that a man resumes his attitude towards God and the world; the thought of his heart comes out of him clean and simple; he takes, in Shakespeare's language, a new acquaintance of himself, and makes of that a new point of departure in belief and conduct. I am tempted to say that a prayer is the highest word of literature. I remember once, after having heard Salvini in a very great performance, the words escaped me in my enthusiasm, 'I should like to pray.' 'You have prayed,' said a friend who was with me. I think with all deference, it was a mistake of words, begun by me, continued by my friend; I had not prayed, I had not wished to pray, I had wished to praise, and sure enough the wish in itself was a sonorous canticle. Prayer issues from another spirit, as warm but considerate and tranquil. As I walked beside my donkey on this voyage, I made a prayer to myself, which I here offer to the reader, as I offer him any other thought that sprung up in me by the way. A voyage is a piece of autobiography at best.

A Prayer

> O God who givest us day by day the support of thy kindly countenance and hopeful spirit among the manifold temptations and adventures of this life, having brought us this far, do not, O God, desert us, but with continued fervour follow us in our path. Keep us upright and humble, and O thou who equally guidest all mankind through sun and rain, give us thy spirit of great mercy.

A Prayer for Mind and Body

Give us peace of mind in our day, O Lord, and a sufficiency of
bodily comfort, that we be not tortured by changing friendships or
opinions nor crucified by disease, but ever in strength, constancy
and pleasantness, walk in a fair way before thy face and in the sight
of men; and if it pleases thee, O Lord, take us soon in health of mind
and human of body into thy eternal rest.

A Prayer for Friends

God, who hast given us the love of women and the friendship of
men, keep alive in our hearts the sense of old fellowship and tenderness; make offences to be forgotten and services remembered; protect those whom we love in all things and follow them with kindness,
so that they may lead simple and unsuffering lives, and in the end
die easily with quiet minds.

The Shakespeare reference is to Sonnet 77, 9–12; Tommaso
Salvini (1830–1915) was an Italian actor, famous especially for
Shakespearian tragedy, whom Stevenson saw play Macbeth in
Edinburgh. The gist of the French song is: 'You do have a lot
of pretty girls ... Love will count them!' From the operetta
Giroflé-Girofla (1874) by Charles Lecocq (1832–1918).

30. *red ribbon*: Wearing a red ribbon signifies membership of the
French Legion of Honour, awarded to civilians as well as soldiers.
31. *Poland ... Carthage*: For the reference to Poland, see 'Velay',
n. 5. Carthage was the North African city that rivalled ancient
Rome, which therefore became committed to destroying it and
succeeded in doing so in 146 BC.
32. *Gambetta's moderation*: Léon Gambetta (1838–82) was a French
Republican leader and patriot. He tried to reconcile some of the
political factions in France, but his strong anticlericalism made
him unpopular with religious people.
33. *Comment, monsieur*: What, sir?
34. *Et vous prétendez mourir dans cette espèce de croyance*: And you
mean to die holding that sort of belief?
35. *Gœtulian lion*: See Horace, *Odes* I.23.10. Gaetulia was the
Roman name for the part of North Africa roughly corresponding
to southern Morocco.
36. *C'est mon conseil ... et celui de monsieur comme prêtre ...*
added the *curé*: That's my advice as an old soldier ... And that
of this gentleman as a priest. (A *curé* is a parish priest.)

37. *grig*: A merry fellow. A grig is also a cricket.
38. *a faddling hedonist*: An unsigned review of Stevenson's first travel book, *An Inland Voyage*, in the 27 June 1878 issue of the Allahabad *Pioneer* said that it was 'decidedly brilliant, but not free from some serious faults: a large amount of affectation founded on the faddling hedonism of the day . . . being the worst' (see *Robert Louis Stevenson: The Critical Heritage*, ed. Paul Maixner (London: Routledge & Kegan Paul, 1981), pp. 56–7).
39. *La parole est à vous*: That's your word for it; you said it.

UPPER GÉVAUDAN (*continued*)

1.   *Old Play*: Stevenson adopts the practice of Sir Walter Scott, who often invented the epigraphs for chapters in his novels, and attributed his own verses to an unidentified source. In a letter to William Henley in March 1879 Stevenson sought his approval of these verses and those he put at the start of 'The Country of the Camisards', saying 'I can't get mottoes for some of my sections and took to making them; for I wish rather to have the precise sense than very elegant verses' (*Letters*, ed. Booth and Mehew, vol. 2, p. 306).
2.   *Père . . . in front of him*: *CJ* (p. 76) adds that Father (*Père*) Apollinaire 'besought me to write him a letter with news of Doctor Pusey, and I duly and solemnly promised; as also a copy of my book, above all if it were illustrated'. For Pusey, see 'Our Lady of the Snows', n. 12.
3.   *Hé, bourgeois; il est cinq heures*: Hey there! It's five o'clock!
4.   *bourrée*: A dance form of French origin, the music for which became the model for a movement in the classical suite; the dance itself apparently survives in the Auvergne, perhaps near enough to the Cévennes to make it possible that Stevenson heard an authentic tune.
5.   *feyness*: A Scots word from the adjective 'fey', meaning 'fated' or 'doomed', with also the suggestion of being unfit for this world. *CJ* (p. 77) uses the word 'lightheartedness' here instead.
6.   *for the winter's firing*: *CJ* (p. 79) adds: 'The carts and the oxen were dwarfed into nothing by the length and bushiness of what they carried; and to see one of them at a steep corner relieved against the sky, was like seeing a dragon half erected on his hind feet with forepaws in the air.'
7.   *In a more sacred or sequestered bower . . . haunted*: Milton, *Paradise Lost*, IV. 705–08 (misquoted).

8. *a hearty meal*: CJ (p. 79) gives the menu: 'bread, sausage, chocolate and brandy and water'.

9. *Montaigne*: Michel Eyquem de Montaigne (1533–92), French essayist; Stevenson has in mind a passage from his essay 'On Experience' (III. 13): 'To the end that even sleep itself should not so stupidly escape from me, I have formerly caused myself to be disturbed in my sleep, so that I might the better and more sensibly relish and taste it.'

10. *Bastille*: The infamous state prison in Paris whose storming by the mob on 14 July 1789 is annually celebrated as a national holiday in France.

11. *the stars*: CJ (p. 80) has: 'the steady sapphires and emeralds of the heavenly bodies'.

12. *A faint wind . . . the most complete and free*: This is a thorough revision of the corresponding passage in CJ (p. 81). The final sentence here replaces these two: 'The woman whom a man has learned to love wholly, in and out, with utter comprehension, is no longer another person in the troublous sense. What there is of exacting in other companionship has disappeared; there is no need to speak; a look or a word stand for such a world of feeling; and where the two watches go so nicely together, beat for beat, thought for thought, there is no call to conform the minute hands and make an eternal trifling compromise of life.' This is a reference to Stevenson's love for Fanny Osbourne, the woman he hoped to marry.

THE COUNTRY OF THE CAMISARDS

1. *Camisards*: The name given, apparently from the Languedoc word *camiso* (shirt), to the Protestant guerrilla fighters of the Cévennes who resisted attempts by Louis XIV to force them to convert to Roman Catholicism, the state religion. The revolt of the Camisards followed about twenty years of persecution during which they worshipped in secret, led by a number of inspired preachers known as prophets, many of whom were executed as heretics. Armed resistance broke out in 1702, with the murder of Abbot du Chayla in Pont de Montvert (as Stevenson describes in 'Across the Lozère'). The war ended in 1705 after negotiations, but outbreaks of violence continued for another ten years. The Protestants of the Cévennes and elsewhere in France received no measure of official recognition until the Edict of Toleration in 1787, which gave Protestants and other non-Catholics the right

to register births, marriages and deaths legally but their religious services remained forbidden. (See the Introduction.)

2. *stone pillars*: Route-markers, known as *monts-joie*, to show the path in snow or fog.

3. *'like stout Cortez when, with eagle eyes, he stared at the Pacific'*: John Keats (1795–1821), 'On First Looking into Chapman's *Homer*' (sonnet, 1816), 11–12.

4. *Cette*: Sète is the modern spelling. On the Mediterranean, today it is an important commercial and fishing port.

5. *the Grand Monarch*: Louis XIV (1638–1715), King of France, and the most powerful European ruler of his time.

6. *Roland ... Cavalier ... Castanet*: Pierre Laporte, called Rolland (1680–1704), was a peasant farmer and one of the Camisard leaders. Jean Cavalier (1681–1740) was the Camisard leader who agreed to the terms, repudiated by many of his followers, that ended the war in 1705. He later left France and fought for the Duke of Savoy and for Britain, eventually becoming a major-general. Stevenson wrote a poem about Cavalier and may have planned a book. He was mistaken in believing that Cavalier died aged fifty-five. André Castanet (captured and executed in 1705) was another Camisard leader.

7. *Florentin*: An inhabitant of St-Florent-sur-Auzonnet. The Florentins responded to a Camisard massacre of Roman Catholics with a massacre of Protestants.

8. *Carlisle ... Dumfries*: The first is a city in northern England, near the border with Scotland; the second, a town in south-west Scotland, near the border with England.

9. *set forth on such another*: *CJ* (p. 90) adds: 'Their patois was much like French; and with luck and close attention, I could follow about half of what passed about the table, not in detail, of course, but in the bulk, as when they discussed the orientation of a neighbouring hill and again when the talk ran upon sheep's cheeses.' The dialect difference Stevenson encounters here derives from the historical division between the Languedoc, the southern part of France, where they spoke the *langue d'oc*, and the northern part, where they spoke the *langue d'oïl*, the source of modern French.

10. *table d'hôte*: Literally, host's table; as today, a fixed-price meal in a public eating-house or restaurant.

11. *performing cow*: *CJ* (p. 91) has the hardly less insulting phrase 'educated cow' instead.

12. *patet dea*: The goddess is revealed (Latin); see Virgil, *Aeneid*

I.405: 'et vera incessu patuit dea' (by her gait she was revealed as a true goddess).

13. *Covenanters slew their Archbishop Sharpe*: In 1638 Scottish Protestants signed a National Covenant as a pledge to defend their religion; in the second half of the seventeenth century the more zealous Covenanters refused to conform to Church doctrines and practices imposed on Scotland by the state and suffered persecution that in turn drove them to violence and rebellion. Stevenson had a long-standing interest in the history of the Covenanters (his first book, written when he was sixteen, was an account of a battle between them and government forces near Edinburgh) and the similarities between the Covenanters and the Camisards intrigued him (see the Introduction). James Sharp (1618–79), Archbishop of St Andrews, was assassinated by Covenanters opposed to the reintroduction of bishops and archbishops to the Scottish Church because they were a feature of Roman Catholicism.

14. *Marshal Villars*: Marshal Claude Louis Hector, Duke of Villars (1653–1734), the last of Louis XIV's great generals. He was given command of operations against the Camisards in 1704, after the failure of his predecessors, the Count of Broglie and Marshal Montrevel. By first defeating and then offering terms to the Camisard leader Cavalier (see n. 6 above) he brought the war to an end.

15. *Lamoignon de Bâvile . . . du Chayla*: Nicolas de Lamoignon de Bâville (1648–1724) was Intendant of Languedoc from about 1685 to 1718. As such he led the persecution of Protestantism in the Cévennes. After serving as a missionary in Siam (modern Thailand), du Chayla became 'inspector of missions' in the Cévennes, where he persecuted the Protestants unmercifully, provoking his own death in 1702, the event which began the Camisard war.

16. *conventicle*: A private or clandestine meeting; the word is particularly applied to the illegal religious services held by the Scottish Covenanters in the seventeenth century, often outdoors. Stevenson transfers the term from the Covenanters to the Camisards.

17. *Séguier*: 'Esprit' (Spirit) Séguier (1650–1702), Camisard preacher.

18. *Scavenger's Daughter*: 'Scavenger' here is said to be a corruption of the surname of Sir William (or Leonard) Skeffington, Master of the Ordnance under Henry VIII, who is thought to have invented this instrument of torture, also called the 'Spanish

A-frame' or 'cicogna' (Italian for 'stork'). It consisted of a metal A-shaped frame four to five feet high, with a collar at the peak, two cuffs for the wrists in the middle of the two side-pieces and two cuffs at the bottom for the ankles, which forced the prisoner into a painfully constricted position.

19. *Baal*: The god of several peoples opposed to the Hebrews in the Old Testament and hence a representative of the heathen idols denounced by Jews and Christians.

20. *Captain Poul*: An officer in the royal army opposing the Camisards. After capturing Séguier in August 1702 he was himself killed a year later.

21. *My soul is like a garden full of shelter and of fountains*: This seems to be a reference to the Song of Solomon 4:12: 'A garden enclosed is my sister, my spouse; a spring shut up, a fountain sealed.'

22. *Killiecrankie*: A pass in the Scottish Highlands where in 1689 a government army was defeated by a force of Highlanders led by James Graham of Claverhouse ('Bonny Dundee'), who was killed in the hour of victory; another reference to the seventeenth-century Scottish religious wars.

23. *Between Modestine's laggard humour . . . afternoon*: A bald summary of the following in *CJ* (pp. 95–6):

> Modestine led me a wretched life all the way; she was perpetually putting about to return to Pont de Montvert, or standing obstinately still on the roadside; blood flowed freely from her poop; but she had a patience, *une endurance*, beyond that of saints. It was horrible to behold her, with her head hanging and an equivocal look upon her face, resisting like a natural object.

The annotators of *CJ* (p. 153, n. 28) comment that 'From this description of Modestine, it appears certain that the donkey was in heat . . . this impression is confirmed by the author's difficulties a week earlier (a she-ass is in heat for one week, once every month) at the beginning of the journey, as well as the male donkey's reaction to Modestine on the road from Goudet.'

24. *Camisard*: *CJ* (p. 96) has 'criminal'.

25. *Joani's . . . Salomon's*: Joani, or Jouany, was a Camisard leader. Salomon Couderc, Camisard leader and preacher (or prophet), participated in the murder of Chayla. He fled to Switzerland after the war, returned and was captured and burned at the stake in 1706.

26. *Antony Watteau*: Antoine Watteau (1684–1721), French rococo painter, famous for pictures of elegant and fanciful picnics.

27. *large ants swarmed upon the ground*: CJ (p. 97) also says they 'walked all over me inside my clothes and bit me several times before the morning'.

28. *I learned next day ... about my neighbours*: This sentence replaces two paragraphs in CJ (p. 98):

> At any rate, the whole business of getting to sleep had to be begun again from the beginning. I perspired by fits, my limbs trembled, fever got into my mind and prevented all continuous and happy thinking; I was only conscious of broken, vanishing thoughts, travelling through my mind as if upon a whirlwind. I could not, however, be sufficiently grateful that I was out here alone in the sweet night air, with nothing but stars and chestnuts around me, and not in a stifling inn room, among chance companions; and although I was unable to fix my attention on this cause for satisfaction, it recurred ever and again in the wanderings of my mind and helped to tranquilise my spirits. I did not wish a companion then; pleasure to be shared, not discomfort.
>
> Suddenly, as if all the troubles had given each other tryst for that night, a great stamping and consequent rolling downhill of the stones awoke me to the recollection of Modestine. I felt persuaded that the brute had broken loose, leaped to my feet, jumped into my boots and started for her terrace. Among these sliding stones in the starlight, it was not possible even for a man to make much head, and this consoled me; it was evident that my donkey could not get far. When at last I arrived, she was still safely fastened, and had not even stirred; only in a fit of obdurate anger with the world, she was stamping and kicking patiently at the stones. I felt pleased and amused, I scarce know why, and sitting down at the root of a chestnut, whence I had a view to the opposite side of the glen, I smoked a cigarette with a nearer approach to contentment than I had yet experienced. Right opposite, a couple of stars rested exactly on the ridge of the hill, and to me, who cannot pardon a want of composition even in nature, this sight was annoying. I averted my eyes; and when I looked up again, the stars in question had gone down. The human mind is a mighty strange contrivance, for this infinitesimal relief caused me great joy; it was like an answer to prayer; the fever seemed to abate from that moment; and when I returned to my sack, it was to drop asleep, as doctors say, with the first intention.

29. *Here was an escape . . . Camisard*: A condensed version of this passage from *CJ* (p. 99):

> Here was a man who had missed, by a hairsbreadth, a sight that would have supplied him with matter for conversation for the rest of his life. It had seemed to me more terrible to be discovered in the evening; now that morning had come, I found my disinclination to an interview not one whit abated, and my imagination became peopled with angry proprietors and local courts of law.
>
> I fed Modestine with all haste I could; but it took me longer than usual, for the minx, smelling hurry, refused to eat except from my hand . . .

30. *C'est bien*: *CJ* (p. 99) has 'All right'.
31. *thrillingly*: *CJ* (p. 100) has 'refreshingly'.
32. *Take it how you please . . . tour*: This sentence is not in *CJ*.
33. *Connaissez-vous le Seigneur*: Do you know the Lord?
34. *Many are called . . . and few chosen*: From Matthew 20:16 and 22:14.
35. *Moravians . . . Gard . . . Derbists*: The Moravians were a Protestant sect, founded at the beginning of the eighteenth century in Saxony by emigrants from Moravia, which spread to England and America. The Gard is the region of France centred on Nîmes, south-east of the Cévennes. Darbyites ('Durbists' (*CJ*, p. 101)) were the followers of John Nelson Darby (1800–82), one of the Plymouth Brethren.
36. *Plymouth Brother*: The Plymouth Brethren are believers in Christ but with no formal church organization; first centred in the 1830s on Plymouth in the south of England.
37. *Christian and Faithful*: The main character and his companion in John Bunyan's *Pilgrim's Progress*.
38. *pretty and engaging girl*: (p. 101) *CJ* adds: 'My knife, my cane, my sack, all my arrangements were cordially admired. "Tout ce que vous avez est joli," said the young man, "et vous l'êtes." [Everything you have is nice, and you are, too.] Did I not say it was a more intelligent population?'
39. *the old castle of Miral*: Begun in the thirteenth century, the seat of the Malbosc-Miral family, who were guillotined during the Revolution and their possessions auctioned off in 1796. Restoration work on the castle began in 1980.
40. *Byron*: George Gordon, Lord Byron (1788–1824), romantic poet; he had a Scottish mother and an English father.

41. *against the approach of winter*: CJ (p. 102) adds: 'I think if the garden of Eden be anywhere, it is here in the valley of the Tarn as it goes down to Florac.' The remainder of this section is not in CJ.

42. *sub-prefecture . . . hill*: A subprefecture is an administrative office of French local government. Apart from a version of this opening sentence, the section on Florac is not present in CJ.

43. *map*: As the annotators of CJ (p. 155, n. 45) point out, 'this is one of the few times that Stevenson mentions the use of a map in his travels, although he surely had one with him because the manuscript [of CJ] contains numerous notations of altitudes'.

44. *Mauchline, Cumnock, or Carsphairn*: Towns in south-west Scotland, the area in which the Covenanters were most active.

45. *Wigtown . . . Muirkirk of Glenluce . . . Prophet Peden*: Wigtown is a town in south-west Scotland, where a number of Protestants were executed in the 1680s. Stevenson possibly means the Moor Kirk of New Luce, another small town in south-west Scotland, where Alexander Peden (1626–86), Scottish Covenanter preacher, was minister from 1659 to 1662.

46. *Cévenols*: The inhabitants of the Cévennes.

47. *Poland*: See 'Velay', n. 5.

48. *Black Camisard . . . Miquelet . . . White Cross*: Members of various bands involved in the Camisard war: the Protestant guerrillas were known as Black Camisards, some of their Catholic opponents called themselves White Camisards, and the Miquelets were light troops from the Pyrenees employed by the King's army. The cadets of the White Cross were Catholic anti-Camisards who wore a white cross on their hats.

49. *valley of the Mimente*: Here a sentence or two of CJ (p. 107) is omitted: 'I had made a very late start, in honour as usual of this disgusting journal; and I think I never had a more unhappy time in my whole journey. The scenery was fair enough . . .'

50. *tourist*: Stevenson omitted the next paragraph in CJ (p. 107):

> But black care was sitting on my knapsack; the thoughts would not flow evenly in my mind; sometimes the stream ceased and left me for a second like a dead man; and sometimes they would spring up upon me without preparation as if from behind a door. I was alternately startled and dull. To say truth, I was now too accomplished a donkey driver; even my pack I had learned to balance so accurately, with stones, that it gave me no further anxiety or preoccupation; I had learned this sort of travel, until it had become

easy and tame; and now, when I made this late start, and had to plod at a wearisome slow pace behind Modestine, the ill humours got uppermost and kept me black and apprehensive. I felt sure I must be going to be ill; and at the same time, I was well aware that a night in the open air and the arrival of holy and healthy dawn would put me all right again with the world and myself.

51. *I beheld a house*: The old mill of Bougès, still standing but now a holiday home beside the remains of the railway built along the Mimente valley in the 1880s, which closed in 1948.

52. *But . . . such a great hotel*: In *CJ* (p. 108) this sentence reads: 'Still it seemed hard in this great caravanserai of the green world and tented heaven, to have to tread softly as if there were a sick man in the next room or as if I were a dissipated student stealing home with a passkey.'

53. *à la belle étoile*: In the open.

54. *with great alacrity*: Stevenson omits here this sentence about the dog: 'I believe I had been causing him agony all night; and now, seeing the day near at hand, he had thought his watch by the house doors well nigh accomplished and had made a reconnaissance in my direction' (*CJ*, p. 109).

55. *Fields of space*: The last sentence of the paragraph in *CJ* (p. 109) is omitted: 'We make such a work about the shadow of a bullet.'

56. *game-bag on a baldric*: Stevenson here omits this sentence in *CJ* (p. 110): 'For some way we walked together, and I found him an agreeable companion.' A baldric is a shoulder-belt.

57. *He is a Catholic . . . change his mind*: Not in *CJ*.

58. *M. de Caladon*: A Protestant who was exiled to England, then Ireland, and left two printed accounts of the Camisards which were consulted by Stevenson in the Advocates' Library in Edinburgh.

59. *Naaman . . . Louis XVI . . . edict*: In 2 Kings 5 Naaman the Syrian is cured of leprosy by the prophet Elisha and then acknowledges the power of God, but asks to be allowed to continue to appear to worship the Syrian god Rimmon when he returns home. Louis XVI, born 1754, King of France 1774–91, was executed in 1793 during the Revolution. The edict referred to is the Edict of Toleration of 1787.

60. *engagements*: A paragraph in *CJ* (p. 112) is omitted here:

Perhaps the bad idea was to enter into them at the first. O, sweet constraint of nature, holy simplicity of our desires and needs. The world gives liberally of things to eat; it is all over spouting fountains; and a man need not travel very far ere he finds a woman to whom his soul may cling. If he can but lay aside some dismal ascetic standards and a few hollow aspirations, in the sweat of his brow, he may live honourably and holily until the day he dies. Alas! and for a dessert, and a carriage and a pair or so, we all go clattering up the wrong road; arduous, unkindly, leading far from peace. And yet, to me at least, nature speaks so plainly, God has so clear a voice!

61. *gendarme*: An armed policeman.

62. *Bruce and Wallace*: Robert the Bruce (1274–1329), King of Scots as Robert I from 1306, and before him Sir William Wallace (1272?–1305), led the Scottish resistance to England that ensured the independence of Scotland in the later Middle Ages. In 1603, however, the crowns of Scotland and England were united when James VI of Scotland succeeded Elizabeth of England to the English throne, and in 1707 a parliamentary union between the two countries took place.

63. *Cependant . . . coucher dehors*: But . . . to sleep outdoors!

64. *tufts of heather*: CJ (p. 114) adds: 'Nothing could equal the deliberation of Modestine; she positively seemed to make steerage way upon this long ascent.'

65. *the Western Ocean*: The Atlantic.

66. *Sir Cloudesley Shovel*: English admiral (1650–1707), commander of a fleet in the Mediterranean. He sent ships to Sète during the Camisard war, but no troops were landed to help the Protestants. He was drowned returning to England when his fleet was wrecked off the Scilly Isles.

67. *Julien*: An officer in Marshal de Broglie's army who took charge of the burning of Protestant villages in the Cévennes.

68. *a profound and quiet shadow*: CJ (pp. 114–15) adds: 'The prospect heartened me. I could have desired, at last, to look down upon a plain, but the hills also were a field of travel; and away across the highest peaks, to the southwest, lay Alais, my destination.'

69. *a black cap of liberty*: A cone-shaped hat given to an emancipated slave in ancient Rome, which became a Republican symbol after the French Revolution.

70. *Rip van Winkle*: The eponymous hero of a story published in 1820 by American essayist and short-story writer Washington Irving (1783–1859); he falls asleep in the mountains and wakes up twenty years later.

71. *my invisible woodland way . . . Pippa*: Instead of the reference to Pippa, *CJ* (p. 115) adds after *way*: 'If a traveller could only sing, he would pay his way literally, it seems to me.' Pippa was the heroine of the poem *Pippa Passes* (1841) by Robert Browning (1812–89); her singing exerts a good influence on the people who overhear her.

72. *How the world . . . distant and strange lands . . . hope, which comes to all*: The first is a reference to Stevenson's feeling of separation from Fanny Osbourne; the quotation is from *Paradise Lost*, I.65.

73. *Volnay*: Wine from a village of the same name near Beaune in Burgundy.

74. *Even Modestine . . . a livelier measure*: Not present in *CJ*.

75. *Louvrelenil*: Jean-Baptiste L'Ouvreleuil (most likely the correct spelling), born 1652, *curé* of St-Germain-de-Calberte. In 1703 he published a book entitled *Histoire du fanatisme renouvelé, où l'on raconte fidèlement les sacrilèges, les incendies, & les meurtres commis dans les Cévennes, & les châtiments qui en ont été faits* (A history of the renewed fanaticism, in which are faithfully recorded the sacrileges, conflagrations and murders committed in the Cévennes, and the punishments exacted).

76. *phylloxera*: A kind of aphid which nearly destroyed the grape-vines of Europe in the nineteenth century.

77. *Aigoal*: The modern spelling is Aigoual.

78. *Mariette*: According to Peyrat's *Histoire des pasteurs du désert* (see 'Upper Gévaudan', n. 10), from which Stevenson took her story, her real name was Marie Planque.

79. *I sold her . . . for five-and-thirty*: Modestine was bought by Eugène Dumas, who used her to pull a small cart. After his death she was purchased by a M. Volpelière of St-Jean-du-Gard.

80. *maire*: Mayor.

81. *Oui, c'est comme ça. Comme dans le nord*: Yes, that's it. Just like up north. (Drinks made from apples are more typical of Normandy, in the north of France.)

82. *And, Oh, / The difference to me*: From Wordsworth's poem, 'She Dwelt Among the Untrodden Ways' (1798), 11–12. Quoting from one of Wordsworth's rather sentimental 'Lucy poems' here is surely ironic.

THE AMATEUR EMIGRANT

Dedication

1. *Robert Alan Mowbray Stevenson*: Stevenson's cousin (1847–1900), known as Bob. He studied painting in Paris, and introduced Stevenson into the artistic circle at Grez, near Fontainebleau, where he met Fanny Osbourne, but realized he lacked talent as a painter and became an art critic and Professor of Fine Art at Liverpool University in 1892.

I. FROM THE CLYDE TO SANDY HOOK

1. *Sandy Hook*: A narrow promontory on the New Jersey coast that dominates a major channel into New York harbour and is the site of the oldest US lighthouse, built in 1764.
2. *Broomielaw*: One of the main quays along the River Clyde in Glasgow.
3. *Greenock . . . the tail of the Bank*: Greenock is a port on the Firth of Clyde about twenty miles west of Glasgow; the Tail of the Bank is an anchorage in the Firth.
4. *junk . . . duff . . . broken meat*: The first consists of lumps of meat, salted and tough as rope; the second is a stiff flour pudding boiled in a bag; the third means 'left-overs'.
5. *two guineas . . . second cabin*: A guinea was equivalent to one pound and one shilling, or £1.05 in modern British currency. Second-cabin passengers were intermediate between steerage and saloon, or first-class, who paid from thirteen to sixteen guineas.
6. *Henry the Third of France*: Henri III (1551–89), last of the Valois, ruled France from 1574 until his assassination during a period of great religious turbulence; to judge from his portrait by François Quesnel, he had a thin face with a pointed chin, a long nose and rather prominent eyes.
7. *Southern readers*: Those who live in England, south of the border with Scotland.
8. *lingua franca . . . feluccas*: The first means, literally, Frankish tongue (Latin); any mixed language used among people, particularly traders and seafarers, who have no other common language. A felucca was a small sailing vessel used in the Mediterranean.
9. *Lough Foyle*: A large inlet of the Atlantic in the north of Ireland. Stevenson here uses the Irish word for 'Lake'; in 'Steerage Types' he uses the Scottish 'Loch' instead.

10. *Marmion*: The eponymous main character of a narrative poem (1808) by Sir Walter Scott (1771–1832); the quotation is from canto 3.XI.5–6.

11. *Tyne*: A river in north-east England, which enters the North Sea at the industrial city of Newcastle.

12. *the French retreat from Moscow*: In 1812 the invasion of Russia by the French Emperor Napoleon ended in a disastrous winter retreat from the capital, Moscow, during which his army, hitherto victorious, suffered terrible losses, mainly caused by the weather.

13. *England*: As in *Travels with a Donkey*, Stevenson uses 'England' when he clearly means the whole of Britain; many of his fellow-passengers, as is already clear, are from Scotland and Ireland, and also from other parts of Europe.

14. *mither . . . Mawmaw*: The first is Scots for 'mother'; the second is presumably stressed on the second syllable and intended as a rather affected pronunciation of 'mamma', a familiar form of address, especially in well-to-do families.

15. *Co' 'way doon to yon dyke*: Keep going down to that wall (Scots).

16. *naming our trades*: It is clear from Stevenson's later remarks in 'Personal Experience and Review' that *his* trade was not easily accounted for, and in 'To the Golden Gates' his occupation seems to have become a source of speculation.

17. *seven bells . . . list*: On board ship a bell was rung with an extra stroke for every half-hour during the four-hour watches; seven bells at night corresponds to 11.30 p.m. To 'list' is to edge with strips of cloth.

18. *hurricane deck*: A light upper deck on a ship.

19. *We don't want to fight, but, by Jingo, if we do*: A music-hall song by George William Hunt (*c.* 1829–1904), very popular during Britain's confrontation with Russia over Turkey in 1878, and the origin of the word 'jingoism', meaning bellicose nationalism.

20. *Platt-Deutsch*: Low German, a loose term for various languages spoken in northern Europe, including the Netherlands and parts of north Germany.

21. *Zululand and Afghanistan*: In January 1879 a British army invaded Zululand in South Africa, was defeated at Isandlwana, but triumphed six months later at the Zulu capital, Ulundi; in November 1878 the British had invaded Afghanistan to counter Russian influence there, and after a bloody campaign they defeated the Afghans in September 1880.

22. *The Anchor's Weighed . . . Auld Lang Syne*: The words of 'The

Anchor's Weighed', about two lovers parting, are by the English dramatist Samuel James Arnold (1774–1852) and the music is by John Braham (1774–1856), a famous opera singer of the time; by 'Rocked on the bosom of the stormy deep' Stevenson may mean 'Rocked in the Cradle of the Deep' by American pioneer of education for women, Emma Hart Willard (1787–1870); 'I'm lonely to-night, love, without you' is the first line of the ballad 'Nora O'Neal' (1866) by American songwriter William Shakespeare Hays (1837–1907); 'Auld Lang Syne' is a traditional song reshaped into the famous song of farewell and parting by Robert Burns, probably in 1788, though not published until 1796.

23. *Christian Agapes*: Meetings held by the early followers of Christ to promote fellowship; the Greek word *agape* (pronounced with three syllables) means 'brotherly love'.

24. *the ship didna gae doon*: The ship did not go down (Scots).

25. *companion*: The stairwell leading from the upper deck to the cabins below.

26. *Strathspey . . . Orpheus*: The first is a moderately slow Scottish country dance, named after the valley of the River Spey in northeast Scotland. Orpheus is the legendary Greek musician.

27. *Mr Darwin*: Charles Darwin (1809–82), whose theory of evolution revolutionized the study of biology.

28. *Merrily danced the Quaker's wife*: A Scots-Irish jig tune to which is sung a comic song, 'The Quaker's Wife Sat Down to Bake'.

29. *sand dance . . . Auld Robin Gray*: The first is another name for the soft-shoe shuffle, a development of step- or tap-dancing, but in shoes without wooden soles or metal taps. The second is a traditional Scottish song to which Lady Anne Lindsay (1750–1825) wrote verses describing the troubles of a girl who marries an older man in the mistaken belief that her young lover has drowned at sea.

30. *Logie o' Buchan*: A song written in 1736 by an Aberdeenshire schoolmaster, George Halkett.

31. *M. Zola*: Émile Zola (1840–1902), French novelist, controversial for his unflinching description of unpleasant aspects of human nature and existence; Stevenson was both appalled and fascinated by Zola's fiction.

32. *Oh why left I my hame . . . Death of Nelson*: The first is from 'The Exile's Song' by the Scottish poet Robert Gilfillan (1798–1850). The second is the most famous song by John Braham and Samuel James Arnold (see n. 22 above), from an opera called *The*

Americans (1811); it makes repeated use of Admiral Horatio Nelson's signal to his fleet before the Battle of Trafalgar (1805), 'England expects that every man will do his duty.'

33. *Theseus*: Though now best known for slaying the Cretan Minotaur, Theseus was regarded by the Greeks as one of their ancient kings and credited with a number of political and social reforms, including the institution of democracy.

34. *Mercury . . . Apollo*: Mercury, the messenger of the Roman gods, was also associated with trickery; Apollo, the Roman sun-god, was also the god of art, literature and music. The whole sentence here allures to the last speech in Shakespeare's comedy *Love's Labour's Lost*.

35. *Caiaphas and Pontius Pilate*: In the New Testament Caiaphas is the High Priest who leads the accusation against Jesus before the Roman Governor of Judea, Pontius Pilate, that results in Jesus's crucifixion.

36. *memoria technica*: A mnemonic, or aid to memory.

37. *fox and goose and cabbage*: The puzzle of the farmer who has to take a fox, a goose and a cabbage across a river in a boat that will carry only himself and one other thing; how does he avoid leaving the fox alone on the riverbank with the goose, or the goose with the cabbage?

38. *hop-step-and-jump* or *push-the-stick*: The first is a common name for what has become known in athletics as the triple jump; the second is a game in which a twig is passed rapidly from hand to hand and then one player in the circle has to guess who has it.

39. *Puss in the Corner*: A game for five players; four each take a corner of a room, and when the fifth calls out they must run to another corner while the fifth player tries to get into one.

40. *Lady-Bountiful air*: Lady Bountiful is a character in *The Beaux' Stratagem* (1707) by the English playwright George Farquhar (1677–1707), who administers her own remedies to the local sick and injured; her name has become proverbial for condescending charity.

41. *Mackay*: See 'Steerage Types' for more information.

42. *Callot*: Jacques Callot (1592?–1635), French engraver, best known for eighteen etchings called *The Miseries of War* (1633) and twenty-five etchings of beggars.

43. *sawder*: Flattery.

44. *Tigg*: Montague Tigg is a swindling character in Charles Dickens's novel *Martin Chuzzlewit* (1843–4), which contains scenes set in America.

45. *Nihilist*: A member of a secret Russian revolutionary movement which was thought to repudiate all social customs and restraints; the name comes from *nihil*, the Latin for 'nothing'.

46. *Ach, ja*: Ah, yes (German).

47. *Kalmuck . . . White Sea*: The Kalmucks are a Mongolian people who live in western Asia, to the north-west of the Caspian Sea; the White Sea is off the north-west coast of Russia; Archangel is its main port.

48. *Neva . . . wie ein feines violin*: The first is a river running into the Baltic Sea; the Russian city of St Petersburg is situated in its delta. The quotation means 'like a fine violin' (German).

49. *Tom Bowling*: An elegiac sea-song by English playwright and songwriter Charles Dibdin (1745–1814).

50. *Abudah*: A merchant, in *Tales of the Genii* (1764) by English novelist James Ridley (1736–65), who nightly dreams of a hag who insists he must seek the talisman of happiness, which he finally learns means he should fear God and keep His commandments.

51. *Cœlum non animam . . . Glenlivet for Bourbon*: The Latin reference is to Horace's *Epistles* I.xi.27: *coelum non animum mutant qui trans mare currunt* (they who hurry across the sea change their surroundings, not their souls); since both *animus* and *anima* can mean 'soul' in Latin, Stevenson's use of *animam* instead of *animum* conforms to the meaning though not the text of Horace's epistle. Glenlivet is a celebrated Scottish single-malt whisky; Bourbon is an American whisky first made in Bourbon County, Kentucky.

52. *teetotal pledge*: Members of the British Association for the Promotion of Temperance, formed in 1835, at first signed pledges to abstain only from alcoholic drinks other than beer or wine, but later the temperance movement advocated total abstinence.

53. *a corporation*: Humorous term for a fat belly, an 'expanding waistline'.

54. *Hoppus's Measurer . . . Juan Fernandez*: The first refers to *Practical Measuring Now Made Easy to the Meanest Capacity* (London, 1736), a quantity surveyor's ready-reckoner by Edward Hoppus (d. 1739); the second, to islands in the Pacific Ocean off the coast of Chile, named after their Spanish discoverer, on one of which a Scottish seaman, Alexander Selkirk (c. 1676–1721), was marooned from 1704 to 1709; his experiences inspired the English novelist and journalist Daniel Defoe's novel *Robinson Crusoe* (1719).

55. *the staff of life*: Usually this biblical phrase refers to bread, but here it seems to mean food in general.

56. *Suffolk*: County in the south-east of England.

57. *Fife*: Eastern county in the lowlands of Scotland, across the Firth of Forth from Edinburgh.

58. *Ye see, he has aye something ayont*: You see, he has always something beyond [the concerns of everyday life] (Scots).

59. *Shorter Catechism*: The series of religious questions and answers, drawn up in 1647, used to teach the doctrine of the Church of Scotland up to and beyond Stevenson's day.

60. *Billy Keogh . . . daffing*: The name is evidently Irish, and possibly a reference to judge and politician William Keogh (1817–78), at first a supporter of Irish Home Rule, but then appointed Solicitor-General by the British government. He became notorious for passing severe sentences on Irish nationalists. No doubt he was the subject of satirical songs and verses. 'Daffing' means 'foolishness', 'merriment' (Scots).

61. *no fish on Friday*: Fish was regarded by the Roman Catholic Church as an acceptable substitute for the meat which its followers should abstain from eating on Fridays.

62. *Captain Burnaby's mind*: Frederick Gustavus Burnaby (1842–85), English soldier, traveller and balloonist, published accounts of his travels in Asia in 1876 and 1877.

63. *divel . . . iver . . . plased*: In this exchange Stevenson attempts to convey in an Irish accent 'devil', 'ever' and 'pleased'.

64. *Sir Philip Sidney . . . a Roland for his Oliver*: Sidney was an English courtier, soldier and poet (1554–86), who, mortally wounded in battle, passed a cup of water to another wounded man with the words, 'Thy necessity is greater than mine.' Roland and Oliver figure in tales of chivalry to do with the Emperor Charlemagne (742–814); their friendship begins when they engage in single combat and find themselves equally matched, so that the phrase Stevenson uses can simply mean 'tit for tat'.

65. *bieldy . . . dinna*: The first means 'sheltered'; the second, 'do not' (both Scots).

66. *Sebastopol . . . the Alabama . . . Tory*: Sebastopol was the Russian naval base besieged by British and French forces in the Crimean War, 1853–6. The *Alabama* was one of several British-built ships used during the American Civil War by the southern states in raiding northern merchant shipping, and after the war the United States demanded compensation from Britain for its losses; in 1871 the British prime minister, William Gladstone, agreed to refer the

dispute to international arbitration and Britain was required to pay the USA over £3 million, about a third of the US demand. Gladstone's approach was unpopular in Britain but the case set a precedent for the peaceful resolution of international disagreements. 'Tory' is the nickname of the British Conservative Party, usually implying strong support for the established Church and state and opposition to political and social change.

67. *hazed*: Harassed with overwork.

68. *Fisherrow to Whitby*: The first is a small harbour on the Firth of Forth just outside Edinburgh; the second is on the coast of Yorkshire in the north-east of England.

69. *by with me*: The end for me (Scots).

70. *Liberton Hill*: A hill south of Edinburgh, now one of the city suburbs; the name is a corruption of 'Leper Town', indicating that there was a leper hospital there in the Middle Ages.

71. *Atlantic Cable*: The first cable across the Atlantic was laid in 1858, but failed after a few weeks; in 1866, however, a lasting link was made between Ireland and Newfoundland, allowing telegrams to be sent from Europe to America.

72. *Nemesis*: The ancient Greek personification of divine resentment and punishment.

73. *smoking-cap*: A cap, often of velvet and with a tassel, worn by gentlemen while smoking to prevent their hair smelling of tobacco.

74. *P. and O. Company . . . Royal Engineers*: The Peninsular and Oriental Steam Navigation Company has been a major British shipping company from the 1830s to the present day. The Corps of Royal Engineers became an independent division of the British army in 1787; their role is to construct defences, roads and bridges.

75. *Homeric*: Powerful and heroic, like the characters in the epics of the Ancient Greek poet Homer.

76. *rodomontade . . . Burns*: Robert Burns (1759–96), Scottish poet, whose conversational powers were admired in polite circles as well as in taverns; 'rodomontade' is boastful talk.

77. *Woolwich . . . Westminster Bridge*: Woolwich was then a town on the River Thames east of London, and the site of a naval dockyard and the Royal Arsenal until 1994. Westminster Bridge spans the Thames near the Houses of Parliament.

78. *We gentlemen . . . at ease*: The first line, with 'we' for 'you', of a song about the hardships of sailors by Martyn Parker, who lived in the middle of the seventeenth century. Each verse of the song ends with the chorus 'When the stormy winds do blow'.

79. *Prison Discipline Act ... Wakefield Jail*: Before the Prisons Act of 1877, which brought all British prisons under the control of a central Prison Commission, there were variations in the treatment of prisoners in county jails. Wakefield is in Yorkshire.

80. *Circassia*: Another ship of the Anchor Line, built in 1878.

81. *before the mast*: That is, as a common sailor, whose quarters were traditionally in the forward part of the ship, whereas the officers' quarters were at the stern.

82. *finger-glasses*: Finger-bowls, dishes of water on the table for diners to rinse their fingers in during a meal, a practice generally regarded as a sign of upper-class refinement.

83. *the West Park*: Perhaps West End Park, the original name for Kelvingrove in Glasgow.

84. *on tick*: On credit.

85. *Sauchiehall Street*: One of the principal and busiest streets of central Glasgow.

86. *reviewing the yeomanry*: Killing time; the yeomanry were volunteer cavalry whose drill exercises any idler might watch for nothing.

87. *sheet*: A rope at the corner of a sail.

88. *Weymouth ... Bristol Channel ... dandy*: The first is a port on the coast of Dorset, a county neighbouring Devon, in the south-west of England; the second is the stretch of water between the south-west peninsula of England and South Wales; the third is a kind of sloop or cutter.

89. *hand, reef, and steer*: Stevenson perhaps had in mind the boast of the captain of HMS *Pinafore* in Gilbert and Sullivan's 1878 opera that 'though related to a peer, I can hand, reef, and steer'.

90. *Glasgow Green*: Once the common land of the ancient burgh of Glasgow, it was taken over as a public park in 1857.

91. *Sailor's Home*: Many major ports had cheap hotels specifically for seamen, where those who were destitute could find accommodation.

92. *Scapin*: The rascally servant in *Les Fourberies de Scapin* (The Double-Dealing of Scapin; 1671) by the French comic dramatist Molière.

93. *the Montyon prize*: Jean-Baptiste Antoine Auget, Baron de Montyon (1733–1820), left money for a prize for virtue to be awarded by the Académie Française, the French institution founded in the seventeenth century to safeguard linguistic and literary standards; it was first awarded in 1836.

94. *C'est Vénus tout entier*: From *Phèdre* (I. 306) by the French tragic

playwright Jean Racine (1639–99): 'C'est Vénus tout entière à sa proie attachée' (It is Venus wholly attached to her prey).

95. *Amadis of Gaul . . . Orson*: The first is the hero of a Spanish and Portuguese romance who performs amazing feats in love and war. In the French romance of *Valentine and Orson* the latter is carried off by bears as a child and brought up as a wild man.

96. *Out of my country and myself I go*: Quoted by English essayist, journalist and critic William Hazlitt (1778–1830) at the end of his essay 'On Going a Journey' (*Table Talk*, 1821), but unattributed and unidentified.

97. *In a former book*: See 'We are Pedlars' in Stevenson's first travel book, *An Inland Voyage* (1878).

98. *the transformed monarch in the story*: Perhaps Stevenson has in mind James V of Scotland, who went about disguised as a private person under the name of the Goodman of Ballengiech, a habit familiarized by Sir Walter Scott's account of it in *Tales of a Grandfather* (1827–9).

99. *Tom Holt's Log*: A novel subtitled 'A Tale of the Deep Sea', by William Stephens Hayward (London, 1868).

100. *anonasume*: Hart, *From Scotland to Silverado* (p. 76), here prints this nonsense word presumably because he had difficulty with Stevenson's handwriting. The reading in Noble, *From the Clyde to California* (p. 93), is 'manoeuvre'.

101. *Barmecide*: Illusory; Barmecide is a character in the *Arabian Nights* who sets empty dishes before a beggar so polite that he pretends he has indeed been given the best of fare.

102. *Arcady . . . brass plate*: Arcady is the classical equivalent of Eden, a land of innocence and simple rural pleasures. For *a gentleman on a brass plate* see the fourth paragraph of 'The Second Cabin'.

103. *Lord Beaconsfield*: Benjamin Disraeli, first Earl of Beaconsfield (1804–81), Conservative politician and twice prime minister of the United Kingdom.

104. *Aberdeen*: A city and port in north-east Scotland.

105. *Von Moltke*: Helmuth, Count von Moltke (1800–91), chief of the Prussian General Staff, who organized victorious wars against Denmark, Austria and France.

106. *Robinson Crusoe*: The novel published in 1719 by Daniel Defoe (1660?–1731) in which the hero describes in detail how he survived and prospered after being shipwrecked on a desert island.

107. *the Cévennes . . . Pradelles*: See *Travels with a Donkey*, 'I Have a Goad'.

108. What looks like a reversed apostrophe (properly, turned comma)

after the first letter of this name represents an abbreviation, now usually spelled 'Mc', of the Gaelic 'Mac', meaning 'son of'. This convention was common in nineteenth-century printing, and was in use into the following century.

109. *with a wild surmise*: From John Keats's sonnet 'On First Looking into Chapman's Homer' (1816), but the seamen there are those of Cortés, not of Vasco Núñez de Balboa (*c*. 1475–1519), another Spanish conquistador and the discoverer of the Pacific Ocean.

110. *Castle Garden*: An island off the south-west tip of Manhattan used as a receiving station for immigrants to the USA from 1855 until 1890, before the more famous Ellis Island.

111. *Westward the march of empire holds its way*: From 'Verses on the Prospect of Planting Arts and Learning in America' which Irish-born English philosopher George Berkeley (1685–1753) wrote before he went to America in 1728 in order to found a missionary college in Bermuda – which failed to materialize – but his ideas for a college were instrumental in founding King's College in New York City, which later became Columbia University; Stevenson substitutes 'march' for 'course' and 'holds' for 'takes'.

112. *costume*: Probably a misprint for 'custom'; or, possibly, Stevenson is using an archaic spelling.

113. *Maine Laws*: In 1846 and 1851 the state of Maine, under the leadership of Neal Dow (1804–97), passed laws prohibiting the manufacture and sale of alcoholic drinks.

114. *the Sierras . . . Whitman*: The Sierra Nevada mountain range is in California. Walt Whitman was an American poet (1819–92).

115. *the navy revolver and the bowie knife . . . when Chicago was burned*: From 1851 the famous American gunsmiths Colt manufactured several handguns called Navy models because a scene depicting a battle between the Texan and Mexican navies was engraved on the cylinder; the long-bladed bowie knife was named after the frontiersman Jim Bowie (1795–1836). A fire raged through the city of Chicago for nearly two days in October 1871.

116. *Uncle Sam*: The personification of the United States because, during the War of 1812, meat-packer Samuel Wilson (1766–1854), known as Uncle Sam, supplied provisions to the American army in barrels marked 'US'.

117. *Mr Lowell*: American poet, journalist and diplomat James Russell Lowell (1819–91) published his essay 'On a Certain Condescension in Foreigners' in 1869.

118. *always best at home . . . Woman Hater . . . We are abroad*:

Stevenson may have had in mind the proverb 'Ill bairns are ay best heard at hame', used by Scottish poet Robert Fergusson (1750–74) in his poem 'To the Principal and Professors of the University of St Andrews, on their superb treat to Dr Samuel Johnson' (line 60). Charles Reade (1814–84), English novelist, playwright and journalist, published his novel *The Woman Hater* in 1874. The quotation is from Chapter 7 (Zoe Vizard is a character in the novel).

119. *non omnia sua secum ... A Bohemian*: The quotation is an allusion to the Latin 'Sapiens omnia sua secum portat' (The wise man carries all he needs in himself), a Stoic maxim derived from Cicero's *Paradoxa* I. 8. In Stevenson's time 'Bohemian' meant someone whose manners, appearance and opinions were unconventional or rebellious. The word derives from the French *bohémien* (gypsy); gypsies were thought to come from Bohemia in Central Europe.

120. *Portman Square*: Fashionable square in central London.

121. *Sabbatarian*: A strict observer of the Sabbath; a Christian who spends Sunday at his devotions, neither working nor playing.

122. *the Prodigal Son*: Luke 15: 11–32.

123. *Benjamin Franklin*: The American writer and politician (1706–90); the quotation comes from a letter of 30 July 1776.

124. *copyright*: The United States did not join the International Copyright Union until 1896; before that, American publishers produced editions of books by British writers, including Stevenson, without permission and without payment to the author.

125. *turret ship ... the old three decker*: Modern warships with guns mounted in revolving turrets were replacing older ships with their tiers of gun-decks.

126. *Liverpool*: City in north-west England, a major port for traffic across the Atlantic.

127. *lights*: Apertures, windows.

128. *He had been ... of the fare*: Note the near-repetition of the end of the paragraph four before this one.

129. *Gymnosophist*: An ancient sect of Hindu ascetics who went naked, ate no meat and spent their time meditating.

130. *seidlitz powder ... Johnson's dictionary*: The first was a laxative, taken dissolved in water, named after Seidlitz in Bohemia, where there is a natural spring whose waters have similar properties. English lexicographer, critic, poet and man of letters Samuel Johnson (1709–84) published his dictionary in 1755; Stevenson would know that the first chapter of William Thackeray's novel

Vanity Fair (1847–8) ends with one of the heroines, Becky Sharp, throwing her presentation copy of the dictionary out of the window of the carriage taking her from school to embark on a life of ambitious social climbing.

131. *true name of my complaint*: It is possible that Stevenson's itching was caused by the parasitic scabies mite; the social stigma of having scabies is probably the reason for his reluctance to name his condition, since it was caused by living in cramped, unhygienic quarters.

132. *red sublimate . . . hence these tears*: Stevenson may have believed it was possible to apply a chemical barrier to the scabies mite which would prevent its movement beyond exposed parts of the body. The last three words are a translation of 'hinc illae lacrimae', from Terence, *Andria*, 126, quoted by Horace in *Epistles*, I.xix.41.

II. ACROSS THE PLAINS

1. *Council Bluffs*: A town in Iowa, on its Omaha border, where several railroads from the east converged and west-bound travellers like Stevenson changed to the Union Pacific for the next stage of their journey. The Union Pacific Railroad Company was formed to build a line west from Nebraska to meet the line from Sacramento built by the Central Pacific Railroad; the link was completed in 1869, enabling passengers to travel across America in ten days.

2. *Bancroft's History of the United States*: American historian and diplomat George Bancroft (1800–91) published his ten-volume history between 1834 and 1873.

3. *Jersey City*: Across the Hudson River from New York.

4. *address the winds*: Waste my breath.

5. *all hands are piped*: Everybody is called together.

6. *cars*: For a description of the American railroad car, see the second paragraph of 'The Emigrant Train'.

7. *Indian corn*: Maize.

8. *Aurora*: The Roman personification of the dawn (and the Latin word for it).

9. *platform*: Open area at either end of a railroad car, outside the covered compartment.

10. *wreck*: Wrack, seaweed.

11. *Susquehanna . . . Adam*: The first is the river in Pennsylvania that was to be the site of the utopian community planned by the

English Romantic poets Samuel Taylor Coleridge (1772–1834) and Robert Southey (1774–1843) in 1794–5. Adam, the first man, names God's creatures in Genesis 1:19.

12. *the same State*: Ohio.

13. *Sloane Square, and the King's Road ... Arkansas*: The first two are a square and a main road in Chelsea, then a suburb of west London. Stevenson's note in the first published version of 'Across the Plains' read: 'Please pronounce Arkansaw, with the accent on the first.'

14. *plague*: There was a serious outbreak of yellow fever in Tennessee and Arkansas in 1879.

15. *Pittsburg*: Pittsburgh – Stevenson's spelling reflects the pronunciation which, as a native of Edinburgh, he would find odd.

16. *Beecher Stowe ... Christy Minstrels*: Harriet Beecher Stowe (1811–96) was the author of *Uncle Tom's Cabin* (1852), the novel which inspired opposition to slavery in the USA. The singer Edwin Pearce Christy (1815–62) founded the most famous black-faced minstrel troupe in 1842; they performed for ten years on Broadway in New York, and toured England.

17. *fag ... Prince Hal with Poins and Falstaff*: A fag is a junior schoolboy who acts as a servant to an older pupil, especially in an English public school. In Shakespeare's *Henry IV* the heir to the throne of England, Prince Hal, consorts with lower-class characters including Edward Poins and with Sir John Falstaff, a disreputable knight, before reforming his ways to become the hero-king Henry V.

18. *Cassell's Family Paper ... Custaloga, an Indian brave*: In the nineteenth century the firm of Cassell's published popular magazines including *Cassell's Family Magazine* and *Cassell's Illustrated Family Paper*; Custaloga was an eighteenth-century chief of the Native American Delaware.

19. *rattle*: Talker, chatterbox.

20. *dîner fin*: Fine dinner (French).

21. *Burlington ... Creston*: The first is a town in Iowa, near the Illinois border; the second is in Union County, Iowa.

22. *boots*: A hotel servant, traditionally employed to clean guests' boots and shoes.

23. *the third to the Chinese*: See the opening paragraph of 'Despised Races' for an explanation of this racial segregation on the train.

24. *Noah's ark*: In Genesis 6–9, warned by God that He intends to flood the world, Noah builds a huge boat to save himself, his family and a collection of other creatures.

25. *Yankeeland*: Specifically New England, though the term could be applied to the northern states of the USA more generally.

26. *Pennsylvania Dutchman*: A descendant of the original German settlers in Pennsylvania.

27. '*Home, sweet Home*': From the opera *Clari, or The Maid of Milan* (1823), music by English composer and conductor Henry Bishop (1786–1855), words by American playwright and actor John Howard Payne (1791–1852).

28. *Timotheus*: The minstrel in 'Alexander's Feast' (1697), an ode by English poet and playwright John Dryden (1631–1700), whose music moves and inspires Alexander the Great.

29. *North Platte . . . The Sweet By-and-bye*: The first is a railroad town founded in 1873 in Nebraska. The second, a hymn (1868) with words by Samuel Fillmore Bennett (1836–98) and tune by Joseph Philbrick Webster (1819–75).

30. *Seven-up or Cascino*: The first was the American name for a popular trick-taking card-game known in England as All Fours, in which the first player to win seven points is the winner; the second is probably cassino, another popular card-game.

31. *Ogden to Sacramento*: The first is not far from the Great Salt Lake in Utah and is where west-bound passengers changed from Union Pacific to Central Pacific trains; the second is in California.

32. *crown-piece*: A crown, a silver coin over an inch in diameter, was worth five shillings (modern 25p), or a quarter of a pound sterling.

33. *cicadæ*: Stevenson uses the Latinized plural of cicada.

34. *sage-brush*: *Artemisia tridentata*, a low, irregular shrub that covers much of the American plains.

35. *cañon*: Stevenson's spelling of canyon.

36. *Laramie*: Town in Wyoming, founded in 1868 as a consequence of the building of the transcontinental railroad.

37. *savage tribes . . . Golden Gates*: Stevenson's careful consideration of the treatment of Native Americans in 'Despised Races' suggests that this reference to them is not to be taken at face value. He consistently and mistakenly makes the Golden Gate, the four-mile strait linking San Francisco Bay with the Pacific Ocean, a plural.

38. *Troy*: The ancient city in Asia Minor (modern Turkey) whose siege and capture by the Greeks is the subject of Homer's *Iliad* and many other classical and modern poems and stories.

39. *a boy of eleven*: 'The writer was Martin Mahoney, brother of Mrs Mary Carson, Stevenson's landlady in San Francisco, from whom he obtained the letter' (note in Hart, *From Scotland to Silverado*, p. 130).

40. *prairie chicken*: The greater prairie chicken (*Tympanuchus cupido*), a kind of grouse, hunted close to extinction for food.

41. *hoop*: Whoop.

42. *Dean Swift*: Irish poet and satirist Jonathan Swift (1667–1745), author of *Gulliver's Travels* (1726), in the fourth part of which Gulliver meets disgusting subhumans called Yahoos; Stevenson, in common with other nineteenth-century readers, confuses Swift with his fictional creatures.

43. *Saratoga . . . Camby*: A Saratoga trunk was a large travelling trunk with a rounded top, named after Saratoga in New York State. By *Prince of Camby* Stevenson perhaps means King Cambyuskan in *The Squire's Tale* in Chaucer's *Canterbury Tales* (c. 1387); at the beginning of the second part of the tale he falls deeply asleep.

44. *Demogorgon*: The name of an ancient god, used by the poet Percy Bysshe Shelley (1792–1822) in *Prometheus Unbound* (1820).

45. *Cornish miners . . . Lady Hester Stanhope*: Between 1861 and 1901 about 20 per cent of the male population of Cornwall in the south-west of England emigrated, mainly as a result of the decline of the tin- and copper-mining industry, taking their skills across the world, notably to Grass Valley in California. Hester Stanhope was an English traveller (1776–1839), who spent the second half of her life in the Lebanon. She lived for a time in Wales, where she tried to help the poor, including miners, but there is no record of her helping Cornish miners.

46. *short commons*: Scanty meals.

47. *El Dorado*: The gilded one (Spanish), the name applied to a land of gold, thought to be in South America but also sought elsewhere.

48. *Sand-lot*: Sand-lots were open spaces in San Francisco, where meetings took place.

49. *a priori*: From that which comes before (Latin); that is, a claim based on an assumption that is not argued for and is often no more than a prejudice.

50. *John Bull . . . Zazel . . . Pat*: John Bull is the personification of Great Britain. Zazel is the name of a demon or fallen angel, translated in the Bible as 'scapegoat', which is Stevenson's meaning here; he is referring to the return of the Mediterranean island of Crete to Turkish rule, a consequence of British support for Turkey against Russia in 1878–9. Pat is a generic name for an Irishman; Stevenson is referring to Irish terrorism following the founding in Dublin in 1879 of the Land League, the key organization of the Land War, a campaign of agrarian protest against landlordism. See also next note.

51. *vulgar fellow*: Dennis Kearney (1847–1907), an Irish immigrant who became involved in San Francisco politics; in 1877 he instigated riots among the unemployed with his speeches attacking bosses and Chinese workers.

52. *Abreham Lincoln . . . dhirty Mongolians*: Born in 1809, assassinated in 1865, Lincoln was the most famous nineteenth-century US president; he led the northern states against the south in the Civil War (1861–5), which he made a campaign to abolish slavery. Both *Abreham* and *dhirty* are meant to convey Irish pronunciation.

53. *Great Wall*: Built over two thousand years ago to protect China from invasion, the wall stretches for four thousand miles north and west of the capital Beijing (formerly 'Pekin[g]').

54. *that old, grey, castled city*: Edinburgh, whose castle is a military headquarters over which flies the flag of the United Kingdom.

55. *Cockney*: Specifically, someone of the working class from central London, but here Stevenson uses it as an adjective meaning brash and ignorant, as of a city know-all.

56. *Cherokees*: Originally a tribe of the Appalachians in the east, in 1835 the Cherokee Nation were forced to move west to Oklahoma; those that survived the journey were subjected to continued oppression and exploitation by the United States until their Nation was officially dissolved in 1906.

57. *Monterey . . . Carmel . . . chaparral*: Fanny Osbourne, the woman Stevenson had crossed the Atlantic to be with, lived in Monterey, north of the Carmel Valley; chapparal (*Larrea tridentata*), also called the 'creosote bush', is a desert plant.

58. *kine . . . ground squirrel*: The first means 'cows', 'cattle'. As its name suggests, the Californian ground squirrel (*Otospermophilus beecheyi*) lives in burrows.

59. *Rancherie*: A rancheria is a Californian Indian settlement.

60. *Toano*: A small town near the border with Utah, Toano was founded as a railroad stop in 1868, had a population of 123 in 1880 and was abandoned in 1906. Today, no buildings are left.

61. *brither*: Brother (Scots).

62. *decimal coinage*: Until the introduction of decimal currency in 1971, British money was complex and idiosyncratic, with twelve pennies to the shilling and twenty shillings to the pound sterling.

63. *bit . . . dime*: A bit is any small coin; the Mexican real was widely used in the south-west United States; the dime was ten cents.

64. *Elko*: Another railroad town, founded in 1868.

65. *The Wearing of the Green*: A traditional Irish song that figures in

the play *Arrah-na-Pogue* (1865), by Dion Boucicault (1820–90). Stevenson's claim that this and 'Auld Lang Syne' are the only songs he knows seems inconsistent with his references to music elsewhere, particularly in 'Early Impressions' and 'Steerage Scenes'.

66. *Blue Cañon, Alta, Dutch Flat*: Three small towns in Placer County, California, on the railroad just west of the border with Nevada.

67. *Oakland ... Tamalpais*: Oakland is on the east side of San Francisco Bay; it was here that Stevenson married Fanny Osbourne in 1880. Tamalpais is a mountain north of San Francisco.

68. *The tall hills Titan discovered*: 'And the high hills Titan discovered', from *The Faerie Queene* (1590), Book I, canto 2.vii.4, by the English poet Edmund Spenser (1552–99); *Titan* means 'the sun', and *discovered* means 'disclosed', 'revealed'.